THE WORLD WITHIN
THE WORLD WITHOUT

Readings for the Christian Student

Ruth H. Givens
William R. Epperson
Betty D. Howard

Kendall/Hunt
Publishing Company
Dubuque, Iowa

Copyright © 1987 Kendall/Hunt Publishing Company

Library of Congress Catalog Card Number: 87–51045

ISBN: 0–8403–4609–3

Printed in the United States of America
10 9 8 7 6 5 4 3 2 1

Contents

Preface, ix

The Writer's World and the Readers' World, 1

PART I: THE SEARCH FOR GOD, 19

    Introduction, 19

Spiritual Authenticity in a Secularized World, 21

    Aleksandr Solszhenitsyn, "The Templeton Address: Men Have Forgotten God," 21
        Christian Perspectives, 26
    Thomas Hardy, "God-Forgotten," 27
        Christian Perspectives, 28
    Emily Dickinson, "Those — Dying Then," 28
        Christian Perspectives, 29
    Percy Shelley, "Ozymandias," 29
        Christian Perspectives, 29
    Matthew Arnold, "Dover Beach," 30
        Christian Perspectives, 31

Spiritual Authenticity in the Religious World, 33

    Will Herberg, "Religiosity and Religion," 33
        Christian Perspectives, 35
    Flannery O'Connor, "Revelation," 36
        Christian Perspectives, 49
    The Apostles' Creed, 50
    Dorothy L. Sayers, "The Dogma Is the Drama," 50
        Christian Perspectives, 53
    Langston Hughes, "Salvation," 53
        Christian Perspectives, 54
    John Updike, "Pigeon Feathers," 55
        Christian Perspectives, 69

Spiritual Authenticity in the Community of God, 71

    Dorothy L. Sayers, "Toward a Christian Esthetic," 71
        Christian Perspectives, 80
    G. K. Chesterton, Excerpt from "Everlasting Man," 81
    C. S. Lewis, "What Are We to Make of Jesus Christ?" 81
    C. S. Lewis, "Theology," 83
        Christian Perspectives, 84
    Psalm 8, 85
        Christian Perspectives, 86
    Gerard Manley Hopkins, "God's Grandeur," 86
        Christian Perspectives, 86

Gerard Manley Hopkins, "Pied Beauty," 87
    Christian Perspectives, 87
George Herbert, "Easter Wings," 87
    Christian Perspectives, 88
George Herbert, "The Pulley," 88
    Christian Perspectives, 89
John Donne, "Holy Sonnet XIV," 89
    Christian Perspectives, 89
Gerald Manley Hopkins, "The Windhover," 90
    Christian Perspectives, 91
Emily Dickinson, "God Is a Distant — Stately — Lover," 91
    Christian Perspectives, 91
Making Connections, 91

PART II: THE SEARCH FOR A MORAL PERSPECTIVE, 93
    Introduction, 93

Responsibility to Self, 95

Mark Twain, Excerpt from *Huckleberry Finn,* 95
    Christian Perspectives, 96
Henry David Thoreau, Excerpt from *Walden,* 97
    Christian Perspectives, 100
Ann Morrow Lindbergh, "The Channelled Whelk," 101
    Christian Perspectives, 105
William Wordsworth, "The World Is Too Much with Us," 105
    Christian Perspectives, 105
C. S. Lewis, Excerpt from *Mere Christianity,* 106
    Christian Perspectives, 107
Making Connections, 107

Responsibility to Others, 109

Margaret Sanger, "The Turbid Ebb and Flow of Misery," 109
    Christian Perspectives, 113
Jonathan Swift, "A Modest Proposal," 113
    Christian Perspectives, 118
Making Connections, 118

Commitment to a Cause, 121

Martin Luther King, Jr., "Letter from Birmingham Jail," 121
    Christian Perspectives, 131
Wilfred Owen, "Dulce et Decorum Est," 132
    Christian Perspectives, 133
Richard Lovelace, "To Lucasta, Going to the Wars," 133
    Christian Perspectives, 133
John Donne, "A Valediction: Forbidding Mourning," 134
    Christian Perspectives, 134
e. e. cummings, "next to of course god america i," 135
    Christian Perspectives, 136

Ecclesiasticus, 136
>   Making Connections, 138

PART III: THE SEARCH FOR INDIVIDUALITY, 139
>   Introducton, 139

Defining Individuality, 141
>   Garrison Keillor, from *Lake Wobegon Days,* 141
>>   Christian Perspectives, 144
>   Malcolm X, Excerpt from *Autobiography of Malcolm X,* 144
>>   Christian Perspectives, 150
>   Emily Dickinson, "I'm Nobody," 150
>>   Christian Perspectives, 150
>   W. H. Auden, "The Unknown Citizen," 151
>>   Christian Perspectives, 152
>   George Herbert, "The Collar," 152
>>   Christian Perspectives, 153

Defining a Personal Philosophy, 155
>   Plato, "Allegory of the Cave," 155
>>   Christian Perspectives, 157
>   John Milton, from *Areopagitica,* 157
>>   Christian Perspectives, 161
>   William Blake, "The Tiger," 162
>>   Christian Perspectives, 162
>>   "The Lamb," 163
>>   Christian Perspectives, 163
>   Anton Checkhov, "The Bet," 163
>>   Christian Perspectives, 167

Adapting to the World Without from Within, 169
>   Paul Tillich, "Riddle of Inequality," 169
>>   Christian Perspectives, 174
>   John Milton, "Sonnet XIX," 174
>>   Christian Perspectives, 175
>   Scott Peck, "The Risk of Loss," 175
>>   Christian Perspectives, 177
>   Dan Wakefield, "Returning to Church," 177
>>   Christian Perspectives, 182
>   Making Connections, 182
>   John Milton, from *Paradise Lost*, 183
>>   Christian Perspectives, 188

Bibliography, 189
Index, 193

Preface

Christians find themselves in a paradoxical position in our society today. Universally, Christianity is a major religion and an influential voice in most cultures. The Christian influence is, in fact, one of the major distinguishing characteristics of the Western world. One only needs to read St. Augustine, Dante, or even Shakespeare to find the influence of Jesus Christ and Christendom on civilization. Individually, however, the Christian does not have it so easy. Theoretically, to profess Christianity is acceptable and even respected, but to embrace Christianity—to regard the Bible as divinely inspired, and to believe in Jesus Christ as the risen son of God—is a different matter. In fact, the primary tenets of Christianity are often rejected by a society that professes Christianity as its major religion.

The editors of this reader feel that one of the reasons for the dichotomy in society's reaction toward fundamental Christianity is the fallacy that it is not a thinking person's religion. The word *faith* implies ignorance in a society of science and technology, but to those of us who truly want to be a part of the "mind of God," our faith requires the best of all of us.

We feel that literature, particularly secular literature, has not always been used by the Christian community as effectively as it could be as a tool for spiritual insight. Yet what greater way can we learn of the dilemmas that have prevailed upon mankind than through common experiences of philosophers, poets, and story tellers. These writers have attempted to express man's condition and give readers insight into their own lives. Herein lies the rationale for this book.

Literature is a valuable tool for learning, for the Christian as well as the non-Christian. God can use the secular writer as well as the religious writer to reveal truth to mankind. C. S. Lewis says it most succinctly: "It [Christianity] was never intended to replace or supercede the ordinary arts and sciences; it is rather a director which will set them all to the right jobs, and a source of energy which will give them all new life, if only they will put themselves at its disposal."

In this textbook we introduce the views of many writers, and all of their views will not necessarily be Christian views. In our analysis of their works we do not wish to circumvent or to pervert the author's original meaning, but our purpose is to view the literature from a Christian perspective—to present questions and applications that provide writing opportunities and that suggest a spiritual dimension for the student.

The uniqueness of this anthology is not in its literary content, even though we have endeavored to maintain high academic standards that would prepare students for college and for life. But rather its uniqueness is in its applications from a Christian perspective. Our goal is that students in a Christian educational environment will see a merging of Christianity with education, rather than a polarizing as is often done in a traditional educational setting. For we feel that all of life, to the Christian, should proclaim the message of God's salvation to the world.

Acknowledgements: We are grateful to all of those who directly or indirectly participated in the development of this book. Combining their talent and vision, each contributed a vital part to the whole. June Hobbs, one of our original editors, provided insightful material and left her creative mark on the project that remains with us even in her absence.

Our special thanks to Renee Valentine who donated her illustrations for this first printing. We are also indebted to the faculty, staff, and students at Oral Roberts University who tested the book two years and who provided honest feedback for its improvement. We would particularly like to thank Linda Gray, Grady Walker, Clyta Harris, and Kathy McCullough for their constructive comments and valuable assistance.

We also profited from the suggestions made by the members of the Christian College Coalition who attended the 1986 summer workshop on "Teaching Values in Literature." We appreciated advice from Pat Ward, Kenneth Shipps, Alan Rose, Annie Stevens, Bill Fry, and Ruth Cameron.

And, finally, we want to thank Kathleen Anderson, Jeff Donaldson, and Belinda Gantt for hours of dedicated assistance.

The Writer's World
and the Reader's World

The Creative Word

The Bible presents God's word as powerful, active, and creative. His word calls all creatures out of nothingness into existence, shaping them into their myriad and particular forms. His word sustains His creation in His love. His word informs the human community with its sustaining virtues: justice, mercy, goodness, and love. And His word conveys to individual persons the judgment, forgiveness, and salvation which open them to their full identities as children of God. Christian faith identifies this Creative Word of God with Jesus, God Incarnate, "in flesh," whose earthly life fully images the creative and sustaining love of God.

Humans, made in the image of God, also use words which shape the human environment. They do not create out of nothing, as God does, but they act as "sub-creators" to order the flow of phenomena their senses respond to, using a language system to know reality. A simple way to understand this shaping power of words on one level is to think of how words affect personal relationships. By a word you can bless, creating trust, friendship, love; and by a word you can curse, destroying relationships by a lie, a betrayal, an insult. Parents' words are especially powerful in shaping their children's personalities: affirming words build confidence and trust; negative words destroy these, breeding doubt and confusion. The capacity to grow in faith and love depends greatly upon the nurturing words parents give to their children.

Storytellers, poets, dramatists, writers of essays, and singers of songs have given shape to our human community through history. The bards of the ancient world celebrated their heroes, telling adventures which would later be written down as *The Iliad, The Odyssey, Beowulf,* and other epic poems which have been preserved for modern readers. By their celebration of the qualities that constituted the hero in their society, they shaped their listeners' imaginations to love those virtues such as courage, friendship, loyalty, hospitality, strength, and skill. The world of the story perpetuated the moral values of the community. The storyteller delighted his listeners with his stories, even as he instructed, reminding them of the way good and evil manifest themselves in the human world.

The Active Writer

Whenever you write or speak, you cause something to happen—your words have effects, evoke responses. By training yourself to be more aware of the elements of any communication event you can make your creative words more purposeful, more powerful in shaping your environment.

The simple act of writing involves a writer, an audience, and a message which is conveyed for a purpose. A diagram of the *rhetorical situation* looks like this:

$$\text{writer} \longrightarrow \text{persona} \begin{cases} \nearrow \text{purpose} \\ \searrow \text{subject} \end{cases} \longrightarrow \text{audience} \qquad \text{reader}$$

Persona

An active writer becomes conscious of each of these elements; he carefully plans a strategy for achieving his purpose. As a craftsman, he shapes material into graceful and useful forms. The active writer critically listens to the sound of his words, noting their rhythms, their style. He becomes aware that the *voice* of his writing is itself a *made* voice; it is not himself, but a *persona,* a voice he creates on the page to carry his message and to effect his purpose. The persona of a personal essay may be very closely linked to the writer's sense of self, and a reader may find it difficult to distinguish the "I" of such an essay from the "I" of the author as a private person, but they are different.

As you write, be aware that you have many options about the persona you choose to speak through. You may use a first person narration which discloses you very openly to your reader. On the other hand, you may create a first person narrator entirely different from yourself. Analyze how Mark Twain purposely creates a naive persona in his novel, *Huckleberry Finn,* and how the detached, objective persona of Jonathan Swift's "A Modest Proposal," effectively conveys the author's own passionate concern.

Each element of the rhetorical situation affects the others. Already you can think of how Twain and Swift made their personas to fit their purposes of satirizing evil aspects of their societies. Your *purpose,* your sense of your *audience,* and your *subject,* will be matters for you to consider as you choose your voice of *persona* for any writing task. The personal "I" of an informal essay or the persona that narrates a short story would be inappropriate as the voice for most academic writing. Do not think a simple rule covers all writing situations. If a teacher warns you against using the pronoun "I" in an essay, it merely indicates that he considers it inappropriate for the audience, purpose, and subject matter of that essay. As you become an *active writer,* you should be able to make such judgments from your own sense of purpose, audience, and subject.

The Active Reader

Becoming an *active reader* requires you to attend to the text with full awareness. Train yourself to distinguish between *purpose, subject, topic,* and *thesis.* Purpose has been discussed above as what an author wishes to accomplish by his writing. The broad area of an author's interest is the subject, and the particular aspect of the subject he focuses on is the topic. Again you are sensitive to the elements of the rhetorical situation. You note the writer's voice, his persona's manner and sound. You look for clues to his purpose. You ask questions as you read. "What is the author seeking to do with this text?" "Does he want to *inform* me, *persuade* me, or *entertain* me?" Perhaps he wants to tell you how to do a task, understand a theory, or correct a problem. Perhaps he wants to move your emotions, exhort you, anger you, make you cry or laugh.

Your understanding of the author's purpose will probably coincide with your growing knowledge of his *subject*. *What* he is saying and *why* he is saying it become clearer as you read. Be sure to be open-minded, hearing what the writer is trying to say to you. A necessary skill of good reading is the ability to suspend judgment until all the information is received. Readers who make quick judgments of a writer's beliefs or information can easily misread the text, mistaking its purpose and even its content.

Thesis

The *thesis* asserts a particular opinion about the topic. Professional writers sometimes do not state their theses directly, giving their readers opportunity to infer them from the whole article or essay. As a student writer, however, you should make your thesis statements explicit, specific, and concise. Aim at containing your thesis statement in one sentence that makes an interesting, arguable stand on your topic. If your thesis is so widely accepted as to invite no critical thought, your reader will see no reason for your writing. Make the thesis statement as specific as possible, indicating by details the order your argument will take and the kind of support it will have.

Examine Dorothy L. Sayers' essay "The Dogma is the Drama," for its purpose, subject, topic, and thesis. A brief analysis reveals Sayers purposes to be several; she wants to convince readers that modern young people in England are ignorant of the fundamental teachings of the Christian faith, and to convince her readers that those teachings are not boring, but shockingly fresh and compelling. In accomplishing these, she has another purpose—she wants her own writing to entertain, so she uses the devices of satire, metaphor, exaggeration, and wit. Her subject is the condition of faith in modern England. Her topic focuses on the contemporary ignorance and misunderstanding of the assertions of the Christian Creeds. Her thesis could be stated like this:

> In modern England, the Christian faith has been so taken for granted that its dogma has been lost, but the central reality that dogma witnesses to—the Incarnate God, Jesus the Christ—remains an exciting wonder to all humans who come to know of Him.

You can become a more active reader by practicing some exercises that require your reacting to the text. If you are using your own book, *underline* what strikes you as significant—statements of the author's thesis, topic sentences, and important supporting details. If you are looking for a particular thing in the text, such as how a character is portrayed in a short story, underline every significant detail.

You should also make *marginal notations* in your own book. Such notes may give clarifying information, definitions, or your personal responses. You may want to note the method the author is using to develop his idea, the kind of persuasive appeals he employs (ethical appeal, logical appeal, emotional appeal), and your responses to his method, his persuasions, or his style. These notes, along with your underlinings, will help you see how the text is structured — the order of its main ideas and supporting details.

Further reactions may come in the form of *paraphrase* and *summary*. Most of the notes you take in doing academic research will be written in the form of paraphrases or summaries. Copying the source text exactly is necessary only when you have clear reason for quoting it, as when the information is very detailed, when the original is stated in an unusual or striking way, or when you feel that any paraphrase would inadequately represent the author's tone or intention.

Paraphrase

When you *paraphrase,* find synonyms for the author's wording and rearrange word order, changing sentences as freely as you can while retaining the sense of the original. This will help you avoid unconscious *plagiarism.* Remember that use of specific information or ideas you obtain from an author must be documented, even if you do not quote his exact wording.

A paraphrase of the Hopkins' poem "God's Grandeur" might be expressed in the following way:

God's glory shines through all the natural world. It glows like the warm reflections off precious metals, and grows like an overflowing barrel of olive oil. But humans continue to ignore God's presence, generation after generation. The earth is dirtied by human commerce, greed, and the misuse of labor. The environment is hurt and made less fertile because of the way humans use it; and the humans themselves are becoming less sensitive to nature, their earthly home.

The earth is not totally exhausted, however. Life still remains within nature. Even when all seems dark, there is hope of rebirth, because the Holy Spirit continues to care for the fallen world.

Summary

Summarize by condensing a text to its main ideas and chief support. For most material, a good summary will be about one fourth the length of the original. In writing both paraphrases and summaries, you must be careful to give full and valid representation of the author's ideas. Although you will be responding to what you are reading, agreeing or disagreeing, you should keep these evaluative responses out of your paraphrase or summary. Other forms, essays of *analysis* and *synthesis,* are appropriate vehicles for your responses.

A summary of the poem paraphrased above, "God's Grandeur," would be much briefer than the poem itself; a strict informational summary, without comment about the author, might look like this:

Nature shines with God's glory, but men ignore it, degrading nature and desensitizing themselves as they do so. But God's Spirit continues to care for His creation, and each morning brings a renewed sense of life to the world.

A *descriptive* summary will introduce the author and his work to your reader. This kind of summary might be expressed like this:

In "God's Grandeur" the poet Gerard Manley Hopkins expresses his faith that God continues to care for His world, even though human sin, as seen in the way people ignore His presence in nature, degrades the beauty and fertility of the earth and desensitizes human life. The poet affirms that new hope comes with each morning's sunrise, because God's Spirit sustains creation in love.

You would use strict informational summaries in most note taking, and descriptive summaries in your essays, where you wish to make your acknowledgements of sources clear.

Finally, to be an active reader, be patient. Reading is not a passive occupation as so much television viewing is. Reading requires concentration. You must let ideas develop as the author puts one piece of information with another; you, in effect, follow the process or reasoning he has placed before you in his text. Some authors provide examples that help you understand their ideas easily; others depend on logical progressions that are relatively free from concrete illustration. When you find a selection difficult to understand, as Hopkins' and Wilbur's poems often are, or Milton's prose is, work with it. Do not blame the author for frustrating you; grant that he *intends* to communicate and that others have comprehended his text — and even enjoyed it. You may simply have to enter his world, his vocabulary, his ideas, by a patient working through what is at first strange territory to you. Only when you have truly *heard* any author, though, are you in a position to begin judging his ideas.

Writing as Creative Response

By the time you have thoughtfully and actively read a text, using the skills of underlining, noting, paraphrasing, and summarizing, you are ready to respond by bringing your own world of experiences, concepts, and values into reaction with the author's world. Your written responses may take many forms, shaped by your purposes in writing.

Personal Response

You may wish to respond to a selection by comparing or contrasting what it tells about with your own experiences. In this case you would write a *personal response* essay, relating something about yourself to something discussed by an author. You may find the Langston Hughes' essay "Salvation" one to which you can make such a personal written response.

Analysis

You may want to *analyze* a selection, dealing with the parts of a text to see how they constitute a whole. You can analyze a literary text from nearly any perspective, so you need to be very clear about your purpose, your topic, and your thesis. When these begin to come into focus, you can write a thoughtful, well supported analytical essay. Some of the selections lend themselves to certain approaches: Henry David Thoreau's *Walden* suggests interesting stylistic and thematic analyses; Martin Luther King, Jr.'s "Letter from Birmingham Jail" invites a rhetorical analysis; and the essays by C. S. Lewis and Paul Tillich make an analysis of reasoning necessary even to read them with understanding.

Synthesis

A *synthesis* essay requires that you use ideas from several sources to support your own idea or thesis. In writing a good synthesis you must do more than simply place the ideas of the sources together, as if they were blocks of wood stacked side by side. You need to relate the ideas, actively moving from one notion to another, letting one comment modify or suggest another. You want to put the ideas from the sources together in such a way as to generate new insights. Good synthetic thinking aims at your arriving at such fresh understanding, from which you can address your audience with assurance and enthusiasm when you begin to write. The arrangements of poems, stories, and essays in this collection have been made to suggest useful approaches for synthesis thinking and writing, and you will find suggestions for synthesizing in "Making Connections."

Evaluation

Academic writing for which you use written material for sources generally requires both analysis and synthesis skills. When these skills are developed well, you can feel more assured in employing *evaluation* skills. An evaluation essay allows you to respond to the quality of the thing you are reviewing. If you are dealing with a literary text, you should determine the author's intention and evaluate how well he fulfills that intention.

Evaluation requires much precision at every step of the process. You must determine exactly what you are judging—for any object may be judged on many levels. Are you weighing the selection under consideration for its logic and reasoning? For its moral value? For its beauty? Remember that different readers may be looking at different things when they make their evaluating comments. Take responses to a movie as an example. You may call a movie "good" because of its technical excellence—its acting, scripting, filming, and editing. Your evaluation would be on the aesthetic level. Your friends may find the movie "good" because it is emotionally compelling, or because it portrays good and evil in a realistic way, or because it illumines something of the life of faith. In various ways your friends are dealing with the movie on different levels, finding it good because of the way it fulfills their categories—emotional, ethical, aesthetic and religious categories they judge it by. Whenever you read an evaluation, and especially when you write evaluations, make clear the intention, the focus, and the perspective of judgment.

Getting Started

It is hard to get those first words of an essay down on your paper. The work does not spring from your pen as a fully developed product. Writing is a creative *process* and has stages which you must progress through to achieve the finished *product: preparation, incubation, illumination* and *execution,* and *verification.* These stages generally go in order, but in actual writing you will find yourself mixing them to some degree—you will be preparing one aspect of the subject while you are writing on another part. Remember that the process is not without frustration; do not expect the outline of your work to be always clear from the start; do not wait to feel inspired.

Preparation

Preparation begins with the careful, open minded reading described above. Read to understand the major ideas held by authorities on your topic. Do not read just to prove a position you have already taken, and do not read simply those sources which agree with you. In choosing a topic, you should have found in it questions which you want answered, areas on which you want to be better informed. When the topic is relevant to you, and open to more inquiry, it will usually be interesting to your readers.

Use this preparation stage as a time to play with ideas—brainstorm the topic, writing down anything that comes into your mind. Ask yourself all the *journalist's questions: who? what? when? where?* and *why?* Expand those to other probing questions:

How does this happen?
What does this feel like?
What senses does it evoke?
What does it compare to?
How is it different from other things in its class?
What are its parts?
What is its value?

Freely asking such questions, and freely discussing the topic with friends, will help you focus on your attitude toward the topic. In the latter part of this preparation stage you will find yourself forming some definite opinions which you should try to state as a *hypothesis,* a tentative thesis which asserts your view. The hypothesis should be specific enough to guide you to the further research or questioning you need to do but not so rigidly committed to as to limit your thinking. Consider the hypothesis flexible, subject to change as your information and understanding of the topic increases.

Incubation

Give yourself time to let your active preparation cease for a day or two, so that the second stage, *incubation,* can occur. This stage allows ideas to settle into place, and lets you relax about your project, and return to it with a fresh eye and renewed imaginative energy. Students who wait until the evening before a paper is due to begin writing it cannot experience this stage of the creative process, and their work suffers as a result.

Illumination and Execution

Illumination and *execution* is the next stage, where you begin putting down ideas on paper. You might start with organizing your note cards into categories, then composing an outline which structures your paper to support your hypothesis. The opening of an essay is often difficult, but you can combat "writer's block" by starting to write at the point you feel most sure about. You can always move paragraphs and sentences around, so you should feel no problem about temporarily ignoring your introduction. In fact, writing your introduction and conclusion *after* you have completed the body of your paper will help you focus on stating your final thesis in these two crucial places.

Verification

The final stage of the creative process, *verification,* is essential to the success of your project. Here you edit, proofread, and polish your style. Do not become impatient with your work. In this stage you can discover the joy of a craftsman taking pride in the final efforts that give his work quality, lifting it above the mediocre, making it worthy of presenting to others. Here again you will do well to give yourself some extra time so that you can approach the project with an objective, critical eye. Let a friend read and comment on your essay, but choose one who will be honest with you and whose judgment and reading ability you trust.

Exposition — Shaping Material

Writers have many methods for shaping their material. The skilled writer knows her purpose and audience as well as her topic and thesis, and is adept at mixing methods — description, narration, definition, classification, and other methods — to communicate most effectively, accomplishing her purpose with her audience.

These methods for shaping material are often referred to as the *modes* of exposition. A writer seldom uses only one mode in an essay, but commonly purpose and audience considerations will cause her to choose one mode as the dominant method of that particular writing task.

Narration and Description

When writers want to involve their readers most directly, giving them what is known as vicarious experience, they will often use methods of *narration* and *description.* Narration tells a story. It proceeds to follow an action through time. Both Langston Hughes' essay "Salvation" and Dan Wakefield's "Returning to Church" are narrative essays. If they were fictional, we would call them "stories," but since they describe actual events in the authors' lives, we refer to them as personal essays in the narrative mode. Description builds in the reader's mind a scene, a particular object, space, or time. This mode may also be quite effective for a personal essay. Much of Thoreau's *Walden* is descriptive, detailing for the reader what Thoreau's life was like while he spent two years at Walden Pond.

Process

If the writer wants to explain how something works, he may use the method called *process.* This mode traces, step by step, the way any process occurs: a cookbook recipe for baking a cake, a set of directions for operating a VCR, a detailed essay on making a garden — these topics would call for a process method. Writers of process descriptions usually have as their purpose the instructing of their readers; they must be very clear about the time sequence of each step, and very specific about each detail. While this method is normally employed for very pragmatic purposes, and is not a typical "literary" mode, Jonathan Swift, the eighteenth century author of satiric prose and poetry, uses process description brilliantly for his bitter satire on the English treatment of the Irish in his day, "A Modest Proposal."

Shaping Exposition to Persuade

As Swift's example shows us, any of the methods may be used by skilled writers to *persuade* readers—another major purpose for writing and speaking. Most of the poems, stories, and essays of these chapters are basically persuasive in purpose. Writers also may proceed from simple explaining, narrating, or describing, to persuading by using other common methods of developing their material:

definition,
cause and effect,
classification,
division,
comparison and contrast,
analogy, and
support and illustration.

Definition

Definition you probably know as the formal type of definitions of things, words, or ideas found in dictionaries. These definitions give the general class the object or phenomenon is in, and then provide its distinctive characteristics. Writers extend this method to provide unusual or elaborate descriptions of the thing being described. They may use concrete examples to define abstract attitudes. Anne Morrow Lindbergh's "Channeled Whelk," for example, becomes an extended definition of the concept "simplicity." Even though she does not formally define it as a dictionary would, she does give us a sense of what simplicity and its opposite do to one as they take root in the soul.

Cause and Effect

Lindbergh also uses *cause and effect* as she writes about her activities. She lists how very specific things about her life, her housing, her clothing, and her relationships and social involvement cause specific effects in her emotions. Similarly, Margaret Sanger combines cause and effect reasoning with impassioned narrative to persuade her readers of the evil effects of ignorance and poverty in her essay, "The Turbid Ebb and Flow of Misery." In using cause and effect reasoning writers try to explain *why* something happens, what causes precede and constitute a later effect. They must be cautious about making assertions of causality though, for it is easy to mistake simple relationship in time for a cause/effect relationship. "A happened; then B happened" becomes interpreted as "A happened, therefore B happened." In logic, this is known as a logical fallacy with the Latin name *"post hoc, ergo propter hoc"* or, more briefly, the *"post hoc"* fallacy. A simple everyday example of this can be seen in the way we so easily blame our poor performance on a test on our being out too late the evening before, or skipping breakfast, or on some other thing that occurred prior to our taking the examination. These may have been factors influencing us, but they may be excuses. The real cause may have been a simple lack of study—so a relationship in time is not sufficient to establish a cause/effect relationship.

Classification

Classification and *division* are similar methods. In classifying, an author breaks a class or group of things into categories. A student writing about an English faculty, for example, might classify them as composition teachers and literature teachers, or as instructors and professors, or as freshman English teachers and upper division course teachers. The writer should be careful to make his classifications by consistent and reasonable principles. Anne Morrow Lindbergh classifies sea shells into their various types, using the suggestions of their shapes and colors to build extended comparisons with human attitudes. Such comparisons are called *analogies,* and may be seen as yet another method of developing material.

Division

In the method of *division,* the writer divides one subject into its component parts. A typical job description is formed by this method: the work of an office manager might be divided into her various tasks: evaluating secretaries, interviewing personnel, researching, and interpreting data. Many of the essays you write fulfilling academic assignments will require you to divide topics into logical parts. For a biology paper on a living organism you may need to divide your topic into parts such as the nervous system, the circulatory system, and the bone and muscle systems. In writing an analysis of a poem, you might divide your topic into metrics, tone, figurative language, and theme.

Comparison and Contrast

Comparison, where you show similarities between several things, and *contrast,* where you show differences, are common methods of developing material. These methods may form the structure of an entire essay, or may be used briefly as you make particular points.

Support and Illustration

Good writers also use abundant *support* and *illustration* as they write, backing their general statements—like their thesis or topic sentences—with details which are specific, relevant, and interesting. Note, for example, the several ways Martin Luther King, Jr., supports his assertions in "Letter From Birmingham Jail." He cites authorities for ethical and legal support of his cause; he draws comparisons and makes analogies; he gives personal examples from his own family's experiences. Moving from highly abstract statements to concrete examples helps the reader "flesh out" the meaning intended by the author, so one mark of good writing is its flexible movement from one level of abstraction to another, from general statements to specific example, from abstract concept to concrete, sense-evoking imagery.

As you can see from the examples above, writers are not confined to a single method of development. They mix the methods freely, but always with reason. The alert writer senses, or experiments and discovers, the clearest way to think through and tell about his topic; he considers the audience he is trying to reach, their level of knowledge, their assumptions or prejudices, their values, their language habits; and finally he determines the methods by which he can best communicate his topic to this audience.

Purpose and Strategy

Readers must be alert as they approach texts, giving them *active* readings. A basic process of active reading requires discerning what method a writer is using and analyzing why he has chosen that method. Knowing Swift's purpose in writing "A Modest Proposal," for example, will allow you to read it rightly, as a powerful protest against national exploitation, rather than as a literal, methodical, and unemotional proposal to reduce the Irish to a kind of livestock, a new type of food supply.

Confrontation or Communication

Student writers need to think critically about their purposes as they choose every element of their writing. The satiric form, as Swift uses, is difficult to write successfully. It tends to set the writer against his material and, often, against the reader, forcing the reader to judge an unpleasant or evil situation from a new, less complacent, point of view. Similarly, certain methods and tones chosen may promote confrontation rather than agreement. The debate model, where two sides of an issue are rigidly lined up against each other, rarely serves to bring persons into agreement.

The diction chosen by a writer can also be confrontational. Using emotionally laden terms, what the semanticist S. I. Hayakawa calls "words with built in judgments," may unfairly bias your reader—either for or against your position. If she already agrees with your basic attitude, your slanted diction will let her unthinkingly agree with your every statement. If your diction reveals your bias to a reader who does not feel in agreement with you, he will be all the more on the defensive against what you have to say. The slogans and cliches you hear constantly in political or religious conversations, the bumper sticker admonitions you see pasted on cars, are more successful as displays of ideological positions than as effective methods of convincing people. In other words, taking confrontational stances in your rhetoric, emphasizing differences between you and your readers, may serve the purpose of asserting what you think, but such confrontations usually fail to convince others to share your viewpoint.

Finding Areas of Agreement

The writer who has active concern for the truth about her subject matter, and who wants to share that for the good of her readers, is a writer who is, at least in a small way, reaching out to her world with love. The *loving* writer or speaker does want to build a bridge with her communication, a bridge over which can be transported all the good, truth, or beauty she has discovered through her research or meditation. Jesus' "Golden Rule" suggests an appropriate attitude for guiding such a writer; she treats her subject with respect and care. She deals fairly with opposing evidence and opinions. She employs a moderate tone, avoiding slanted wording or other devices to inflame emotion in a manipulative manner. Basically, the writer who seeks to persuade starts by establishing areas of agreement with her reader, proceeds with moderate language, presents opposing views or evidence fully and fairly, accounts for it in her own argument, and relies on reason—her own and that of her reader—to bring the desired agreement.

King's "Letter From Birmingham Jail" presents a model for effective persuasive writing. He reminds those Birmingham clergymen who had objected to his civil rights demonstrations of their religious and political ideals. In doing this he establishes areas of agreement, for he cites moral authorities from the tradition he shares with them—the Old Testament prophets, Jesus and the early Christians, great Jewish, Catholic, and Protestant theologians, and the founding documents and political thinkers of our nation. By invoking such high ideals, King manages to call out the noblest motives in his readers, to set the contemporary conflict in a context of the historic struggle for justice, and to portray himself as a man of ethical significance.

In ancient Greece, Aristotle described three kinds of appeal speakers use in persuading their audience: *ethos,* which is basically a moral appeal; *logos,* which is the appeal to logic and reason; and *pathos*, which is an appeal to the emotions. In these terms, King has established an ethos, a view of himself as a writer/speaker of integrity, whose words carry a moral power because of his character. As he builds his *ethos,* linking himself with those who are perceived as moral leaders, he also gives searching analysis of the justice of his cause, he *reasons* on the nature of law, and on the duty of free citizens to judge specific laws according to a high ideal of justice. In this reasoning, King is invoking reasoning to establish the appeal of *logos.* Only after he has appealed to his readers by his moral power (ethos) and by his reasoning (logos), does King tell the personal examples of prejudice, like his daughter's painful questioning, which move readers' emotions (*pathos*).

Presenting yourself as a persuasive writer who can be trusted requires more than just finding areas of agreement on which discussion can begin. You must win trust by your *knowledge.* Having researched your topic, meditated on it, weighed differing views, you are ready to establish your *hypothesis*—a tentative *thesis* that can be changed as your understanding of your data changes. When you are confident of your knowledge, you can select details which are relevant to your topic and which support your thesis. Be careful to avoid bias in your selection of data, for the evidence you choose to present can be misleading. You have a moral responsibility to your material and to your readers, a responsibility that requires you to gather all the pertinent information within the limits of your time and your assignment, to interpret it fairly, to review important views on the topic, and to present your own view with reasonable support, concrete examples, and moderate language.

Fiction and Poetry

Fiction and poetry may employ the methods of development discussed above, but what sets them apart from exposition is the way they present direct images of reality. The expository writer talks *about* his topics; the writer of fiction, drama, or poetry gives his readers experiences which mirror life. John Updike tells a story of a young boy's search for reassurance that he will have the resurrected life promised by orthodox Christianity. Wilfred Owen tells of death, with vivid imagery that causes us to experience with our senses the horrors of modern war. Gerard Manley Hopkins relates his joy of serving his God. In each of these examples, the writer has not told his reader directly what attitudes to hold, but has given the reader a chance to share an experience from which attitudes, emotions, ideas, values, and questions can emerge.

Elements of Fiction

Plot

Writers of fiction have some fundamental concerns as they shape their stories. They may emphasize *plot,* a series of events which occur in time, with each event influencing or causing the following event. The plot's movement usually goes from a section of *exposition,* where background is revealed, to a *conflict* which builds to a *climax* and ends in a sense of *resolution.* The conflicts of stories vary greatly. Some stories tell of simple struggles—one man against another, or man against nature. Other stories develop more complex conflicts, the psychological struggle of a man against himself, or a man against his society.

Character

Character is another major concern of a writer shaping a story. He may develop his characters by telling directly about them, as a kind of commentary given by an omniscient author. He may provide many details about the character's physical appearance, revealing personality through such clues as dress and mannerisms. Other characters' comments can inform readers, as can a character's own thoughts—if the author chooses to reveal them. Probably the best guide to our evaluation of a character comes from his actions; what he *does* shapes our sense of what he *is.* Authors may create characters who are *dynamic,* changing in response to events that occur to them, or characters who are *static,* remaining unchanged throughout the plot. Characters may also be described as *round,* portraying many dimensions in their personalities, or as *flat,* one-dimensional personalities who respond in predictable ways to nearly all events.

Setting

Writers take great care in describing the *setting* of their stories—the particular place and time of the events. In their descriptions, they use sense imagery to bring alive the sights, sounds, smells, tastes, and textures of the setting. Flannery O'Connor, for example, in her story "Revelation," provides many physical details which allow her readers to imagine the doctor's office at the beginning of the tale, and the pig parlor at the ending. Thoughtful readers often find the setting of stories and poems to have thematic significance—as these from the O'Connor story do. When setting suggests meaning or significance beyond itself, it may be serving a symbolical function.

Narrative Point of View

Writers choose from a variety of *points of view* by which they relate their stories. They may be able to enter any character's mind and reveal background from the past or events of the future—such an all-knowing point of view is called the *omniscient author* narrative technique. The point of view may be limited to varying degrees. A *central consciousness* narration reveals events from the knowledge of one character, but the story is told in third person, referring to every character as "he" or "she." *First person* narration has one of the characters telling the story in his own voice, the "I" of the story having his distinct diction and attitudes.

Reading for Style

The narrative point of view chosen by an author will determine some important aspects of his *style*. Mark Twain uses his character Huck Finn to relate the adventures Huck and Jim have on their journey down the Mississippi River. Huck's voice, with its distinctive dialect and diction, vividly creates the world of the mid-nineteenth century rural South for Twain's readers. *Huckleberry Finn* has been praised for its authentic style, for Twain here captured the sound of spoken American English better than any previous author who experimented with dialect. By employing the rather naive, but observant and objective, consciousness of Huck, and by telling the story through Huck's words, Twain created effects of irony and humor that would have been difficult to achieve through other methods.

Diction

A reader analyzes *style* by paying close attention to words, sentences, and figures of speech. When you are reading any selection, be aware of the wording the author uses. What about the level of diction? Is it formal or informal? Do you think the vocabulary conforms to a certain time or place, to a particular class or society, to an ethnic group? Is the writer using the level of diction employed by journalists and academic writers, what is called Edited American English? Do the writer's characters have their own speech characteristics? Is jargon used for special effects, like humor or satire—as in the e. e. cummings' poem "next to of course god america i." Answering these questions will give you a good start toward understanding the writer's style.

Sentences

You should consider sentences next. Note how the writer varies the length and type of sentences, creating a rhythm in his prose or poetry. This flexible rhythm helps him shade his meanings, for he can imitate the very process of developing ideas by the way he shapes his phrases, by his *syntax* (word order), and by the patterns of *subordination* and *coordination* he uses.

Figures of Speech, Images, Symbols

Finally, look for the figures of speech and other literary devices the writer uses. Identify *images,* words which evoke sense impressions—these add concreteness to writing, giving colors, shapes, odors, textures, and sounds to your imagination. Do such images center around one dominant sense, such as sight? Or do they form patterns or motifs which suggest wider significance, thus serving as *symbols?*

Allusions

Henry David Thoreau uses many Biblical and classical *allusions* in *Walden*. These allusions help constitute his style even as they persuade his readers of his meanings. Thoreau also plays with the figurative langauge and paradoxes he finds in common American speech, making literal some of the forgotten ideas and metaphors stated in cliches, punning with words like *sleepers,* and bringing out unexpected meaning from etymologies of words. Thoreau achieves a style that is playful, making readers smile while they give serious consideration to the point he is making. His style thereby contributes to his success in fulfilling the traditional goals of literature, *delighting* and *instructing*.

Reading for Structure

Structure: Repetition

Readers analyze *structure* by finding the patterns formed in the text by *repetition* and *juxtaposition*. As you read you may notice certain words or phrases repeated in ways that suggest a building emotion or a developing significance. Martin Luther King uses repetition of phrases to intensify emotion, to increase that quality (pathos), in his oratory and writing. King employs this powerful structural device in the same way the writers of Biblical poetry do, for Hebrew verse is characterized by a rhythm created by repeated phrasing, called *parallelism*, rather than by rhyme. Notice the opening of Psalm 149, a clear example of the parallelism of Hebrew poetry:

> O sing unto the Lord a new song; let the congregation
> of saints praise him.
> Let Israel rejoice in him that made him, and let the
> children of Sion be joyful in their King.
> Let them praise his Name in the dance: let them sing
> praises unto him with tabret and harp.

Structure: Juxtaposition

Juxtaposition refers to the way words, phrases, or other elements of the writing, such as scenes, incidents, or characters, are placed together in the text. A writer may place ideas together, or combine words together, in surprising or paradoxical juxtapositions. Jesus often used such unusual combinations to shock his hearers into new ways of looking at things, provoking new insights into spiritual values they had misperceived: the "meek" are called the "inheritors of the earth," the outwardly pious are placed below the "tax collectors" and "sinners." Note how Flannery O'Connor draws on this kind of juxtaposition of spiritual values in her story "Revelation," in which Mrs. Turpin has a vision which reveals her own spiritual pride as she sees the kind of people she has judged to be inferior to herself preceding the "quality folk" in the procession into heaven.

Structure and Theme

O'Connor has also juxtaposed scenes in this story in such a way as to support her *theme,* the meaning that the reader reaches as the text is thoughtfully considered. O'Connor begins her story with the setting of a doctor's office, a place for healing. Significantly, Mrs. Turpin is not there to seek healing for herself, but for her husband, whom she dominates as she tends to dominate all her environment by her judgmental attitudes. The last scene of the story has a "pig parlor" as its setting. You may be reminded here of the story of the prodigal son, who was reduced to tending swine—animals considered by the Jews to be ritually unclean. In this humbled state he came to insight, knowing his depraved condition and longing for his father's house. O'Connor has Mrs. Turpin called a "wart hog from hell" in the doctor's office, the place for diagnosis and treatment. She tends her pampered pigs in the well-kept "parlor." Even if O'Connor is not directly alluding to the story of the prodigal son, she is using the general symbolic connotations associated with pigs to support her theme and to provide meaning for the settings she juxtaposes.

The Game of Poetry

A major reason unskilled readers make statements like "I can't read poetry. It doesn't make sense!" is that the forms they see do not meet their expectations. They look at a poem like e. e. cummings' "next to of course god america i" and see that it is not divided properly into sentences, it has no capital letters, and it doesn't sound "beautiful" or "poetic" when read aloud. So, they conclude, it makes no sense. Ironically, those parts of the poem which make it seem hardest to read are the ones which carry its meaning. The words to the poem are all jargon; the form *is* the meaning. What does saying patriotic-sounding phrases all in a rush, with no attention to meaning, show us about the speaker anyway? What do you think of his patriotism?

Form in Poetry

Anticipating the unexpected requires that you have some knowledge of the various forms or structures of poetry. When you know what makes the kind of poem we call a sonnet, fourteen lines of strictly rhyming and accented verse, you can recognize, and be pleased by, the variations made by poets like e. e. cummings and Gerard Manley Hopkins. However unusual "next to of course god america i" or "The Windhover" strike us as being, they are both sonnets.

In many ways, poetry is a game—a game played with words, with sounds, with sense images. Good poets, like cummings and Hopkins, play the game well and enjoy creating new strategies—just as any game player likes to surprise others, and himself perhaps, with daring new moves on the playing field. But the writers are not the only players in this game of poetry. When you read a poem you become a participant in the game, too. You become a skilled player as you practice, getting used to the "rules"—the conventions of the art—and having patience with yourself as you get used to the "action" of this game.

Robert Frost believed that the good poem brings surprises to both the writer and the reader. "No surprise for the writer, no surprise for the reader," he said in his brief essay "The Figure a Poem Makes." To him, the poem was not completely thought out before the poet put his pen to paper; instead, the poem was a process; composing brought insights and conclusions not known beforehand. The poem, Frost said, "finds its own name as it goes and discovers the best waiting for it in some final phrase at once wise and sad." Frost too enjoyed the game of poetry, and knew it—like love—to bring both pleasure and wisdom, the traditional ends of poetry recognized since the day of the Greeks and Romans:

> The figure a poem makes. It begins in delight and ends in wisdom. The figure is the same as for love. No one can really hold that the ecstasy should be static and stand still in one place. It begins in delight, in inclines to the impulse, it assumes direction with the first line laid down, it runs a course of lucky events, and ends in a clarification of life—not necessarily a great clarification . . . but in a momentary stay against confusion. ("The Figure a Poem Makes")

Even if poetry is considered a kind of game, it remains an unfamiliar and difficult game to many modern students. Skilled poets throw unusual images and diction at their readers, challenging their ability to read with a highly condensed, metaphoric wording that too often seems to end not in Frost's "clarification," but in confusion. English teachers seem to have a mysterious interpretive key to these poetic puzzles, but students feel defeated by them and doubt that the struggle to read them is really worthwhile. Part of the problem may come with the technical jargon teachers use when talking about poetry. Like any profession, from computer programming to electrical engineering, literary criticism has its own vocabulary. Phrases like "iambic pentameter" or "feminine rhyme" may provide shortcuts to communication for those who know this language, but, like all technical jargon, this vocabulary excludes those who are unfamiliar with it. As a student reader you will want to learn some of the basic terminology which will help you analyze and explain the processes you observe in your reading.

Other frustrations in reading difficult texts may lead students to decide that literary meaning is simply subjective—it can mean anything one wants it to. Nothing is more frustrating than a game whose rules keep changing or are unclear, but many students read poetry with that kind of uncertainty. Instead of thinking of the meaning of poetry, and other literature, as being either objective or subjective, think of it as being contextual: every writer has his own physical, intellectual, and spiritual world. He shares the experiences and the knowledge of his own time; he is acquainted with the popular authors and arts of his day; he is educated in a certain way, worships in a certain way, and shares values, customs, beliefs, and conventions with his contemporaries. All these factors, plus his personal experiences, comprise his context of meaning. Similarly, readers come to a literary text with their own contexts—the meanings they share with others, what we can call the communal meanings, and those that are more private and individual. The words of a text must bridge the contextual meanings of the author and those of the reader. When these contexts are separated, as they often are, by many years, or by cultures, readers must work hard to recapture the intended meanings of the authors they are reading. For example, the title of the Wilfred Owen poem, "Dulce et Decorum Est," was familiar enough for his audience that he felt no need to translate it. The "interpretive community" Owen was a part of, educated Englishmen of the first decades of the twentieth century, knew precisely what he meant, and his bitter sarcasm was direct and powerful. Contemporary American students need to have the Latin motto translated, and perhaps explained, before they can properly read the poem. They must, that is, enter the context of meanings Owen possessed in order to understand his text.

As you read the selections in these units, learn what you can about the authors' personal experiences and about their historical contexts. Think of whom Martin Luther King, Jr., would consider his moral and spiritual authorities as he speaks to modern American from the jail cell in Birmingham; think of the relationship between England and Ireland during the time of Jonathan Swift. In the discipline of enlarging your context to take in that of the authors you are reading, you are actively educating yourself.

PART I

The Search for God

Introduction

To many who are outside the Christian faith, Christianity is just one more religion, one more attempt to search for God among many attempts made by the religions of the world. Yet the Christian would argue that Christianity is based on a personal relationship with Christ, rather than a mere set of beliefs or religious dogmas. Still, even with our claim to uniqueness among other religions, the fact remains that even the Christian's "search for God" is often tainted with inaccuracy and misrepresentation.

Part of this inaccuracy results from the secularization of Western thinking. Aleksandr Solzhenitsyn, the Nobel Prize winner and Russian dissident, warns us against "the destructive spirit of secularism," which has inundated modern society and threatens to destroy faith from within. In a secularized society such as ours, it is difficult to identify authentic Christianity. In their poetry, Emily Dickinson and Matthew Arnold lament the loss of faith, cautioning us that the "abdication of belief" makes the world a place that "hath really neither joy, nor love, nor light."

In Part I we see the religious world fosters its own inaccuracies regarding Christianity. Several writers vocalize criticism of "modern" religious thought which is often characterized by self-centeredness, mental laziness, and external behavior. The writers confront ignorance of scriptural principles, ignorance which damages the Christian faith and destroys the credibility of Christianity to an unbelieving world. Another weakness in the religious community is its emphasis on a type of cultural religion that often excludes a personal encounter with God. In this selection's two short stories, both Mrs. Turpin and David have inherited cultural ideas about God; however, a moment of epiphany for each changes the impersonality of their cultural religion into their own transforming spiritual experience.

The concluding selections provide definitive direction for the authentic Christian who is living in a post-Christian world. Whereas modern thinking demands entertainment in its expression of art, and scientific proof in its study of theology, the Christian alternative demands a relentless search for truth that employs both.

C. S. Lewis tells us that our search for God is much like our search for an unknown destination. If we rely on a map, we are much more likely to arrive at our true destination than if we rely on heresay or hunches. Finding spiritual authenticity *is* possible when we recognize the truth that really sets us free.

Spiritual Authenticity in a Secularized World

THE TEMPLETON ADDRESS:
Men Have Forgotten God

Aleksandr Solzhenitsyn

More than half a century ago, while I was still a child, I recall hearing a number of older people offer the following explanation for the great disasters that had befallen Russia: "Men have forgotten God; that's why all this has happened."

Since then I have spent well-nigh fifty years working on the history of our Revolution; in the process I have read hundreds of books, collected hundreds of personal testimonies, and have already contributed eight volumes of my own toward the effort of clearing away the rubble left by that upheaval. But if I were asked today to formulate as concisely as possible the main cause of the ruinous Revolution that swallowed up some sixty million of our people, I could not put it more accurately than to repeat: "Men have forgotten God; that's why all this has happened."

What is more, the events of the Russian Revolution can only be understood now, at the end of the century, against the background of what has since occurred in the rest of the world. What emerges here is a process of universal significance. And if I were called upon to identify briefly the principal trait of the *entire* twentieth century, here too I would be unable to find anything more precise and pithy than to repeat once again: "Men have forgotten God." The failings of human consciousness, deprived of its divine dimension, have been a determining factor in all the major crimes of this century. The first of these was World War I, and much of our present predicament can be traced back to it. That war (the memory of which seems to be fading) took place when Europe, bursting with health and abundance, fell into a rage of self-mutilation that could not but sap its strength for a century or more, and perhaps forever. The only possible explanation for this war is a mental eclipse among the leaders of Europe due to their lost awareness of a Supreme Power above them. Only a godless embitterment could have moved ostensibly Christian states to employ poison gas, a weapon so obviously beyond the limits of humanity.

The same kind of defect, the flaw of a consciousness lacking all divine dimension, was manifested after World War II when the West yielded to the satanic temptation of the nuclear umbrella. It was equivalent to saying: "Let's cast off our worries, let's free the younger genera-

21

tion from its duties and obligations, let's make no effort to defend ourselves, to say nothing of defending others—let's stop our ears to the groans emanating from the East, and let us live instead in the pursuit of happiness. If danger should threaten us, we shall be protected by the nuclear bomb; if not, then let the world be burned in Hell for all we care. The pitifully helpless state to which the contemporary West has sunk is in large measure due to this fatal error: the belief that the defense of peace depends not on stout hearts and steadfast men, but solely on the nuclear bomb.

Only the loss of that higher intuition which comes from God could have allowed the West to accept calmly, after World War I, the protracted agony of Russia as she was being torn apart by a band of cannibals, or to accept, after World War II, the similar dismemberment of Eastern Europe. The West did not perceive that this was in fact the beginning of a lengthy process that spells disaster for the whole world; indeed the West has done a good deal to help the process along. Only once in this century did the West gather its strength—for the battle against Hitler. But the fruits of that victory have long since been lost. Faced with cannibalism, our godless age has discovered the perfect anaesthetic—trade! Such is the pathetic pinnacle of contemporary wisdom.

Today's world has reached a stage that, if it has been described to preceding centuries, would have called forth the cry: "This is the Apocalypse!"

Yet we have grown used to this kind of world; we even feel at home in it.

Dostoevsky warned that "great events could come upon us and catch us intellectually unprepared." That is precisely what has happened. And he predicted that "the world will be saved only after a visitation by the demon of evil." Whether it really will be saved we shall have to wait and see; this will depend on our conscience, on our spiritual lucidity, on our individual and combined efforts in the face of catastrophic circumstances. But it has already come to pass that the demon of evil, like a whirlwind, triumphantly circles all five continents of the earth.

We are witness to the devastation of the world, be it imposed or voluntarily undergone. The entire twentieth century is being sucked into the vortex of atheism and self-destruction. This plunge into the abyss has aspects that are unquestionably global, dependent neither on political systems, nor on levels of economic and cultural development, nor yet on national peculiarities. And present-day Europe, seemingly so unlike the Russia of 1913, is today on the verge of the same collapse, for all that it has been reached by a different route. Different parts of the world have followed different paths, but today they are all approaching the threshold of a common ruin.

In its past, Russia did know a time when the social ideal was not fame, or riches, or material success, but a pious way of life. Russia was then steeped in an Orthodox Christianity that remained true to the Church of the first centuries. The Orthodoxy of that time knew how to safeguard its people under the yoke of a foreign occupation that lasted more than two centuries, while at the same time fending off iniquitous blows from the swords of Western crusaders. During those centuries the Orthodox faith in our country became part of the very patterns of thought and the personality of our people, the forms of daily life, the work calendar, the priorities in every undertaking, the organization of the week and of the year. Faith was the shaping and unifying force of the nation.

But in the seventeenth century Russian Orthodoxy was gravely weakened by an internal schism. In the eighteenth, the country was shaken by Peter's forcibly imposed transformations, which favored the economy, the state, and the military at the expense of the religious spirit and national life. And along with this lopsided Petrine enlightenment, Russia felt the first whiff of secularism; its subtle poisons permeated the educated classes in the course of the nineteenth century and opened the path to Marxism. By the time of the Revolution, faith had virtually disappeared in Russian educated circles; among the uneducated, too, faith had declined.

It was Dostoevsky, once again, who drew from the French Revolution and its seething hatred of the Church the lesson that "revolution must necessarily begin with atheism." That is absolutely true. But the world had never before known a godlessness as organized, militarized, and tenaciously malevolent as that practiced by Marxism. Within the philosophical system of Marx and Lenin, and at the heart of their psychology, hatred of God is the principal driving force, more fundamental than all their political and economic pretensions. Militant atheism is not merely incidental or marginal to Communist policy; it is not a side effect, but the central pivot. To achieve its diabolical ends, Communism needs to control a population devoid of religious and national feeling, and this entails the destruction of faith and nationhood. Communists proclaim both of these objectives openly, and just as openly go about carrying them out. The degree to which the atheistic world longs to annihilate religion, the extent to which religion sticks in its throat, was demonstrated by the web of intrigue surrounding the recent attempts on the life of the Pope.

The 1920s in the USSR witnessed an uninterrupted procession of victims and martyrs among the Orthodox clergy. Two metropolitans were shot, one of whom, Veniamin of Petrograd, had been elected by the popular vote of his diocese. Patriarch Tikhon himself passed through the hands of the Cheka-GPU and then died under suspicious circumstances. Scores of archbishops and bishops perished. Tens of thousands of priests, monks, and nuns, pressured by the Chekists to renounce the word of God, were tortured, shot in cellars, sent to camps, exiled to the desolate tundra of the far north, or turned out into the streets in their old age without food or shelter. All these Christian martyrs went unswervingly to their deaths for the faith; instances of apostasy were few and far between.

For tens of millions of laymen access to the Church was blocked, and they were forbidden to bring up their children in the faith; religious parents were wrenched from their children and thrown into prison, while the children were turned from the faith by threats and lies. One could argue that the pointless destruction of Russia's rural economy in the 1930s—the so-called dekulakization and collectivization, which brought death to 15 million peasants while making no economic sense at all—was enforced with such cruelty, first and foremost, for the purpose of destroying our national way of life and of extirpating religion from the countryside. The same policy of spiritual perversion operated throughout the brutal world of the Gulag Archipelago, where men were encouraged to survive at the cost of the lives of others. And only atheists bereft of reason could have decided upon the ultimate brutality—against the Russian land itself—that is being planned in the USSR today: The Russian north is to be flooded, the flow of the northern rivers reversed, the life of the Arctic Ocean disrupted, and the water channeled southward, toward lands already devastated by earlier, equally foolhardy "feats of Communist construction."

For a short period of time, when he needed to gather strength for the struggle against Hitler, Stalin cynically adopted a friendly posture toward the Church. This deceptive game, continued in later years by Brezhnev with the help of showcase publications and other window dressing, has unfortunately tended to be taken at face value in the West. Yet the tenacity with which hatred of religion is rooted in Communism may be judged by the example of its most liberal leader, Khrushchev: for though he undertook a number of significant steps to extend freedom, Khrushchev simultaneously rekindled the frenzied Leninist obsession with destroying religion.

But there is something they did not expect: that in a land where churches have been leveled, where a triumphant atheism has rampaged uncontrolled for two-thirds of a century, where the clergy is utterly humiliated and deprived of all independence, where what remains of the Church as an institution is tolerated only for the sake of propaganda directed at the West, where even today people are sent to labor camps for their faith and where, within the camps themselves, those who gather to pray at Easter are clapped in punishment cells—they could not suppose that beneath this Communist steamroller the Christian tradition would survive in Russia. It is true that millions of our countrymen have been corrupted and spiritually devastated by an officially imposed atheism, yet there remain many millions of believers; it is only external pressures that keep them from speaking out, but, as is always the case in times of persecution and suffering, the awareness of God in my country has attained great acuteness and profundity.

It is here that we see the dawn of hope: for no matter how formidably Communism bristles with tanks and rockets, no matter what successes it attains in seizing the planet, it is doomed never to vanquish Christianity.

The West has yet to experience a Communist invasion; religion here remains free. But the West's own historical evolution has been such that today it too is experiencing a drying up of religious consciousness. It too has witnessed racking schisms, bloody religious wars, and rancor, to say nothing of the tide of secularism that, from the late Middle Ages onward, has progressively inundated the West. This gradual sapping of strength from within is a threat to faith that is perhaps even more dangerous than any attempt to assault religion violently from without.

Imperceptibly, through decades of gradual erosion, the meaning of life in the West has ceased to be seen as anything more lofty than the "pursuit of happiness," a goal that has even been solemnly guaranteed by constitutions. The concepts of good and evil have been ridiculed for several centuries; banished from common use, they have been replaced by political or class considerations of short-lived value. It has become embarrassing to appeal to eternal concepts, embarrassing to state that evil makes its home in the individual human heart before it enters a political system. Yet is it not considered shameful to make daily concessions to an integral evil. Judging by the continuing landslide of concessions made before the eyes of our own generation alone, the West is ineluctably slipping toward the abyss. Western societies are losing more and more of their religious essence. If a blasphemous film about Jesus is shown throughout the United States, reputedly one of the most religious countries in the world, or a major newspaper publishes a shameless caricature of the Virgin Mary, what further evidence of godlessness does one need? When external rights are completely unrestricted, why should one make an inner effort to restrain oneself from ignoble acts?

Or why should one refrain from burning hatred, whatever its basis—race, class, or ideology? Such hatred is in fact corroding many hearts today. Atheist teachers in the West are bringing up a younger generation in a spirit of hatred of their own society. Amid all the vituperation we forget that the defects of capitalism represent the basic flaws of human nature, allowed unlimited freedom together with the various human rights; we forget that under Communism (and Communism is breathing down the neck of all moderate forms of socialism, which are unstable) the identical flaws run riot in any person with the least degree of authority; while everyone else under that system does indeed attain "equality"—the equality of destitute slaves.

This eager fanning of the flames of hatred is becoming the mark of today's free world. Indeed, the broader the personal freedoms are, the higher the level of prosperity or even of abundance—the more vehement, paradoxically, does this blind hatred become. The contemporary developed West thus demonstrates by its own example that human salvation can be found neither in the profusion of material goods nor in merely making money.

This deliberately nurtured hatred then spreads to all that is alive, to life itself, to the world with its colors, sounds, and shapes, to the human body. The embittered art of the twentieth century is perishing as a result of this ugly hate, for art is fruitless without love. In the East art has collapsed because it has been knocked down and trampled upon, but in the West the fall has been voluntary, a decline into a contrived and pretentious quest where the artist, instead of attempting to reveal the divine plan, tries to put himself in the place of God.

Here again we witness the single outcome of a worldwide process, with East and West yielding the same results, and once again for the same reason: Men have forgotten God.

Confronted by the onslaught of worldwide atheism, believers are disunited and frequently bewildered. And yet the Christian (or post-Christian) world would do well to note the example of the Far East. I have recently had an opportunity to observe in Free China and in Japan how, despite their apparently less clearly defined religious concepts, and despite the same unassailable "freedom of choice" that exists in the West, both the younger generation and society as a whole have preserved their moral sensibility to a greater degree than the West; has, and have been less affected by the destructive spirit of secularism.

What can one say about the lack of unity among the various religions, if Christianity has itself become so fragmented? In recent years the major Christian churches have taken steps toward reconciliation. But these measures are far too slow; the world is perishing a hundred times more quickly. No one expects the churches to merge or to revise all their doctrines, but only to present a common front against atheism. Yet even for such a purpose the steps taken are much too slow.

There does exist an organized movement for the unification of the churches, but it presents an odd picture. The World Council of Churches seems to care more for the success of revolutionary movements in the Third World, all the while remaining blind and deaf to the persecution of religion where this is carried through most consistently—in the USSR. No one can fail to see the facts; must one conclude, then, that it is deemed expedient not to see, not to get involved? But if that is the case, what remains of Christianity?

It is with profound regret that I must note here something which I cannot pass over in silence. My predecessor in the receipt of this prize last year—in the very month that the award was made—lent public support to Communist lies by his deplorable statement that he had not noticed the persecution of religion in the USSR. Before the multitude of those who have perished and who are oppressed today, may God be his judge.

It seems more and more apparent that even with the most sophisticated of political maneuvers, the noose around the neck of mankind draws tighter and more hopeless with every passing decade, and there seems to be no way out for anyone—neither nuclear, nor political, nor economic, nor ecological. That is indeed the way things appear to be.

With such global events looming over us like mountains, nay, like entire mountain ranges, it may seem incongruous and inappropriate to recall that the primary key to our being or non-being resides in each individual human heart, in the heart's preference for specific good or evil. Yet this remains true even today, and it is, in fact, the most reliable key we have. The social theories that promised so much have demonstrated their bankruptcy, leaving us at a dead end. The free people of the West could reasonably have been expected to realize that they are beset by numerous freely nurtured falsehoods, and not to allow lies to be foisted upon them so easily.

All attempts to find a way out of the plight of today's world are fruitless unless we redirect our consciousness, in repentance, to the Creator of all: without this, no exit will be illumined, and we shall seek it in vain. The resources we have set aside for ourselves are too impoverished for the task. We must first recognize the horror perpetrated not by some outside force, not by class or national enemies, but within each of us individually, and within every society. This is especially true of a free and highly developed society, for here in particular we have surely brought everything upon ourselves, of our own free will. We ourselves, in our daily unthinking selfishness, are pulling tight that noose.

Let us ask ourselves: Are not the ideals of our century false? And is not our glib and fashionable terminology just as unsound, a terminology that offers superficial remedies for every difficulty? Each of them, in whatever sphere, must be subjected to a clear-eyed scrutiny while there is still time. The solution of the crisis will not be found along the well-trodden paths of conventional thinking.

Our life consists not in the pursuit of material success but in the quest for worthy spiritual growth. Our entire earthly existence is but a transitional stage in the movement toward something higher, one rung of the ladder: Material laws alone do not explain our life or give it direction. The laws of physics and physiology will never reveal the indisputable manner in which the Creator constantly, day in and day out, participates in the life of each of us, unfailingly granting us the energy of existence; when this assistance leaves us, we die. And in the life of our entire planet the Divine Spirit surely moves with no less force: this we must grasp in our dark and terrible hour.

To the ill-considered hopes of the last two centuries, which have reduced us to insignificance and brought us to the brink of nuclear and non-nuclear death, we can propose only a determined quest for the warm hand of God, which we have so rashly and self-confidently spurned. Only in this way can our eyes be opened to the errors of this unfortunate twentieth century and our hands be directed to setting them right. There is nothing else to cling to in the landslide: the combined vision of all the thinkers of the Enlightenment amount to nothing.

Our five continents are caught in a whirlwind. But it is during trials such as these that the highest gifts of the human spirit are manifested. If we perish and lose this world, the fault will be ours alone.

Christian Perspectives

1. Solzhenitsyn's historical evidence supports his premise that men have forgotten God. Although he spends a great deal of time identifying the global effects of forgetting God, Solzhenitsyn holds the individual ultimately responsible. What must each person do to reverse the direction our society is going?
2. Solzhenitsyn quotes Dostoevsky's warning that "great events could come upon us and catch us intellectually unprepared." Identify such an event. What is the event? Do you think we are intellectually unprepared?"
3. Trace Solzhenitsyn's use of love as a creative force and hatred as a diabolical force in the essay. What are the specific products of love? of hatred?
4. Identify the danger signs of our own society that parallel those of other societies that have forgotten God.

5. Solzhenitsyn uses the causes and effects of history to develop his argument. See how many examples of cause and effect you can find.

The search for meaning in life does not lead every person to God. Many find the world dissatisfying and become cynical rather than turning to the true source for meaning. The following poems illustrate our inability to find meaning by ourselves.

GOD FORGOTTEN

Thomas Hardy

I towered far, and lo! I stood within
The presence of the Lord Most High,
Sent thither by the sons of Earth, to win
Some answer to their cry.

'The Earth, sayest thou? The Human race?
By Me created? Sad is lot?
Nay: I have no remembrance of such place:
Such world I fashioned not.'—

'O Lord, forgive me when I say
Thou spakest the word that made it all.'—
The Earth of men—let me bethink me. . . . Yea!
I dimly do recall

'Some tiny sphere I built long back
(Mid millions of such shapes of mine)
So named. . . . It perished, surely—not a wrack
Remaining, or a sign?

'It lost my interest from the first,
My aims therefor succeeding ill;
Haply it died of doing as it durst?'—
'Lord, it existeth still.'—

'Dark, then, its life! For not a cry
Of aught it bears do I now hear;
Of its own act the threads were snapt whereby
Its plaints[1] had reached mine ear.

It used to ask for gifts of good,
Till came its severance, self-entailed,
When sudden silence on that side ensued,
And has till now prevailed.

---

1. plaints— complaints, lamentations

'All other orbs have kept in touch;
Their voicings reach me speedily:
Thy people took upon them overmuch
In sundering them from me!

'And it is strange — though sad enough —
Earth's race should think that one whose call
Frames, daily, shining spheres of flawless stuff
Must heed their tainted ball! . . .

'But sayest it is by pangs distraught,
And strife, and silent suffering? —
Sore grieved am I that injury should be wrought
Even on so poor a thing!

'Thou shouldst have learnt that "Not to Mend"
For me could mean but "Not to Know":
Hence, Messengers! and straightway put an end
To what men undergo.'. . .

Homing at dawn, I thought to see
One of the Messengers standing by.
— Oh, childish thought! . . . Yet often it comes to me
When trouble hovers nigh.

Christian Perspective

1. The conversation between the persona and God reveals the reasons why God has "forgotten" the world. What are the reasons? Are they valid reasons?
2. This poem presents a disturbing view about God. What would you say in response to this view?

THOSE — DYING THEN

Emily Dickinson

Those — dying, then
Knew where they went
They went to God's Right Hand —
The Hand is amputated now
And God cannot be found —

The abdication of Belief
Makes the Behavior small—
Better an ignis fatuus[1]
Than no illume[2] at all—

Christian Perspective

Dickinson's statement, "The hand is amputated now" refers to God's inability to reach man. Dickinson uses irony to suggest that God exercises his influence through man's choice. What scripture parallels with Dickinson's view?

OZYMANDIAS

Percy Shelley

I met a traveler from an antique land
Who said: Two vast and trunkless legs of stone
Stand in the desert. Near them, on the sand,
Half sunk, a shattered visage[3] lies, whose frown,
And wrinkled lip, and sneer of cold command,
Tell that its sculptor well those passions read
Which yet survive, stamped on these lifeless things,
The hand that mocked them and the heart that fed:
And on the pedestal these words appear:
"My name is Ozymandias, king of kings:
Look on my works, ye Mighty, and despair!"
Nothing beside remains. Round the decay
Of that colossal wreck, boundless and bare
The lone and level sands stretch far away.

Christian Perspective

1. This poem also uses irony to warn about men like Ozymandias. What is the message?
2. The message in this poem is similar to Jesus' parable of the rich man who tore down his barns to build larger ones. (See Luke 12:16–20.) What happened to both of them?
3. Write a brief paragraph using this poem and the verse "Pride goeth before a fall."

---

1. ignis fatuus—a "will-o'-the-whisp," a phosphorescent light that appears over swampy ground
2. illume—light
3. visage—the face or appearance

DOVER BEACH

Matthew Arnold

The sea is calm tonight.
The tide is full, the moon lies fair
Upon the straits, on the French coast the light
Gleams and is gone; the cliffs of England stand,
Glimmering and vast, out in the tranquil bay.
Come to the window, sweet is the night air!
Only, from the long line of spray
Where the sea meets the moon-blanched land,
Listen! you hear the grating roar
Of pebbles which the waves draw back, and fling,
At their return, up the high stand,
Begin, and cease, and then again begin,
With tremulous cadence slow, and bring
The eternal note of sadness in.

Sophocles long ago
Heard it on the Aegean, and it brought
Into his mind the turbid ebb and flow
Of human misery; we
Find also in the sound a thought,
Hearing it by this distant northern sea.

The Sea of Faith
Was once, too, at the full, and round earth's shore
Lay like the folds of a bright girdle furled.[1]
But now I only hear
Its melancholy, long, withdrawing roar,
Retreating, to the breath
Of the night wind, down the vast edges drear
And naked shingles[2] of the world.

Ah, love let us be true
To one another! for the world, which seems
To lie before us like a land of dreams,
So various, so beautiful, so new,
Hath really neither joy, nor love, nor light,
No certitude, nor peace, nor help for pain;
And we are here as on a darkling plain
Swept with confused alarms of struggle and flight,
Where ignorant armies class by night.

1. furled — at high tide the sea covers the beach
2. shingles — pebbled beach

Christian Perspective

1. The melancholy tone of this poem shows the poet's despair over the unending struggles of life. What does he want to do?
2. The poet refers to the sea of faith that was once "at the full, and round earth's shore." What does he see has happened to faith?
3. What does the last line imply about society? Do you agree with this view?
4. For added insight, you might want to read about Matthew Arnold's life and his quarrel with faith. Obviously the tone reveals his ambivalence, but further study might tell you why.

Spiritual Authenticity in the Religious World

RELIGIOSITY AND RELIGION
Will Herberg

Religion is taken very seriously in present-day America, in a way that would have amazed and chagrined the "advanced" thinkers of half a century ago, who were so sure that the ancient superstition was bound to disappear very shortly in the face of the steady advance of science and reason. Religion has not disappeared; it is probably more pervasive today, and in many ways more influential, than it has been for generations. The only question is: What kind of religion is it? What is its content? What is it that Americans believe in when they are religious?

"The 'unknown God' of Americans seems to be faith itself." What Americans believe in when they are religious is . . . religion itself. Of course, religious Americans speak of God and Christ, but what they seem to regard as really redemptive is primarily religion, the "positive" attitude of believing. It is this faith in faith, this religion that makes religion its own object, that is the outstanding characteristic of contemporary American religiosity. Daniel Poling's formula: "I began saying in the morning two words, 'I believe' — those two words with nothing added . . ." may be taken as the classic expression of this aspect of American faith.

On the social level, this faith in religion involves the conviction, quite universal among Americans today, that every decent and virtuous nation is religious, that religion is the true basis of natural existence and therefore presumably the one sure resource for the solution of all national problems. On the level of personal life, the American faith in religion implies not only that every right-minded citizen is religious, but also that religion (or faith) is a most efficacious device for getting what one wants in life. "Jesus," the Rev. Irving E. Howard assures us, "recommended faith as a way to heal the body and to remove any of the practical problems that loom up as mountains in a man's path."

As one surveys the contemporary scene, it appears that the "results" Americans want to get out of faith are primarily "peace of mind," happiness, and success in worldly achievement. Religion is valued too as a means of cultural enrichment.

Prosperity, success, and advancement in business are the obvious ends for which religion, or rather the religious attitude of "believing," is held to be useful. There is ordinarily no criticism of the ends themselves in terms of the ultimate loyalties of a God-centered faith, nor is there much concern about what the religion or the faith is all about, since it is not the content of the belief but the attitude of believing that is felt to be operative.

Almost as much as worldly success, religion is expected to produce a kind of spiritual euphoria, the comfortable feeling that one is all right with God. Roy Eckardt calls this the cult of "divine-human chumminess" in which God is envisioned as the "Man Upstairs," a "Friendly Neighbor," who is always ready to give you the pat on the back you need when you happen to feel blue. "Fellowship with the Lord is, so to say, an extra emotional jag that keeps [us] happy. The 'gospel' makes [us] 'feel real good.'" Again, all sense of the ambiguity and precariousness of human life, all sense of awe before the divine majesty, all sense of judgment before the divine holiness, is shut out; God is, in Jane Russell's inimitable phrase, a "Livin' Doll." What relation has this kind of god to the biblical God Who confronts sinful man as an enemy before He comes out to meet repentant man as a Saviour? Is this He of Whom we are told, "It is a fearful thing to fall into the hands of the living God" (Heb. 10:31)? The message of how far contemporary American religiosity falls short of the authentic tradition of Jewish-Christian faith is to be found in the chasm that separates Jane Russell's "livin' Doll" from the living God of Scriptures.

The cultural enrichment that is looked for in religion varies greatly with the community, the denomination, and the outlook and status of the church members. Liturgy is valued as aesthetically and emotionally "rewarding," sermons are praised as "interesting" and "enjoyable," discussions of the world relations of the church are welcomed as "educational," even theology is approved of as "thought provoking." On another level, the "old-time religion" is cherished by certain segments of the population because it so obviously enriches their cultural life.

But, in the last analysis, it is "peace of mind" that most Americans expect of religion. "Peace of mind" is today easily the most popular gospel that goes under the name of religion; in one way or another it invades and permeates all other forms of contemporary religiosity. It works in well with the drift toward other-direction characteristic of large sections of American society, since both see in adjustment the supreme good in life. What is desired, and what is promised, is the conquest of insecurity and anxiety, the overcoming of inner conflict, the shedding of guilt and fear, the translation of the self to the painless paradise of "normality" and "adjustment"! Religion, in short, is a spiritual anodyne designed to allay the pains and vexations of existence.

It is this most popular phase of contemporary American religiosity that has aroused the sharpest criticism in more sophisticated theological circles. The Most Rev. Patrick A. O'Boyle, Catholic archbishop of Washington, has warned that although "at first glance piety seems to be everywhere . . ." many persons appear to be "turning to religion as they would to a benign sedative to soothe their minds and settle their nerves." Liston Pope emphasizes that the approach of the "peace of mind" school is not only "very dubious on psychological ground," but its "identification [with] the Christian religion . . . is of questionable validity." Roy Eckardt describes it as "religious narcissism," in which "the individual and his psycho-spiritual state occupy the center of the religious stage" and piety is made to "concentrate on its own navel." I have myself spoken of it as a philosophy that would "dehumanize man and reduce his life to the level of subhuman creation which knows neither sin nor guilt." It encourages moral insensitivity and social irresponsibility, and cultivates an almost lascivious preoccupation with self. The church becomes a kind of emotional service to relieve us of our worries: "Go to church—you'll feel better," "Bring your troubles to church and leave them there" (slogans on subway posters urging church attendance). On every ground, this type of religion is poles apart from authentic Jewish-

Christian spirituality which, while it knows of the "peace that passeth understanding" as the gift of God, promotes a "divine discontent" with things as they are and a "passionate thirst for the future," in which all things will be renewed and restored to their right relation to God.

The burden of this criticism of American religion from the point of view of Jewish-Christian faith is that contemporary religion is so naively, so innocently man-centered. Not God, but man—man in his individual and corporate being—is the beginning and end of the spiritual system of much of present-day American religiosity. In this kind of religion there is no sense of transcendence, no sense of the nothingness of man and his works before a holy God; in this kind of religion the values of life, and life itself, are not submitted to Almighty God to judge, to shatter, and to reconstruct; on the contrary, life, and the values of life, are given an ultimate sanction by being identified with the divine. In this kind of religion it is not man who serves God, but God who is mobilized and made to serve man and his purposes—whether these purposes be economic prosperity, free enterprise, social reform, democracy, happiness, security, or "peace of mind." God is conceived as man's "omnipotent servant," faith as a sure-fire device to get what we want. The American is a religious man, and in many cases personally humble and conscientious. But religion as he understands it is not something that makes humility or the easy conscience: it is something that reassures him about the essential rightness of everything American, his nation, his culture, and himself; something that validates his goals and his ideals instead of calling them into question; something that enhances his self-regard instead of challenging it; something that feeds his self-sufficiency instead of shattering it; something that offers him salvation on easy terms instead of demanding repentance and a "broken heart." Because it does all these things, his religion, however sincere and well-meant, is ultimately vitiated by a strong and pervasive idolatrous element.

Christian Perspectives

1. In II Timothy 4:3,4, Paul talks about religion that "tickles our ears." What does he mean? How does this Scripture verse relate to Herberg's essay?
2. Herberg believes that the typical American's "chumminess" with God is inconsistent with the scriptural description of the personality of God (Hebrews 10:31); yet Jesus calls us his friends. Do you agree or disagree with Herberg? Explain your answer.
3. Jesus tells us that He has come to give us an abundant life (John 10:10). In fact, it is from this statement that we base many of our beliefs about "economic prosperity, free enterprise, social reform, democracy, happiness, security, or 'peace of mind.'" Do we, as Christians, have a right to expect these things? If not, what did Jesus mean when He talked about the abundant life?
4. Christians are the salt of the earth and a light to the world (Matthew 5:13,14). We have the responsibility to demonstrate the true gospel to the unbelieving world, rather than to offend the world with our self-centeredness. What would you say to Herberg in defense of modern Christianity?

REVELATION

Flannery O'Conner

The doctor's waiting room, which was very small, was almost full when the Turpins entered. Mrs. Turpin, who was very large, made it look even smaller by her presence. She stood looming at the head of the magazine table set in the center of it, a living demonstration that the room was inadequate and ridiculous. Her little bright black eyes took in all the patients as she sized up the seating situation. There was one vacant chair and a place on the sofa occupied by a blond child in a dirty blue romper who should have been told to move over and make room for the lady. He was five or six, but Mrs. Turpin saw at once that no one was going to tell him to move over. He was slumped down in the seat, his arms idle at his sides and his eyes idle in his head; his nose ran unchecked.

Mrs. Turpin put a firm hand on Claud's shoulder and said in a voice that included anyone who wanted to listen, "Claud, you sit in that chair there," and gave him a push down into the vacant one. Claud was florid and bald and sturdy, somewhat shorter than Mrs. Turpin, but he sat down as if he were accustomed to doing what she told him to.

Mrs. Turpin remained standing. The only man in the room besides Claud was a lean stringy old fellow with a rusty hand spread out on each knee, whose eyes were closed as if he were asleep or dead or pretending to be so as not to get up and offer her his seat. Her gaze settled agreeably on a well-dressed grey-haired lady whose eyes met hers and whose expression said: If that child belonged to me, he would have some manners and move over—there's plenty of room there for you and him too.

Claud looked up with a sigh and made as if to rise.

"Sit down," Mrs. Turpin said. "You know you're not supposed to stand on that leg. He has an ulcer on his leg," she explained.

Claud lifted his foot onto the magazine table and rolled his trouser leg up to reveal a purple swelling on a plump marble-white calf.

"My!" the pleasant lady said. "How did you do that?"

"A cow kicked him," Mrs. Turpin said.

"Goodness!" said the lady.

Claud rolled his trouser leg down.

"Maybe the little boy would move over," the lady suggested, but the child did not stir.

"Somebody will be leaving in a minute," Mrs. Turpin said. She could not understand why a doctor—with as much money as they made charging five dollars a day to just stick their head in the hospital door and look at you—couldn't afford a decent-sized waiting room. This one was hardly bigger than a garage. The table was cluttered with limp-looking magazines and at one end of it there was a big green glass ash tray full of cigarette butts and cotton wads with little blood spots on them. If she had had anything to do with the running of the place, that would have been emptied every so often. There were no chairs against the wall at the head of the room. It had a rectangular-shaped panel in it that permitted a view of the office where the nurse came and went and the secretary listened to the radio. A plastic fern in a gold pot sat in the opening and trailed its fronds down almost to the floor. The radio was softly playing gospel music.

Just then the inner door opened and a nurse with the highest stack of yellow hair Mrs. Turpin had ever seen put her face in the crack and called for the next patient. The woman sitting beside Claud grasped the two arms of her chair and hoisted herself up; she pulled her dress free from her legs and lumbered through the door where the nurse had disappeared.

Mrs. Turpin eased into the vacant chair, which held her tight as a corset. "I wish I could reduce," she said, and rolled her eyes and gave a comic sigh.

"Oh, you aren't fat," the stylish lady said.

"Ooooo I am too." Mrs. Turpin said. "Claud he eats all he wants to and never weighs over one hundred and seventy-five pounds, but me I just look at something good to eat and I gain some weight," and her stomach and shoulders shook with laughter. "You can eat all you want to, can't you, Claud?" she asked, turning to him.

Claud only grinned.

"Well, as long as you have such a good disposition," the stylish lady said. "I don't think it makes a bit of difference what size you are. You just can't beat a good disposition."

Next to her was a fat girl of eighteen or nineteen, scowling into a thick blue book which Mrs. Turpin saw was entitled *Human Development*. The girl raised her head and directed her scowl at Mrs. Turpin as if she did not like her looks. She appeared annoyed that anyone should speak while she tried to read. The poor girl's face was blue with acne and Mrs. Turpin thought how pitiful it was to have a face like that at that age. She gave the girl a friendly smile but the girl only scowled the harder. Mrs. Turpin herself was fat but she had always had good skin, and, though she was forty-seven years old, there was not a wrinkle in her face except around her eyes from laughing too much.

Next to the ugly girl was the child, still in exactly the same position, and next to him was a thin leathery old woman in a cotton print dress. She and Claud had three sacks of chicken feed in their pump house that was in the same print. She had seen from the first that the child belonged to the old woman. She could tell by the way they sat — kind of vacant and white-trashy, as if they would sit there until Doomsday if nobody called and told them to get up. And at right angles but next to the well-dressed pleasant lady was a lank-faced woman who was certainly the child's mother. She had on a yellow sweat shirt and wine-colored slacks, both gritty-looking, and the rims of her lips were stained with snuff. Her dirty yellow hair was tied behind with a little piece of red paper ribbon. Worse than niggers any day, Mrs. Turpin thought.

The gospel hymn playing was, "When I looked up and He looked down," and Mrs. Turpin, who knew it, supplied the last line mentally, "And wona these days I know I'll we-eara crown."

Without appearing to, Mrs. Turpin always noticed people's feet. The well-dressed lady had on red and grey suede shoes to match her dress. Mrs. Turpin had on her good black patent leather pumps. The ugly girl had on Girl Scout shoes and heavy socks. The old woman had on tennis shoes and the white-trashy mother had on what appeared to be bedroom slippers, black straw with gold braid threaded through them — exactly what you would have expected her to have on.

Sometimes at night when she couldn't go to sleep, Mrs. Turpin would occupy herself with the question of who she would have chosen to be if she couldn't have been herself. If Jesus had said to her before he made her, "There's only two places available for you. You can either be a nigger or white-trash," what would she have said? "Please, Jesus, please," she would have said, "just let me wait until there's another place available," and he would have said, "No you have to go right now and I have only those two places so make up your mind." She would have wiggled and squirmed and begged and pleaded but it would have been no use and finally she would have said, "All right, make me a nigger then—but that don't mean a trashy one." And he would have made her a neat clean respectable Negro woman, herself but black.

Next to the child's mother was a red-headed youngish woman, reading one of the magazines and working on a piece of chewing gum, hell for leather, as Claud would say. Mrs. Turpin could not see the woman's feet. She was not white-trash, just common. Sometimes Mrs. Turpin occupied herself at night naming the classes of people. On the bottom of the heap were most colored people, not the kind she would have been if she had been one, but most of them; then next to them—not above, just far from—were the white-trash; then above them were the home-owners, and above them the home-and-land owners, to which she and Claud belonged. Above she and Claud were people with a lot of money and much bigger houses and much more land. But here the complexity of it would begin to bear in on her, for some of the people with a lot of money were common and ought to be below she and Claud and some of the people who had good blood had lost their money and had to rent and then there were colored people who owned their homes and land as well. There was a colored dentist in town who had two red Lincolns and a swimming pool and a farm with registered white-face cattle on it. Usually by the time she had fallen asleep all the classes of people were moiling and roiling around in her head, and she would dream they were all crammed in together in a box car, being ridden off to be put in a gas oven.

"That's a beautiful clock," she said and nodded to her right. It was a big wall clock, the face encased in a brass sunburst.

"Yes, it's very pretty," the stylish lady said agreeably. "And right on the dot too," she added, glancing at her watch.

The ugly girl beside her cast an eye upward at the clock, smirked, then looked directly at Mrs. Turpin and smirked again. Then she returned her eyes to her book. She was obviously the lady's daughter because, although they didn't look anything alike as to disposition, they both had the same shape of face and the same blue eyes. On the lady they sparkled pleasantly but in the girl's seared face they appeared alternately to smolder and to blaze.

What if Jesus had said, "All right, you can be white-trash or a nigger or ugly!"

Mrs. Turpin felt an awful pity for the girl, though she thought it was one thing to be ugly and another to act ugly.

The woman with the snuff-stained lips turned around in her chair and looked up at the clock. Then she turned back and appeared to look a little to the side of Mrs. Turpin. There was a cast in one of her eyes. "You want to know wher you can get one of themther clocks?" she asked in a loud voice.

"No, I already have a nice clock," Mrs. Turpin said. Once somebody like her got a leg in the conversation, she would be all over it.

"You can get you one with green stamps," the woman said. "That's most likely wher he got hisn. Save you up enough, you can get you most anythang. I got me some joo'ry."

Ought to have got you a wash rag and some soap, Mrs. Turpin thought.

"I get contour sheets with mine," the pleasant lady said.

The daughter slammed her book shut. She looked straight in front of her, directly through Mrs. Turpin and on through the yellow curtain and the plate glass window which made the wall behind her. The girl's eyes seemed lit all of a sudden with a peculiar light, an unnatural light like night road signs give. Mrs. Turpin turned her head to see if there was anything going on outside that she should see, but she could not see anything. Figures passing cast only a pale shadow through the curtain. There was no reason the girl should single her out for her ugly looks.

"Miss Finley," the nurse said, cracking the door. The gum-chewing woman got up and passed in front of her and Claud and went into the office. She had on red high-heeled shoes.

Directly across the table, the ugly girl's eyes were fixed on Mrs. Turpin as if she had some very special reason for disliking her.

"This is wonderful weather, isn't it?" the girl's mother said.

"It's good weather for cotton if you can get the niggers to pick it," Mrs. Turpin said, "but niggers don't want to pick cotton any more. You can't get the white folks to pick it and now you can't get the niggers—because they got to be right up there with the white folks."

"They gonna try anyways," the white-trash woman said, leaning forward.

"Do you have one of those cotton-picking machines?" the pleasant lady asked.

"No," Mrs. Turpin said, "they leave half the cotton in the field. We don't have much cotton anyway. If you want to make it farming now, you have to have a little of everything. We got a couple of acres of cotton and a few hogs and chickens and just enough white-face that Claud can look after them himself."

"One thing I don't want," the white-trash woman said, wiping her mouth with the back of her hand. "Hogs. Nasty stinking things, a-grunting and a-rootin all over the place."

Mrs. Turpin gave her the merest edge of her attention. "Our hogs are not dirty and they don't stink," she said. "They're cleaner than some children I've seen. Their feet never touch the ground. We have a pig-parlor—that's where you raise them off concrete," she explained to the pleasant lady, "and Claud scoots them down with the hose every afternoon and washes off the floor." Cleaner by far than that child right there, she thought. Poor nasty little thing. He had not moved except to put the thumb of his dirty hand into his mouth.

The woman turned her face away from Mrs. Turpin. "I know I wouldn't scoot down no hog with no hose," she said to the wall.

You wouldn't have no hog to scoot down, Mrs. Turpin said to herself.

"A-gruntin and a-rootin and a-groanin," the woman muttered.

"We got a little of everything," Mrs. Turpin said to the pleasant lady. "It's no use in having more than you can handle yourself with help like it is. We found enough niggers to pick our cotton this year but Claud he has to go after them and take them home again in the evening. They can't walk that half a mile. No they can't. I tell you," she said and laughed merrily, "I sure am tired of buttering up niggers, but you got to love em if you want em to work for you. When they come in the morning, I run out and I says, 'Hi yawl this morning?' and when Claud drives them off to the field I just wave to beat the band and they just wave back." And she waved her hand rapidly to illustrate.

"Like you read out of the same book," the lady said, showing she understood perfectly.

"Child, yes," Mrs. Turpin said. "And when they come in from the field, I run out with a bucket of icewater. That's the way it's going to be from now on," she said. "You may as well face it."

"One thang I know," the white-trash woman said. "Two thangs I ain't going to do: love no niggers or scoot down no hog with no hose." And she let out a bark of contempt.

The look that Mrs. Turpin and the pleasant lady exchanged indicated they both understood that you had to have certain things before you could know certain things. But every time Mrs. Turpin exchanged a look with the lady, she was aware that the ugly girl's peculiar eyes were still on her, and she had trouble bringing her attention back to the conversation.

"When you got something," she said, "you got to look after it." And when you ain't got a thing but breath and britches, she added to herself, you can afford to come to town every morning and just sit on the Court House coping and spit.

A grotesque revolving shadow passed across the curtain behind her and was thrown palely on the opposite wall. Then a bicycle clattered down against the outside of the building. The door opened and a colored boy glided in with a tray from the drug store. It had two large red and white paper cups on it with tops on them. He was a tall, very black boy in discolored white pants and green nylon shirt. He was chewing gum slowly, as if to music. He set the tray down in the office opening next to the fern and stuck his head through to look for the secretary. She was not in there. He rested his arms on the ledge and waited, his narrow bottom stuck out, swaying slowly to the left and right. He raised a hand over his head and scratched the base of his skull.

"You see that button there, boy?" Mrs. Turpin said. "You can punch that and she'll come. She's probably in the back somewhere."

"Is that right?" the boys said agreeably, as if he had never seen the button before. He leaned to the right and put his finger on it. "She sometime out," he said and twisted around to face his audience, his elbows behind him on the counter. The nurse appeared and he twisted back again. She handed him a dollar and he rooted in his pocket and made the change and counted it out to her. She gave him fifteen cents for a tip and he went out with the empty tray. The heavy door swung so slowly and closed at length with the sound of suction. For a moment no one spoke.

"They ought to send all them niggers back to Africa," the white-trash woman said. "That's wher they come from in the first place."

"Oh, I couldn't do without my good colored friends," the pleasant lady said.

"There's a heap of things worse than a nigger," Mrs. Turpin agreed. "It's all kinds of them just like it's all kinds of us."

"Yes, and it takes all kinds to make the world go round," the lady said in her musical voice. As she said it, the raw-complexioned girl snapped her teeth together. Her lower lip turned downwards and inside out, revealing the pale pink inside of her mouth. After a second it rolled back up. It was the ugliest face Mrs. Turpin had ever seen anyone make and for a moment she was certain that the girl had made it at her. She was looking at her as if she had known and disliked her all her life—all of Mrs. Turpin's life, it seemed too, not just all the girl's life. Why girl, I don't even know you, Mrs. Turpin said silently.

She forced her attention back to the discussion. "It wouldn't be practical to send them back to Africa," she said. "They wouldn't want to go. They got it too good here."

"Wouldn't be what they wanted—if I had anythang to do with it," the woman said.

"It wouldn't be a way in the world you could get all the niggers back over there," Mrs. Turpin said. "They'd be hiding out and lying down and turning sick on you and wailing and hollering and raring and pitching. It wouldn't be a way in the world to get them over thee."

"They got over here," the trashy woman said. "Get back like they got over."

"It wasn't so many of them then," Mrs. Turpin explained.

The woman looked at Mrs. Turpin as if here was an idiot indeed but Mrs. Turpin was not bothered by the look, considering where it came from.

"Noooo," she said, "they're going to stay here where they can go to New York and marry white folks and improve their color. That's what they all want to do, every one of them, improve their color."

"You know what comes of that, don't you?" Claud asked.

"No, Claud, what?" Mrs. Turpin said.

Claud's eyes twinkled. "White-faced niggers," he said with never a smile.

Everybody in the office laughed except the white-trash and the ugly girl. The girl gripped the book in her lap with white fingers. The trashy woman looked around her from face to face as if she thought they were all idiots. The old woman in the feed sack dress continued to gaze expressionless across the floor at the high-top shoes of the man opposite her, the one who had been pretending to be asleep when the Turpins came in. He was laughing heartily, his hands still spread out on his knees. The child had fallen to the side and was lying now almost face down in the old woman's lap.

While they recovered from their laughter, the nasal chorus on the radio kept the room from silence.

You go to blank blank
And I'll go to mine
But we'll all blank along
To-geth-ther,

And all along the blank
We'll hep each other out
Smile-ling in any kind of
Weath-ther!"

Mrs. Turpin didn't catch every word but she caught enough to agree with the spirit of the song and it turned her thoughts sober. To help anybody out that needed it was her philosophy of life. She never spared herself when she found somebody in need, whether they were white or black, trash or decent. And of all she had to be thankful for, she was most thankful that this was so. If Jesus had said, "You can be high society and have all the money you want and be thin and svelte-like, but you can't be a good woman with it," she would have had to say, "Well don't make me that then. Make me a good woman and it don't matter what else, how fat or how ugly or how poor!" Her heart rose. He had not made her a nigger or white-trash or ugly! He had made her herself and given her a little of everything. Jesus, thank you! she said. Thank you thank you thank you! Whenever she counted her blessings she felt as buoyant as if she weighed one hundred and twenty-five pounds instead of one hundred and eighty.

"What's wrong with your little boy?" the pleasant lady asked the white-trashy woman.

"He has a ulcer," the woman said proudly. "He ain't give me a minute's peace since he was born. Him and her are just alike," she said, nodding at the old woman, who was running her leathery fingers through the child's pale hair. "Look like can't get nothing down them two but Co-Cola and candy."

That's all you try to get down em, Mrs. Turpin said to herself. Too lazy to light the fire. There was nothing you could tell her about people like them that she didn't know already. And it was not just that they didn't have anything. Because if you gave them everything, in two weeks it would be all broken or filthy or they would have chopped it up for lightwood. She knew all this from her own experience. Help them you must, but help them you couldn't.

All at once the ugly girl turned her lips inside out again. Her eyes were fixed like two drills on Mrs. Turpin. This time there was no mistaking that there was something urgent behind them.

41

Girl, Mrs. Turpin exclaimed silently, I haven't done a thing to you! The girl might be confusing her with somebody else. There was no need to sit by and let herself be intimidated. "You must be in college," she said boldly, looking directly at the girl. "I see you reading a book there."

The girl continued to stare and pointedly did not answer.

Her mother blushed at this rudeness. "The lady asked you a question, Mary Grace," she said under her breath.

"I have ears," Mary Grace said.

The poor mother blushed again. "Mary Grace goes to Wellesley College," she explained. She twisted one of the buttons on her dress. "In Massachusetts," she added with a grimace. "And in the summer she just keeps right on studying. Just reads all the time, a real book worm. She's done real well at Wellesley; she's taking English and Math and History and Psychology and Social Studies," she rattled on, "and I think it's too much. I think she ought to get out and have fun."

The girl looked as if she would like to hurl them all through the plate glass window.

"Way up north," Mrs. Turpin murmured and thought, Well, it hasn't done much for her manners.

"I'd almost rather to have him sick," the white-trash woman said, wrenching the attention back to herself. "He's so mean when he ain't. Look like some children just take natural to meanness. It's some gets bad when they get sick but he was the opposite. Took sick and turned good. He don't give me no trouble now. It's me waiting to see the doctor," she said.

If I was going to send anybody back to Africa, Mrs. Turpin thought, it would be your kind, woman. "Yes, indeed," she said aloud, but looking up at the ceiling, "It's a heap of things worse than a nigger." And dirtier than a hog, she added to herself.

"I think people with bad dispositions are more to be pitied than anyone on earth," the pleasant lady said in a voice that was decidedly thin.

"I thank the Lord he has blessed me with a good one," Mrs. Turpin said. "The day has never dawned that I couldn't find something to laugh at."

"Not since she married me anyways," Claud said with a comical straight face.

Everybody laughed except the girl and the white-trash.

Mrs. Turpin's stomach shook. "He's such a caution," she said, "that I can't help but laugh at him."

The girl made a loud ugly noise through her teeth.

Her mother's mouth grew thin and tight. "I think the worst thing in the world," she said, "is an ungrateful person. To have everything and not appreciate it. I know a girl," she said, "who has parents who would give her anything, a little brother who loves her dearly, who is getting a good education, who wears the best clothes, but who can never say a kind word to anyone, who never smiles, who just criticizes and complains all day long."

"Is she too old to paddle?" Claud asked.

The girl's face was almost purple.

"Yes," the lady said, "I'm afraid there's nothing to do but leave her to her folly. Some day she'll wake up and it'll be too late."

"It never hurt anyone to smile," Mrs. Turpin said. "It just makes you feel better all over."

"Of course," the lady said sadly, "but there are just some people you can't tell anything to. They can't take criticism."

"If it's one thing I am," Mrs. Turpin said with feeling, "it's grateful. When I think who all I could have been besides myself and what all I got, a little of everything, and a good disposition besides, I just feel like shouting, 'Thank you, Jesus, for making everything the way it is!' It could have been different." For one thing, somebody else could have got Claud. At the thought of this, she was flooded with gratitude and a terrible pang of joy ran through her. "Oh thank you, Jesus, thank you" she cried aloud.

The book struck her directly over her left eye. It struck almost at the same instant that she realized the girl was about to hurl it. Before she could utter a sound, the raw face came crashing across the table toward her, howling. The girl's fingers sank like clamps into the soft flesh of her neck. She heard the mother cry out and Claud shout, "Whoa!" There was an instant when she was certain that she was about to be in an earthquake.

All at once her vision narrowed and she saw everything as if it were happening in a small room far away, or as if she were looking at it through the wrong end of a telescope. Claud's face crumpled and fell out of sight. The nurse ran in, then out, then in again. Then the gangling figure of the doctor rushed out of the inner door. Magazines flew this way and that as the table turned over. The girl fell with a thud and Mrs. Turpin's vision suddenly reversed itself and she saw everything large instead of small. The eyes of the white-trashy woman were staring hugely at the floor. There the girl, held down on one side by the nurse and on the other by her mother, was wrenching and turning in their grasp. The doctor was kneeling astride her, trying to hold her arm down. He managed after a second to sink a long needle into it.

Mrs. Turpin felt entirely hollow except for her heart which swung from side to side as if it were agitated in a great empty drum of flesh.

"Somebody that's not busy call for the ambulance," the doctor said in the off-hand voice young doctors adopt for terrible occasions.

Mrs. Turpin could not have moved a finger. The old man who had been sitting next to her skipped nimbly into the office and made the call, for the secretary still seemed to be gone.

"Claud!" Mrs. Turpin called.

He was not in his chair. She knew she must jump up and find him but she felt like someone trying to catch a train in a dream, when everything moves in slow motion and the faster you try to run the slower you go.

"Here I am," a suffocated voice, very unlike Claud's, said.

He was doubled up in the corner on the floor, pale as paper, holding his leg. She wanted to get up and go to him but she could not move. Instead, her gaze was drawn slowly downward to the churning face on the floor, which she could see over the doctor's shoulder.

The girl's eyes stopped rolling and focused on her. They seemed a much lighter blue than before, as if a door that had been tightly closed behind them was now open to admit light and air.

Mrs. Turpin's head cleared and her power of motion returned. She leaned forward until she was looking directly into the fierce brilliant eyes. There was no doubt in her mind that the girl did know her, knew her in some intense and personal way, beyond time and place and condition. "What you got to say to me?" she asked hoarsely and held her breath, waiting, as for a revelation.

The girl raised her head. Her gaze locked with Mrs. Turpin's. "Go back to hell where you came from, you old wart hog," she whispered. Her voice was low but clear. Her eyes burned for a moment as if she saw with pleasure that her message had struck its target.

Mrs. Turpin sank back in her chair.

43

After a moment the girl's eyes closed and she turned her head wearily to the side.

The doctor rose and handed the nurse the empty syringe. He leaned over and put both hands for a moment on the mother's shoulders, which were shaking. She was sitting on the floor, her lips pressed together, holding Mary Grace's hand in her lap. The girl's fingers were gripped like a baby's around her thumb. "Go on to the hospital," he said. "I'll call and make the arrangements.

"Now let's see that neck," he said in a jovial voice to Mrs. Turpin. He began to inspect her neck with his first two fingers. Two little moon-shaped lines like pink fish bones were indented over her windpipe. There was the beginning of an angry red swelling above her eye. His fingers passed over this also.

"Lea' me be," she said thickly and shook him off. "See about Claud. She kicked him."

"I'll see about him in a minute," he said and felt her pulse. He was a thin grey-haired young man, given to pleasantries. "Go home and have yourself a vacation the rest of the day," he said and patted her on the shoulder.

Quit your pattin me, Mrs. Turpin growled to herself.

"And put an ice pack over that eye," he said. Then he went and squatted down beside Claud and looked at his leg. After a moment he pulled him up and Claud limped after him into the office.

Until the ambulance came, the only sounds in the room were the tremulous moans of the girls' mother, who continued to sit on the floor. The white-trash woman did not take her eyes off the girl. Mrs. Turpin looked straight ahead at nothing. Presently the ambulance drew up, a long dark shadow, behind the curtain. The attendants came in and set the stretcher down beside the girl and lifted her expertly onto it and carried her out. The nurse helped the mother gather up her things. The shadow of the ambulance moved silently away and the nurse came back in the office.

"That girl is going to be a lunatic, ain't she?" the white-trash woman asked the nurse, but the nurse kept on to the back and never answered her.

"Yes, she's going to be a lunatic," the white-trash woman said to the rest of them.

"Po' critter," the old woman murmured. The child's face was still in her lap. His eyes looked idly out over her knees. He had not moved during the disturbance except to draw one leg under him.

"I thank Gawd," the white-trash woman said fervently, "I ain't a lunatic."

Claud came limping out and the Turpins went home.

As their pick-up truck turned into their own dirt road and made the crest of the hill, Mrs. Turpin gripped the window ledge and looked out suspiciously. The land sloped gracefully down through a field dotted with lavender weeds and at the start of the rise their small yellow frame house, with its little flower beds spread out around it like a fancy apron, sat primly in its accustomed place between two giant hickory trees. She would not have been startled to see a burnt wound between two blackened chimneys.

Neither of them felt like eating so they put on their house clothes and lowered the shade in the bedroom and lay down, Claud with his leg on a pillow and herself with a damp washcloth over her eye. The instant she was flat on her back, the image of a razor-backed hog with warts on its face and horns coming out behind its ears snorted into her head. She moaned, a low quiet moan.

"I am not," she said tearfully, "a wart hog. From hell." But the denial had no force. The girl's eyes and her words, even the tone of her voice, low but clear, directed only to her, brooked no repudiation. She had been singled out for the message, though there was trash in the room to whom it might justly have been applied. The full force of this fact struck her only now. There was a woman there who was neglecting her own child but she had been overlooked. The message had been given to Ruby Turpin, a respectable, hard-working, church-going woman. The tears dried. Her eyes began to burn instead with wrath.

She rose on her elbow and the washcloth fell into her hand. Claud was lying on his back, snoring. She wanted to tell him what the girl had said. At the same time, she did not wish to put the image of herself as a wart hog from hell into his mind.

"Hey, Claud," she muttered and pushed his shoulder.

Claud opened one pale baby blue eye.

She looked into it warily. He did not think about anything. He just went his way.

"Wha, whasit?" he said and closed the eye again.

"Nothing," she said. "Does your leg pain you?"

"Hurts like hell," Claud said.

"It'll quit terreckly," she said and lay back down. In a moment Claud was snoring again. For the rest of the afternoon they lay there. Claud slept. She scowled at the ceiling. Occasionally she raised her fist and made a small stabbing motion over her chest as if she were defending her innocence to invisible guests who were like the comforters of Job, reasonable-seeming but wrong.

About five-thirty Claud stirred. "Got to go after those niggers," he sighed, not moving.

She was looking straight up as if there were unintelligible handwriting on the ceiling. The protuberance over her eye had turned a greenish-blue. "Listen here," she said.

"What?"

"Kiss me."

Claud leaned over and kissed her loudly on the mouth. He pinched her side and their hands interlocked. Her expression of ferocious concentration did not change. Claud got up, groaning and growling, and limped off. She continued to study the ceiling.

She did not get up until she heard the pick-up truck coming back with the Negroes. Then she rose and thrust her feet in her brown oxfords, which she did not bother to lace, and stumped out onto the back porch and got her red plastic bucket. She emptied a tray of ice cubes into it and filled it half full of water and went out into the back yard. Every afternoon after Claud brought the hands in, one of the boys helped him put out hay and the rest waited in the back of the truck until he was ready to take them home. The truck was parked in the shade under one of the hickory trees.

"Hi yawl this evening?" Mrs. Turpin asked grimly, appearing with the bucket and the dipper. There were three woman and a boy in the truck.

"Us doin nicely," the oldest woman said. "Hi you doin?" and her gaze stuck immediately on the dark lump on Mrs. Turpin's forehead. "You done fell down, ain't you?" she asked in a solicitous voice. The old woman was dark and almost toothless. She had on an old felt hat of Claud's set back on her head. The other two women were younger and lighter and they both had new bright green sun hats. One of them had hers on her head; the other had taken hers off and the boy was grinning beneath it.

Mrs. Turpin set the bucket down on the floor of the truck. "Yawl hep yourselves," she said. She looked around to make sure Claud had gone. "No. I didn't fall down," she said, folding her arms. "It was something worse than that."

"Ain't nothing bad happen to you!" the old woman said. She said it as if they all knew that Mrs. Turpin was protected in some special way by Divine Providence. "You just had you a little fall."

"We were in town at the doctor's office for where the cow kicked Mr. Turpin," Mrs. Turpin said in a flat tone that indicated they could leave off their foolishness. "And there was this girl there. A big fat girl with her face all broke out. I could look at that girl and tell she was peculiar but I couldn't tell how. And me and her mama were just talking and going along and all of a sudden WHAM! She throws this big book she was reading at me. . . ."

"Naw!" the old woman cried out.

"And then she jumps over the table and commences to choke me."

"Naw!" they all exclaimed, "naw!"

"Hi come she do that?" the old woman asked. "What ail her?"

Mrs. Turpin only glared in front of her.

"Something ail her," the woman said.

"They carried her off in an ambulance," Mrs. Turpin continued, "but before she went she was rolling on the floor and they were trying to hold her down to give her a shot and she said something to me." She paused. "You know what she said to me?"

"What she say?" they asked.

"She said," Mrs. Turpin began, and stopped, her face very dark and heavy. The sun was getting whiter and whiter, blanching the sky overhead so that the leaves of the hickory tree were black in the face of it. She could not bring forth the words. "Something real ugly," she muttered.

"She sho shouldn't have said nothing ugly to you," the old woman said. "You so sweet. You the sweetest lady I know."

"She pretty too," the one with the hat on said.

"And stout," the other one said. "I never knowed no sweeter white lady."

"That's the truth befo' Jesus," the old woman said.

"Amen! You des as sweet and pretty as you can be."

Mrs. Turpin knew just exactly how much Negro flattery was worth and it added to her rage. "She said," she began again and finished this time with a fierce rush of breath, "that I was an old wart hog from hell."

There was an astounded silence.

"Where she at!" the youngest woman cried in a piercing voice. "Lemme see her. I'll kill her!"

"I'll kill her with you!" the other one cried.

"She b'long in the sylum," the old woman said emphatically. "You the sweetest white lady I know."

"She pretty too," the other two said. "Stout as she can be and sweet. Jesus satisfied with her!"

"Deed he is," the old woman declared.

Idiots! Mrs. Turpin growled to herself. You could never say anything intelligent to a nigger. You could talk to them but not with them. "Yawl ain't drunk your water," she said shortly. "Leave the bucket in the truck when you're finished with it. I got more to do than just stand around and pass the time of day," and she moved off and into the house.

She stood for a moment in the middle of the kitchen. The dark protuberance over her eye looked like a miniature tornado cloud which might any moment sweep across the horizon of her brow. Her lower lip protruded dangerously. She squared her massive shoulders. Then she marched into the front of the house and out the side door and started down the road to the pig parlor. She had the look of a woman going single-handed, weaponless, into battle.

The sun was a deep yellow now like a harvest moon and was riding westward very fast over the far tree line as if it meant to reach the hogs before she did. The road was rutted and she kicked several good-sized stones out of her path as she strode along. The pig parlor was on a little knoll at the end of a lane that ran off from the side of the barn. It was a square of concrete as large as a small room, with a broad fence about four feet high around it.The concrete floor sloped slightly so that the hog wash could drain off into a trench where it was carried to the field for fertilizer. Claud was standing on the outside, on the edge of the concrete, hanging onto the top board, hosing down the floor inside. The hose was connected to the faucet of a water trough nearby.

Mrs. Turpin climbed up beside him and glowered down at the hogs inside. There were seven long-snouted bristly shoats in it—tan with liver-colored spots—and an old sow a few weeks off from farrowing. She was lying on her side grunting. The shoats were running about shaking themselves like idiot children, their little slit pig eyes searching the floor for anything left. She had read that pigs were the most intelligent animal. She doubted it. They were supposed to be smarter than dogs. There had even been a pig astronaut. He had performed his assignment perfectly but died of a heart attack afterwards because they left him in his electric suit, sitting upright throughout his examination when naturally a hog should be on all fours.

A-gruntin and a-rootin and a-groanin.

"Gimme that hose," she said, yanking it away from Claud. "Go on and carry them niggers home and then get off that leg."

"You look like you might have swallowed a mad dog," Claud observed, but he got down and limped off. He paid no attention to her humors.

Until he was out of earshot, Mrs. Turpin stood on the side of the pen, holding the hose and pointing the stream of water at the hind quarters of any shoat that looked as if it might try to lie down. When he had had time to get over the hill, she turned her head slightly and wrathful eyes scanned the path. He was nowhere in sight. She turned back again and seemed to gather herself up. Her shoulders rose and she drew in her breath.

"What do you send me a message like that for?" she said in a low fierce voice, barely above a whisper but with the force of a shout in its concentrated fury. "How am I a hog and me both? How am I saved and from hell too?" Her free fist was knotted and with the other she gripped the hose, blindly pointing the stream of water in and out of the eye of the old sow whose outraged squeal she did not hear.

The pig parlor commanded a view of the back pasture where their twenty beef cows were gathered around the haybales Claud and the boy had put out. The freshly cut pasture sloped down to the highway. Across it was their cotton field and beyond that a dark green dusty wood which they owned as well. The sun was behind the wood, very red, looking over the paling of trees like a farmer inspecting his own hogs.

"Why me?" she rumbled. "It's no trash around here, black or white, that I haven't given to. And break my back to the bone every day working. And do for the church."

She appeared to be the right size woman to command the arena before her. "How am I a hog?" she demanded. "Exactly how am I like them?" and she jabbed the stream of water at the shoats. "There was plenty of trash there. It didn't have to be me.

"If you like trash better, go get yourself some trash then," she railed. "You could have made me trash. Or a nigger. If trash is what you wanted why didn't you make me trash?" She

47

shook her fist with the hose in it and a watery snake appeared momentarily in the air. "I could quit working and take it easy and be filthy," she growled. "Lounge about the sidewalks all day drinking root beer. Dip snuff and spit in every puddle and have it all over my face. I could be nasty.

"Or you could have made me a nigger. It's too late for me to be a nigger," she said with deep sarcasm, "but I could act like one. Lay down in the middle of the road and stop traffic. Roll on the ground."

In the deepening light everything was taking on a mysterious hue. The pasture was growing a peculiar glassy green and the streak of highway had turned lavender. She braced herself for a final assault and this time her voice rolled out over the pasture. "Go on," she yelled, "call me a hog! Call me a hog again. From hell. Call me a wart hog from hell. Put the bottom rail on top. There'll still be a top and bottom!"

A garbled echo returned to her.

A final surge of fury shook her and she roared, "Who do you think you are?"

The color of everything, field and crimson sky, burned for a moment with a transparent intensity. The question carried over the pasture and across the highway and the cotton field and returned to her clearly like an answer from beyond the wood.

She opened her mouth but no sound came out of it.

A tiny truck, Claud's, appeared on the highway, heading rapidly out of sight. Its gears scraped thinly. It looked like a child's toy. At any moment a bigger truck might smash into it and scatter Claud's and the niggers' brains all over the road.

Mrs. Turpin stood there, her gaze fixed on the highway, all her muscles rigid, until in five or six minutes the truck reappeared, returning. She waited until it had had time to turn into their own road. Then like a monumental statue coming to life, she bent her head slowly and gazed, as if through the very heart of mystery, down into the pig parlor at the hogs. They had settled all in one corner around the old sow who was grunting softly. A red glow suffused them. They appeared to pant with a secret life.

Until the sun slipped finally behind the tree line, Mrs. Turpin remained there with her gaze bent to them as if she were absorbing some abysmal life-giving knowledge. At last she lifted her head. There was only a purple streak in the sky, cutting through a field of crimson and leading, like an extension of the highway, into the descending dusk. She raised her hands from the side of the pen in a gesture hieratic and profound. A visionary light settled in her eyes. She saw the streak as a vast swinging bridge extending upward from the earth through a field of living fire. Upon it a vast horde of souls were rumbling toward heaven. There were whole companies of white-trash, clean for the first time in their lives, and bands of black niggers in white robes, and battalions of freaks and lunatics shouting and clapping and leaping like frogs. And bringing up the end of the procession was a tribe of people whom she recognized at once as those who, like herself and Claud, had always had a little of everything and the God-given wit to use it right. She leaned forward to observe them closer. They were marching behind the others with great dignity, accountable as they had always been for good order and common sense and respectable behavior. They alone were on key. Yet she could see by their shocked and altered faces that even their virtues were being burned away. She lowered her hands and gripped the rail of the hog pen, her eyes small but fixed unblinkingly on what lay ahead. In a moment the vision faded but she remained where she was, immobile.

At length she got down and turned off the faucet and made her slow way on the darkening path to the house. In the woods around her the invisible cricket choruses had struck up, but what she heard were the voices of the souls climbing upward into the starry field and shouting hallelujah.

LUKE 18:10–14

(King James Version)

Two men went up into the temple to pray; the one a Pharisee, and the other a publican. The Pharisee stood and prayed thus with himself, God, I thank thee, that I am not as other men are, extortioners, unjust, adulterers, or even as this publican. I fast twice in the week; I give tithes of all that I possess. And the publican, standing afar off, would not lift so much as his eyes unto heaven, but smote upon his breast, saying, God be merciful to me a sinner. I tell you, this man went down to his house justified rather than the other: for every one that exalteth himself shall be abased; and he that humbleth himself shall be exalted.

Christian Perspective

1. Parallel the description of the Pharisee's prayer to Mrs. Turpin's statement that she felt like shouting, "Thank you, Jesus, for making everything the way it is!"
2. O'Connor's statement, "She was looking at her as if she [the girl] had known and disliked her all her life," foreshadows not only a confrontation but also a mysterious connection between Mrs. Turpin and Mary Grace. What is the connection?
3. In her vision, Mrs. Turpin sees herself and those like her—honest, decent folk—at the end of the procession line into heaven. She sees that "even their virtues were being burned away." Is O'Connor suggesting that Mrs. Turpin's salvation is just beginning?
4. When Mrs. Turpin goes toward the pig parlor, she has "the look of a woman going single-handed, weaponless, into battle." Once there, she dismisses Claud, uses the hose as a weapon against the pigs, and talks to herself "in a low fierce voice." What is she battling, besides the pigs?
5. Upon looking closely at O'Connor's style, we can see patterns that are used throughout the story. One pattern seems to be her use of pigs; another pattern is eyes. Can you find other patterns?
6. About herself, Flannery O'Connor wrote, "I see from the standpoint of Christian orthodoxy. This means that for me the meaning of life is centered in our redemption by Christ, and what I see in the world I see in relation to that." How does this statement affect your response to the story?
7. Write a character analysis of one of the characters from "Revelation." Remember that an author may use many devices to reveal character: direct authorial comment, physical details, the character's own thoughts and actions, and the other characters' comments and reactions. Also keep in mind that a narrator's comments may be ironic.

THE APOSTLES' CREED[1]

I believe in God the Father Almighty, Maker of heaven and earth:

And in Jesus Christ his only Son our Lord: Who was conceived by the Holy Ghost, Born of the Virgin Mary: Suffered under Pontius pilate, Was crucified, died, and rose again from the dead: He ascended into heaven, And sittest on the right hand of God the Father Almighty: From thence he shall come to judge the quick and the dead.

I believe in the Holy Ghost: The holy Catholic[2] Church; The Communion of Saints: The Forgiveness of sins: the Resurrection of the body: and the Life everlasting. Amen.

THE DOGMA IS THE DRAMA

Dorothy Sayers

"Any stigma," said a witty tongue, "will do to beat a dogma"; and the flails of ridicule have been brandished with such energy of late on the threshing floor of controversy that the seed of the Word has become well-nigh lost amid the whirling of chaff. Christ, in His divine innocence, said to the woman of Samaria, "Ye worship ye know not what" — being apparently under the impression that it might be desirable, on the whole, to know what one was worshipping. He thus showed himself sadly out of touch with the twentieth-century mind, for the cry today is: "Away with the tedious complexities of dogma — let us have the simple spirit of worship; just worship, no matter of what!" The only drawback to this demand for a generalized and undirected worship is the practical difficulty of arousing any sort of enthusiasm for the worship of nothing in particular.

It would not perhaps be altogether surprising if, in this nominally Christian country, where the Creeds are daily recited, there were a number of people who knew all about Christian doctrine and disliked it. It is more startling to discover how many people there are who heartily dislike and despise Christianity without having the faintest notion what it is. If you tell them, they cannot believe you. I do not mean that they cannot believe the doctrine; that would be understandable enough since it takes some believing. I mean that they simply cannot believe that anything so interesting, so exciting, and so dramatic can be the orthodox creed of the Church.

That this is really the case was made plain to me by the questions asked me, mostly by young men, about my Canterbury play, *The Zeal of Thy House*. The action of the play involves a dramatic presentation of a few fundamental Christian dogmas — in particular, the application to human affairs of the doctrine of the Incarnation. That the Church believed Christ to be in any real sense God, or that the eternal word was supposed to be associated in any way with the word of creation; that Christ was held to be at the same time man in any real sense of the word; that the doctrine of the Trinity could be considered to have any relation to fact or any bearing on psychological truth; that the Church considered pride to be sinful, or indeed took notice of

1. Several authors in this section refer to the Christian creeds. These are ancient statements of belief expressing what early Christians agreed were essentials of orthodox doctrine. "The Apostles' Creed" and the later "Nicene Creed" are commonly used by the Roman Catholic, Anglican (Episcopal), and Lutheran churches.
2. The word <u>Catholic</u> means "universal."

any sin beyond the more disreputable sins of the flesh:—all these things were looked upon as astonishing and revolutionary novelties, imported into the faith by the feverish imagination of a playwright. I protest in vain against this flattering tribute to my powers of invention, referring my inquirers to the creeds, to the gospels, and to the offices of the Church; I insisted that if my play were dramatic it was so, not in spite of the dogma, but because of it—that, in short, the dogma was the drama. The explanation was, however, not well received: it was felt that if there were anything attractive in Christian philosophy I must have put it there myself.

Judging by what my young friends tell me, and also by what is said on the subject of anti-Christian literature written by people who ought to have taken a little trouble to find out what they are attacking before attacking it, I have come to the conclusion that a short examination paper on the Christian religion might be very generally answered as follows:

Q.: What does the Church think of God the Father?

A.: He is omnipotent and holy. He created the world and imposed on man conditions impossible of fulfillment; he is very angry if these are not carried out. He sometimes interferes by means of arbitrary judgments and miracles, distributed with a good deal of favoritism. He likes to be truckled to and is always ready to pounce on anybody who trips up over a difficulty in the law or is having a bit of fun. He is rather like a dictator, only larger and more arbitrary.

Q.: What does the Church think of God the Son?

A.: He is in some way to be identified with Jesus of Nazareth. It was not his fault that the world was made like this, and, unlike God the Father, he is friendly to man and did his best to reconcile man to God (see atonement). He has a good deal of influence with God, and if you want anything done, it is best to apply to him.

Q.: What does the Church think of God the Holy Ghost?

A.: I don't know exactly. He was never seen or heard of till Whitsunday. There is a sin against him that damns you for ever, but nobody knows what it is.

Q.: What is the doctrine of the trinity?

A.: "The Father incomprehensible, the Son incomprehensible, and the whole thing incomprehensible." Something put in by theologians to make it more difficult—nothing to do with daily life or ethics.

Q.: What was Jesus Christ like in real life?

A.: He was a good man—so good as to be called the Son of God. He is to be identified in some way with God the Son (q.v.). He was meek and mild and preached a simple religion of love and pacifism. He had no sense of humor. Anything in the Bible that suggests another side to his character must be an interpolation, or a paradox invented by G. K. Chesterton. If we try to live like him, God the Father will let us off being damned hereafter and only have us tortured in this life instead.

Q.: What is meant by the atonement?

A.: God wanted to damn everybody, but his vindictive sadism was sated by the crucifixion of his own Son, who was quite innocent, and therefore, a particularly attractive victim. He now only damns people who don't follow Christ or who never heard of him.

Q.: What does the Church think of sex?

A.: God made it necessary to the machinery of the world, and tolerates it, provided the parties (a) are married, and (b) get no pleasure out of it.

Q.: What does the Church call sin?

→ sex is anything fun or pleasurable.

A.: Sex (otherwise than as excepted above); getting drunk; saying "damn"; murder; and cruelty to dumb animals; not going to church; most kinds of amusement. "Original sin" means that anything we enjoy doing is wrong.

Q.: What is faith?

A.: Resolutely shutting your eyes to scientific fact.

Q.: What is human intellect? *God gave you a mind as your enemy*

A.: A barrier of faith.

Q.: What are seven Christian virtues?

A.: Respectability; childishness; mental timidity; dullness; sentimentality; censoriousness; and depression of spirits.

Q.: Wilt thou be baptized in this faith?

A.: No fear!

I cannot help feeling that as a statement of Christian orthodoxy, these replies are inadequate, if not misleading. But I also cannot help feeling that they do fairly accurately represent what many people take Christian orthodoxy to be.

Whenever an average Christian is represented in a novel or a play, he is pretty sure to be shown practicing one or all of the Seven Deadly Virtues just enumerated, and I am afraid that this is the impression made by the average Christian upon the world at large.

Perhaps we are not following Christ all the way or in quite the right spirit. We are likely, for example, to be a little sparing of the palms and the hosannas. We are chary of wielding the scourge of small cords, lest we should offend somebody or interfere with trade. We do not furnish up our wits to disentangle knotty questions about Sunday observance and tribute money, nor hasten to sit at the feet of the doctors, both hearing them and asking them questions. We pass hastily over disquieting jests about making friends with the mammon of unrighteousness and alarming observations about bringing not peace but a sword; nor do we distinguish ourselves by the graciousness with which we sit at meal with publicans and sinners. Somehow or other, and with the best intentions, we have shown the world the typical Christian in the likeness of a crashing and rather ill-natured bore—and this in the name of one who assuredly never bored a soul in those thirty-three years during which he passed through the world like a flame.

Let us, in heaven's name, drag out the divine drama from under the dreadful accumulation of slipshod thinking and trashy sentiment heaped upon it, and set it on an open stage to startle the world into some sort of vigorous reaction. If the pious are the first to be shocked, so much worse for the pious—others will pass into the kingdom of heaven before them. If all men are offended because of Christ, let them be offended; but where is the sense of their being offended at something that is not Christ and is nothing like him? We do him singularly little honor by watering down his personality till it could not offend a fly. Surely it is not the business of the Church to adapt Christ to men, but to adapt men to Christ.

It is the dogma that is the drama—not beautiful phrases, nor comforting sentiments, nor vague aspirations to lovingkindness and uplift, nor the promise of something nice after death—but the terrifying assertion that the same God who made the world, lived in the world and passed through the grave and gate of death. Show that to the heathen, and they may not believe it; but at least they may realize that here is something that a man might be glad to believe.

It is belief that is exciting in Christianity.
Having something worth believing in.

52

Christian Perspectives

1. Sayers observes that "the true seed of the Word has become well-nigh lost amid the whirling of chaff." (See Matthew 3:12.) What is the chaff that she refers to?
2. Sayers' "examination" of the Christian religion reveals the non-Christian's view. What does she say the "typical Christian" has done to misrepresent Christ?
3. Give your own interpretation of Sayers' statement: "Surely it is not the business of the church to adapt Christ to men, but to adapt men to Christ."

SALVATION

Langston Hughes

I was saved from sin when I was going on thirteen. But not really saved. It happened like this. There was a big revival at my Auntie Reed's church. Every night for weeks there had been much preaching, singing, praying, and shouting, and some very hardened sinners had been brought to Christ, and the membership of the church had grown by leaps and bounds. Then just before the revival ended, they held a special meeting for children, "to bring the young lambs to the fold." My aunt spoke of it for days ahead. That night I was escorted to the front row and placed on the mourners' bench with all the other young sinners, who had not yet been brought to Jesus.

My aunt told me that when you were saved you saw a light, and something happened to you inside! And Jesus came into your life! And God was with you from then on! She said you could see and hear and feel Jesus in your soul. I believed her. I had heard a great many old people say the same thing and it seemed to me they ought to know. So I sat there calmly in the hot, crowded church, waiting for Jesus to come to me.

The preacher preached a wonderful rhythmical sermon, all moans and shouts and lonely cries and dire pictures of hell, and then he sang a song about the ninety and nine safe in the fold, but one little lamb was left out in the cold. Then he said: "Won't you come? Won't you come to Jesus? Young lambs, won't you come?" And he held out his arms to all us young sinners there on the mourners' bench. And the little girls cried. And some of them jumped up and went to Jesus right away. But most of us just sat there.

A great many old people came and knelt around us and prayed, old women with jet-black faces and braided hair, old men with work-gnarled hands. And the church sang a song about the lower lights are burning, some poor sinners to be saved. And the whole building rocked with prayer and song.

Still I kept waiting to see Jesus.

Finally all the young people had gone to the altar and were saved, but one boy and me. He was a rounder's son named Westley. Westley and I were surrounded by sisters and deacons praying. It was very hot in the church, and getting late now. Finally Westley said to me in a whisper: "God damn! I'm tired o' sitting here. Let's get up and be saved." So he got up and was saved.

Then I was left all alone on the mourners' bench. My aunt came and knelt at my knees and cried, while prayers and songs swirled all around me in the little church. The whole congregation prayed for me alone, in a mighty wail of moans and voices. And I kept waiting serenely for Jesus, waiting, waiting—but he didn't come. I wanted to see him, but nothing happened to me. Nothing! I wanted something to happen to me, but nothing happened.

I heard the songs and the minister saying: "Why don't you come? My dear child, why don't you come to Jesus? Jesus is waiting for you. He wants you. Why don't you come? Sister Reed, what is this child's name?"

"Langston," my aunt sobbed.

"Langston, why don't you come? Why don't you come and be saved? Oh, Lamb of God! Why don't you come?"

Now it was really getting late. I began to be ashamed of myself, holding everyone up so long. I began to wonder what God thought about Westley, who certainly hadn't seen Jesus either, but who was now sitting proudly on the platform, swinging his knickerbockered legs and grinning down at me, surrounded by deacons and old women on their knees praying. God had not struck Westley dead for taking his name in vain or for lying in the temple. So I decided that maybe to save further trouble, I'd better lie, too, and say that Jesus had come, and get up and be saved.

So I got up.

Suddenly the whole room broke into a sea of shouting, as they saw me rise. Waves of rejoicing swept the place. Women leaped in the air. My aunt threw her arms around me. The minister took me by the hand and led me to the platform.

When things quieted down, in a hushed silence, punctuated by a few ecstatic "Amens," all the new young lambs were blessed in the name of God. Then joyous singing filled the room.

That night, for the first time in my life but one—for I was a big boy twelve years old—I cried, in bed alone, and couldn't stop. I buried my head under the quilts, but my aunt heard me. She woke up and told my uncle I was crying because the Holy Ghost had come into my life, and because I had seen Jesus. But I was really crying because I couldn't bear to tell her that I had lied, that I had deceived everybody in the church, and hadn't seen Jesus, and that now I didn't believe there was a Jesus any more, since he didn't come to help me.

Christian Perspective

1. Hughes' personal experiences reveal serious weaknesses among Christians in churches. Identify some of those weaknesses.
2. It is obvious that Hughes' experience made a permanent impression on him as a child and even later. What does the Bible say about our responsibility to children? (See Matthew 18:6.)
3. Even though we can identify with Hughes' experience at the beginning, something unexpected still happens. What is it?
4. How does Hughes' style build the momentum and lead to the climax?

PIGEON FEATHERS

John Updike

When they moved to Firetown, things were upset, displaced, rearranged. A red cane-back sofa that had been the chief piece in the living room at Olinger was here banished, too big for the narrow country parlor, to the barn, and shrouded under a tarpaulin. Never again would David lie on its length all afternoon eating raisins and reading mystery novels and science fiction and P.G. Wodehouse. The blue wing chair that had stood for years in the ghostly, immaculate guest bedroom, gazing through the windows curtained with dotted swiss toward the telephone wires and horse-chestnut trees and opposite houses, was here established importantly in front of the smutty little fireplace that supplied, in those first cold April days, their only heat. As a child, David had been afraid of the guest bedroom—it was there that he, lying sick with the measles, had seen a black rod the size of a yardstick jog along at a slight slant beside the edge of the bed and vanish when he screamed—and it was disquieting to have one of the elements of its haunted atmosphere basking by the fire, in the center of the family, growing sooty with use. The books that at home had gathered dust in the case beside the piano were here hastily stacked, all out of order, in the shelves that the carpenters had built along one wall below the deep-silled windows. David, at fourteen, had been more moved than a mover; like the furniture, he had to find a new place, and on the Saturday of the second week he tried to work off some of his disorientation by arranging the books.

It was a collection obscurely depressing to him, mostly books his mother had acquired when she was young: college anthologies of Greek plays and Romantic poetry, Will Durant's *Story of Philosophy*, a soft-leather set of Shakespeare with string bookmarks sewed to the bindings, *Green Mansions* boxed and illustrated with woodcuts, *I, the Tiger*, by Manuel Komroff, novels by names like Galsworthy and Ellen Glasgow and Irvin S. Cobb and Sinclair Lewis and "Elizabeth." The odor of faded taste made him feel the ominous gap between himself and his parents, the insulting gulf of time that existed before he was born. Suddenly he was tempted to dip into this time. From the heaps of books piled around him on the worn old floorboards, he picked up Volume II of a four-volume set of *The Outline of History*, by H. G. Wells. Once David had read *The Time Machine* in an anthology; this gave him a small grip on the author. The book's red binding had faded to orange-pink on the spine. When he lifted the cover, there was a sweetish, attic-like smell, and his mother's maiden name written in unfamiliar handwriting on the flyleaf—an upright, bold, yet careful signature, bearing a faint relation to the quick scrunched backslant that flowed with marvellous consistency across her shopping lists and budget accounts and Christmas cards to college friends from this same, vaguely menacing long ago.

He leafed through, pausing at drawings, done in an old-fashioned stippled style, of bas-reliefs, masks, Romans without pupils in their eyes, articles of ancient costume, fragments of pottery found in unearthed homes. He knew it would be interesting in a magazine, sandwiched between ads and jokes, but in this undiluted form history was somehow sour. The print was determinedly legible, and smug, like a lesson book. As he bent over the pages, yellow at the edges, they seemed rectangles of dusty glass through which he looked down into unreal and irrelevant worlds. He could see things sluggishly move, and an unpleasant fullness came into his throat. His mother and grandmother fussed in the kitchen; the puppy, which they had just acquired, for "protection in the country," was cowering, with a sporadic panicked scrabble of claws, under the dining table that in their old home had been reserved for special days but that here was used for every meal.

Then before he could halt his eyes, David slipped into Well's account of Jesus. He had been an obscure political agitator, a kind of hobo, in a minor colony of the Roman Empire. By an accident impossible to reconstruct, he (the small *h* horrified David) survived his own crucifixion and presumably died a few weeks later. A religion was founded on the freakish incident. The credulous imagination of the times retrospectively assigned miracles and supernatural pretensions to Jesus; a myth grew, and then a church, whose theology at most points was in direct contradiction of the simple, rather communistic teachings of the Galilean.

It was as if a stone that for weeks and even years had been gathering weight in the web of David's nerves snapped them and plunged through the page and a hundred layers of paper underneath. These fantastic falsehoods—plainly untrue; churches stood everywhere, the entire nation was founded "under God"—did not at first frighten him; it was the fact that they had been permitted to exist in an actual human brain. This was the initial impact—that at a definite spot in time and space a brain black with the denial of Christ's divinity had been suffered to exist; that the universe had not spit out this ball of tar but allowed it to continue in its blasphemy, to grow old, win honors, wear a hat, write books that, if true, collapsed everything into a jumble of horror. The world outside the deep-silled windows—a rutted lawn, a whitewashed barn, a walnut tree frothy with fresh green—seemed a haven from which he was forever sealed off. Hot washrags seemed pressed against his cheeks.

He read the account again. He tried to supply out of his ignorance objections that would defeat the complacent march of these black words, and found none. Survivals and misunderstandings more far-fetched were reported daily in the papers. But none of them caused churches to be built in every town. He tried to work backwards through the churches, from their brave high fronts through their shabby, ill-attended interiors back into the events at Jerusalem, and felt himself surrounded by shifting gray shadows, centuries of history, where he knew nothing. The thread dissolved in his hands. Had Christ ever come to him, David Kern, and said, "Here. Feel the wound in My side?" No; but prayers had been answered. What prayers? He had prayed that Rudy Mohn, whom he had purposely tripped so he cracked his head on their radiator, not die, and he had not died. But for all the blood, it was just a cut; Rudy came back the same day, wearing a bandage and repeating the same teasing words. He could never have died. Again, David had prayed for two separate war-effort posters he had sent away for to arrive tomorrow, and though they did not, they did arrive, some days later, together, popping through the clacking letter slot like a rebuke from God's mouth: *I answer your prayers in My way, in My time.* After that, he had made his prayers less definite, less susceptible of being twisted into a scolding. But what a tiny, ridiculous coincidence this was, after all, to throw into battle against H. G. Wells's engines of knowledge! Indeed, it proved the enemy's point: Hope based vast premises on foolish accidents, and reads a word where in fact only a scribble exists.

His father came home. Though Saturday was a free day for him, he had been working. He taught school in Olinger and spent all his days performing, with a curious air of panic, needless errands. Also, a city boy by birth, he was frightened of the farm and seized any excuse to get away. The farm had been David's mother's birthplace; it had been her idea to buy it back. With an ingenuity and persistence unparalleled in her life, she had gained that end, and moved them all here—her son, her husband, her mother. Granmom, in her prime, had worked these fields alongside her husband, but now she dabbled around the kitchen futilely, her hands waggling with Parkinson's disease. She was always in the way. Strange, out in the country, amid eighty acres, they were crowded together. His father expressed his feelings of discomfort by conducting with Mother an endless argument about organic farming. All through dusk, all through supper, it rattled on.

"Elsie, I *know,* I know from my education, the earth is nothing but chemicals. It's the only damn thing I got out of four years of college, so don't' tell me it's not true."

"George, if you'd just walk out on the farm you'd know it's not true. The land has a *soul.*"

"Soil, has, no, soul," he said enunciating stiffly, as if to a very stupid class. To David he said, "You can't argue with a femme. Your mother's a real femme. That's why I married her, and now I'm suffering for it."

"*This* soil has no soul," she said, "because it's been killed with superphosphate. It's been burned bare by Boyer's tenant farmers." Boyer was the rich man they had bought the farm from. "It used to have a soul, didn't it, Mother? When you and Pop farmed it?"

"Ach, yes; I guess," Granmom was trying to bring a forkful of food to her mouth with her less severely afflicted hand. In her anxiety she brought the other hand up from her lap. The crippled fingers, dull red in the orange light of the kerosene lamp in the center of the table, were welded by paralysis into one knobbed hook.

"Only human indi-vidu-als have souls," his father went on, in the same mincing, lifeless voice. "Because the Bible tells us so." Done eating, he crossed his legs and dug into his ear with a match miserably; to get at the thing inside his head he tucked in his chin, and his voice came out low-pitched at David. "When God made your mother, He made a real femme."

"George, don't you read the papers? Don't you know that between the chemical fertilizers and the bug sprays we'll all be dead in ten years? Heart attacks are killing every man in the country over forty-five."

He sighed wearily; the yellow skin of his eyelids wrinkled as he hurt himself with the match. "There's no connection," he stated, spacing his words with pained patience, "between the heart — and chemical fertilizers. It's alcohol that's doing it. Alcohol and milk. There is too much — cholesterol — in the tissues of the American heart. Don't tell me about chemistry, Elsie; I majored in the damn stuff for four years."

"Yes and I majored in Greek and I'm not a penny wiser. Mother, put your waggler *away!*" The old woman started, and the food dropped from her fork. For some reason, the sight of her bad hand at the table cruelly irritated her daughter. Granmom's eyes, worn bits of crazed crystal embedded in watery milk, widened behind her cockeyed spectacles. Circles of silver as fine as thread, they clung to the red notches they had carved over the years into her little white beak. In the orange flicker of the kerosene lamp her dazed misery seemed infernal. David's mother began, without noise, to cry. His father did not seem to have eyes at all; just jaundiced sockets of wrinkled skin. The steam of food clouded the scene. It was horrible but the horror was particular and familiar, and distracted David from the formless dread that worked, sticky and sore, within him, like a too large wound trying to heal.

He had to go to the bathroom, and took a flashlight down through the wet grass to the outhouse. For once, his fear of spiders there felt trivial. He set the flashlight, burning, beside him, and an insect alighted on its lens, a tiny insect, a mosquito or flea, made so fine that the weak light projected its X-ray onto the wall boards; the faint rim of its wings, the blurred strokes, magnified, of its long hinged legs, the dark cone at the heart of its anatomy. The tremor must be its heart beating. Without warning, David was visited by an exact vision of death: a long hole in the ground, no wider than your body, down which you are drawn while the white faces above recede. You try to reach them but your arms are pinned. Shovels pour dirt into your face. There you will be forever, in an upright position (blind and silent), and in time no one will remember you, and you will never be called. As strata of rock shift, your fingers elongate, and your teeth are distended sideways in a great underground grimace undistinguishable from a strip of chalk. And the earth tumbles on, and the sun expires, and unaltering darkness reigns where once there were stars.

Sweat broke out on his back. His mind seemed to rebound off a solidness. Such extinction was not another threat, a graver sort of danger, a kind of pain; it was qualitatively different. It was not even a conception that could be voluntarily pictured; it entered him from outside. His protesting nerves swarmed on its surface like lichen on a meteor. The skin of his chest was soaked with the effort of rejection. At the same time that the fear was dense and internal, it was dense and all around him; a tide of clay had swept up to the stars; space was crushed into a mass. When he stood up, automatically hunching his shoulders to keep his head away from the spider webs, it was with a numb sense of being cramped between two huge volumes of rigidity. That he had even this small freedom to move surprised him. In the narrow shelter of that rank shack, adjusting his pants, he felt — his first spark of comfort — too small to be crushed.

But in the open, as the beam of the flashlight skidded with frightened quickness across the remote surfaces of the barn and the grape arbor and the giant pine that stood by the path to the woods, the terror descended. He raced up through the clinging grass pursued, not by one of the wild animals the woods might hold, or one of the goblins his superstitious grandmother had communicated to his childhood, but by specters out of science fiction, where gigantic cinder moons fill half the turquoise sky. As David ran, a gray planet rolled inches behind his neck. If he looked back, he would be buried. And in the momentum of his terror, hideous possibilities — the dilation of the sun, the triumph of the insects, the crabs on the shore in *The Time Machine* — wheeled out of the vacuum of make-believe and added their weight to his impending oblivion.

He wrenched the door open; the lamps within the house flared. The wicks burning here and there seemed to mirror one another. His mother was washing the dishes in a little pan of heated pump-water; Granmom fluttered near her elbow apprehensively. In the living room — the downstairs of the little square house was two long rooms — his father sat in front of the black fire place restlessly folding and unfolding a news paper as he sustained his half of the argument. "Nitrogen, phosphorus, potash: these are the three replaceable constituents of the soil. One crop of corn carries away hundreds of pounds of" — he dropped the paper into his lap and ticked them off on three fingers — "Nitrogen, phosphorus, potash."

"Boyer didn't grow corn."

"*Any* crop, Elsie. The human animal —"

"You're killing the *earth*worms, George!"

"The human animal, after thousands and *thou*sands of years, learned methods whereby the chemical balance of the soil may be maintained. Don't carry me back to the Dark Ages."

"When we moved to Olinger the ground in the garden was like slate. Just one summer of my cousin's chicken dung and the earthworms came back."

"I'm sure the Dark Ages were a fine place to the poor devils born in them, but I don't want to go there. They give me the creeps." Daddy stared into the cold pit of the fireplace and clung to the rolled newspaper in his lap as if it alone were keeping him from slipping backwards and down, down.

Mother came into the doorway brandishing a fistful of wet forks. "And thanks to your DDT there soon won't be a bee left in the country. When I was a girl here you could eat a peach without washing it."

"It's primitive, Elsie. It's Dark Age stuff."

"Oh what do *you* know about the Dark Ages?"

"I know I don't want to go back to them."

David took from the shelf, where he had placed it this afternoon, the great unabridged Webster's Dictionary that his grandfather had owned. He turned the big thin pages, floppy as cloth, to the entry he wanted, and read:

> soul . . . I. An entity conceived as the essence, substance, animating principle, or actuating cause of life, or of the individual life, esp. of life manifested in physical activities; the vehicle of individual existence, separate in nature from the body and usually held to be separable in existence.

The definition went on, into Greek and Egyptian conceptions, but David stopped short on the treacherous edge of antiquity. He needed to read no further. The careful overlapping words shingled a temporary shelter for him. "Usually held to be separable in existence" — what could be fairer, more judicious, surer?

His father was saying, "The modern farmer can't go around sweeping up after his cows. The poor devil has thousands and *thou*sands of acres on his hands. Your modern farmer uses a scientifically-arrived-at mixture, like five-ten-five, or six-twelve-six, or *three*-twelve-six, and spreads it on with this wonderful modern machinery which of course we can't afford. Your modern farmer can't *afford* medieval methods."

Mother was quiet in the kitchen; her silence radiated waves of anger.

"No now Elsie; don't play the femme with me. Let's discuss this calmly like two rational twentieth-century people. Your organic farming nuts aren't attacking five-ten-five; they're attacking the chemical fertilizer crooks. The monster firms."

A cup clinked in the kitchen. Mother's anger touched David's face; his cheeks burned guiltily. Just by being in the living room he was associated with his father. She appeared in the doorway with red hands and tears in her eyes, and said to the two of them, "I knew you didn't want to come here but I didn't know you'd torment me like this. You talked Pop into his grave and now you'll kill me. Go ahead, George, more power to you; at least I'll be buried in good ground." She tried to turn and met an obstacle and screamed, "Mother, stop hanging on my *back!* Why don't you go to *bed?*"

"Let's all go to bed," David's father said, rising from the blue wing chair and slapping his thigh with a newspaper. "This reminds me of death." It was a phrase of his that David had heard so often he never considered its sense.

Upstairs, he seemed to be lifted above his tears. The sheets on his bed were clean. Granmom had ironed them with a pair of flatirons saved from the Olinger attic; she plucked them hot off the stove alternately, with a wooden handle called a goose. It was a wonder, to see how she managed. In the next room, his parents grunted peaceably; they seemed to take their quarrels less seriously than he did. They made comfortable scratching noises as they carried a little lamp back and forth. Their door was open a crack, so he saw the light shift and swing. Surely there would be, in the last five minutes, in the last second, a crack of light, slowing the door from the dark room to another, full of light. Thinking of it this vividly frightened him. His own dying, in a specific bed in a specific room, specific walls mottled with wallpaper, the dry whistle of his breathing, the murmuring doctors, the nervous relatives going in and out, but for him no way out but down into the funnel. *Never touch a doorknob again.* A whisper, and his parents' light was blown out. David prayed to be reassured. Though the experiment frightened him, he lifted his hands high into the darkness above his face and begged Christ to touch them. Not hard or long: the faintest, quickest grip would be final for a lifetime. His hands waited in the air, itself a substance, which seemed to move through his fingers; or was it the pressure of his pulse? He returned his hands to beneath the covers uncertain if they had been touched or not. For would not Christ's touch *be* infinitely gentle?

Through all the eddies of its aftermath, David clung to this thought about his revelation of extinction: that there, in the outhouse, he had struck a solidness qualitatively different, a rock of horror firm enough to support any height of construction. All he needed was a little help; a word, a gesture, a nod of certainty, and he would be sealed in, safe. The assurance from the dictionary had melted in the night. Today was Sunday, a hot fair day. Across a mile of clear air the church bells called, *Celebrate, celebrate.* Only Daddy went. He put on a coat over his rolled-up shirtsleeves and got into the little old black Plymouth parked by the barn and went off, with the same pained hurried grimness of all his actions. His churning wheels, as he shifted too hastily into second, raised plumes of red dust on the dirt road. Mother walked to the far field, to see what bushes needed cutting. David, though he usually preferred to stay in the house, went with her. The puppy followed at a distance, whining as it picked its way through the stubble but floundering off timidly if one of them went back to pick it up and carry it. When they reached the crest of the far field, his mother asked, "David, what's troubling you?"

"Nothing. Why?"

She looked at him sharply. The greening woods crosshatched the space beyond her half-gray hair. Then she showed him her profile, and gestured toward the house, which they had left a half-mile behind them. "See how it sits in the land? They don't know how to build with the land any more. Pop always said the foundations were set with the compass. We must try to get a compass and see. It's supposed to face due south; but south feels a little more *that* way to me." From the side, as she said these things, she seemed handsome and young. The smooth sweep of her hair over her ear seemed white with a purity and calm that made her feel foreign to him. He had never regarded his parents as consolers of his troubles; from the beginning they had seemed to have more troubles than he. Their confusion had flattered him into an illusion of strength; so now on this high clear ridge he jealously guarded the menace all around them, blowing like a breeze on his fingertips, the possibility of all this wide scenery sinking into darkness. The strange fact that though she came to look at the brush she carried no clippers, for she had a fixed prejudice against working on Sundays, was the only consolation he allowed her to offer.

As they walked back, the puppy whimpering after them, the rising dust behind a distant line of trees announced that Daddy was speeding home from church. When they reached the house he was there. he had brought back the Sunday paper and the vehement remark, "Dobson's too intelligent for these farmers. They just sit there with their mouths open and don't hear a thing the poor devil's saying."

"What makes you think farmers are unintelligent? This country was made by farmers. George Washington was a farmer."

"They are, Elsie. They are unintelligent. George Washington's dead. In this day and age only the misfits stay on the farm. The lame, the halt, the blind. The morons with one arm. Human garbage. They remind me of death, sitting there with their mouths open.

"My *father* was a farmer."

60

"He was a frustrated man, Elsie. He never knew what hit him. The poor devil meant so well, and he never knew which end was up. Your mother'll bear me out. Isn't that right, Mom? Pop never knew what hit him?"

"Ach, I guess not," the old woman quavered, and the ambiguity for the moment silenced both sides.

David hid in the funny papers and sport section until one-thirty. At two, the catechetical class met at the Firetown church. He had transferred from the catechetical class of the Lutheran church in Olinger, a humiliating comedown. In Olinger they met on Wednesday nights, spiffy and spruce, in the atmosphere of a dance. Afterwards, blessed by the brick-faced minister from those lips the word "Christ" fell like a burning stone, the more daring of them went with their Bibles to a luncheonette and smoked. Here in Firetown, the girls were dull white cows and the boys narrow-faced brown goats in old men's suits, herded on Sunday afternoons into a threadbare church basement that smelled of stale hay. Because his father had taken the car on one of his endless errands to Olinger, David walked, grateful for the open air and the silence. The catechetical class embarrassed him, but today he placed hope in it, as the source of the nod, the gesture, that was all he needed.

Reverend Dobson was a delicate young man with great dark eyes and small white shapely hands that flickered like protesting doves when he preached; he seemed a bit misplaced in the Lutheran ministry. This was his first call. It was a split parish; he served another rural church twelve miles away. His iridescent green Ford, new six months ago, was spattered to the windows with red mud and rattled from bouncing on the rude back roads, where he frequently got lost, to the malicious satisfaction of many. But David's mother liked him, and, more pertinent to his success, the Haiers, the sleek family of feed merchants and innkeepers and tractor salesmen who dominated the Firetown church, liked him. David liked him, and felt liked in turn; sometimes in class, after some special stupidity, Dobson directed toward him out of those wide black eyes a mild look of disbelief, a look that, though flattering, was also delicately disquieting.

Catechetical instruction consisted of reading aloud from a work booklet answers to problems prepared during the week, problems like, "I am the _____, the _____, and the _____, saith the Lord." Then there was a question period in which no one ever asked any questions. Today's theme was the last third of the Apostles' Creed. When the time came for questions, David blushed and asked, "About the Resurrection of the Body—are we conscious between the time when we die and the Day of Judgment?"

Dobson blinked, and his fine little mouth pursued, suggesting that David was making difficult things more difficult. The faces of the other students went blank, as if an indiscretion had been committed.

"No, I suppose not," Reverend Dobson said.

"Well, where is our soul, then, in this gap?"

The sense grew, in the class, of a naughtiness occurring. Dobson's shy eyes watered, as if he were straining to keep up the formality of attention, and one of the girls, the fattest, simpered toward her twin, who was a little less fat. Their chairs were arranged in a rough circle. The current running around the circle panicked David. Did everybody know something he didn't know?

"I suppose you could say our souls are asleep," Dobson said.

"And then they wake up, and there is the earth like it always is, and all the people who have ever lived? Where will Heaven be?"

61

Anita Haier giggled. Dobson gazed at David intently, but with an awkward, puzzled flicker of forgiveness, as if there existed a secret between them that David was violating. But David knew of no secret. All he wanted was to hear Dobson repeat the words he said every Sunday morning. This he would not do. As if these words were unworthy of the conversational voice.

"David, you might think of Heaven this way: as the way the goodness Abraham Lincoln did lives after him."

"But is Lincoln conscious of it living on?" He blushed no longer with embarrassment but in anger; he had walked here in good faith and was being made a fool.

"Is he conscious now? I would have to say no; but I don't think it matters." His voice had a coward's firmness; he was hostile now.

"You don't."

"Not in the eyes of God, no." The unction, the stunning impudence, of this reply sprang tears of outrage in David's eyes. He bowed them to his book, where short words like Duty, Love, Obey, Honor, were stacked in the form of a cross.

"Were there any other questions, David?" Dobson asked with renewed gentleness. The others were rustling, collecting their books.

"No." He made his voice firm, though he could not bring up his eyes.

"Did I answer your question fully enough?"

"Yes."

In the minister's silence the shame that should have been his crept over David: the burden and fever of being a fraud were placed upon *him*, who was innocent, and it seemed, he knew, a confession of this guilt that on the way out he was unable to face Dobson's stirred gaze, though he felt it probing the side of his head.

Anita Haier's father gave him a ride down the highway as far as the dirt road. David said he wanted to walk the rest, and figured that his offer was accepted because Mr. Haier did not want to dirty his bright blue Buick with dust. This was all right; everything was all right, as long as it was clear. His indignation at being betrayed, at seeing Christianity betrayed, had hardened him. The straight dirt road reflected his hardness. Pink stones thrust up through its packed surface. The April sun beat down from the center of the afternoon half of the sky; already it had some of summer's heat. Already the fringes of weeds at the edges of the road were bedraggled with dust. From the reviving grass and scuff of the fields he walked between, insects were sending up a monotonous, automatic chant. In the distance a tiny figure in his father's coat was walking along the edge of the woods. His mother. He wondered what joy she found in such walks; to him the brown stretches of slowly rising and falling land expressed only a huge exhaustion.

Flushed with fresh air and happiness, she returned from her walk earlier than he had expected, and surprised him at his grandfather's Bible. It was a stumpy black book, the boards worn thin where the old man's fingers had held them; the spine hung by one weak hinge of fabric. David had been looking for the passage where Jesus says to the one thief on the cross, "Today shalt thou be with me in paradise." He had never tried reading the Bible for himself before. What was so embarrassing about being caught at it, was that he detested the apparatus of piety. Fusty churches, creaking hymns, ugly Sunday-school teachers and their stupid leaflets— he hated everything about them but the promise they held out, a promise that in the most perverse way, as if the homeliest crone in the kingdom were given the Prince's hand, made every good and real thing, ball games and jokes and pert-breasted girls, possible. He couldn't explain this to his mother. There was no time. Her solicitude was upon him.

"David, what are you doing?"

"Nothing."

"What are you doing at Grandpop's Bible?"

"Trying to read it. This is supposed to be a Christian country, isn't it?"

She sat down on the green sofa, which used to be in the sun parlor at Olinger, under the fancy mirror. A little smile still lingered on her face from the walk. "David, I wish you'd talk to me."

"What about?"

"About whatever it is that's troubling you. Your father and I have both noticed it."

"I asked Reverend Dobson about Heaven and he said it was like Abraham Lincoln's goodness living after him."

He waited for the shock to strike her. "Yes?" she said, expecting more.

"That's all."

"And why didn't you like it?"

"Well, don't you see? It amounts to saying there isn't any Heaven at all."

"I don't see that it amounts to that. What do you want Heaven to be?"

"Well, I don't know. I want it to be *some*thing. I thought he'd tell me what it was. I thought that was his job." He was becoming angry, sensing her surprise at him. She had assumed that Heaven had faded from his head years ago. She had imagined that he had already entered, in the secrecy of silence, the conspiracy that he now knew to be all around him.

"David," she asked gently, "don't you ever want to rest?"

"No. Not forever."

"David, you're so young. When you get older, you'll feel differently."

"Grandpa didn't. Look how tattered this book is."

"I never understood your grandfather."

"Well I don't understand ministers who say it's like Lincoln's goodness going on and on. Suppose you're not Lincoln?"

"I think Reverend Dobson made a mistake. You must try to forgive him."

"It's not a *question* of his making a mistake! It's a question of dying and never moving or seeing or hearing anything ever again."

"But"—in exasperation—"darling, it's so *greedy* of you to want more. When God has given us this wonderful April day, and given us this farm, and you have your whole life ahead of you—"

"You think, then, that there is God?"

"Of course I do"—with deep relief, that smoothed her features into a reposeful oval. He had risen and was standing too near her for his comfort. He was afraid she would reach out and touch him.

"He made everything? You feel that?"

"Yes."

"Then who made Him?"

"Why, Man. Man." The happiness of this answer lit up her face radiantly, until she saw his gesture of disgust. She was so simple, so illogical; such a femme.

"Well that amounts to saying there is none."

Her hand reached for his wrist but he backed away. "David, it's a mystery. A miracle. It's a miracle more beautiful than any Reverend Dobson could have told you about. You don't say houses don't exist because Man made them."

"No, God has to be different."

"But, David, you have the *evidence*. Look out the window at the sun; at the fields."

"Mother, good grief. Don't you see"—he rasped away the roughness in his throat—"if when we die there's nothing, all your sun and fields and what not are all, ah, *horrors?* It's just an ocean of horror."

"But David, it's not. It's so clearly not that." And she made an urgent opening gesture with her hands that expressed, with its suggestions of a willingness to receive his helplessness, all her grace, her gentleness, her love of beauty, gathered into a passive intensity that made him intensely hate her. He would not be wooed away from the truth. *I am the Way, the Truth....*

"No," he told her. "Just let me alone."

He found his tennis ball behind the piano and went outside to throw it against the side of the house. There was a patch high up where the brown stucco that had been laid over the sandstone masonry was crumbling away; he kept trying with the tennis ball to chip more pieces off. Superimposed upon his deep ache was a smaller but more immediate worry; that he had hurt his mother. He heard his father's car rattling on the straightaway, and went into the house, to make peace before he arrived. To his relief, she was not giving off the stifling damp heat of her anger, but instead was cool, decisive, maternal. She handed him an old green book, her college text of Plato.

"I want you to read the 'Parable of the Cave'," she said.

"All right," he said, though he knew it would do no good. Some story by a dead Greek just vague enough to please her. "Don't worry about it, Mother."

"I *am* worried. Honestly, David, I'm sure there will be something for us. As you get older, these things seem to matter a great deal less."

"That may be. It's a dismal thought, though."

His father bumped at the door. The locks and jambs stuck here. But before Granmom could totter to the latch and let him in, he had knocked it open. He had been in Olinger dithering with track meet tickets. Although Mother usually kept her talks with David a confidence, a treasure between them, she called instantly, "George, David is worried about death!"

He came to the doorway of the living room, his shirt pocket bristling with pencils holding in one hand a pint box of melting ice cream and in the other the knife with which he was about to divide it into four sections, their Sunday treat. "Is the kid worried about death? Don't give it a thought, David. I'll be lucky if I live till tomorrow, and I'm not worried. If they'd taken a buckshot gun and shot me in the cradle I'd be better off. The *world*'d be better off. Hell, I think death is a wonderful thing. I look forward to it. Get the garbage out of the way. If I had the man here who invented death, I'd pin a medal on him."

"Hush, George. You'll frightened the child worse than he is."

This was not true; he never frightened David. There was no harm in his father, no harm at all. Indeed, in the man's steep self-disgust the boy felt a kind of ally. A distant ally. He saw his position with a certain strategic coldness. Nowhere in the world of other people would he find the hint, the nod, he needed to begin to build his fortress against death. They none of them believed. He was alone. In that deep hole.

In the months that followed, his position changed little. School was some comfort. All those sexy, perfumed people, wisecracking, chewing gum, all of them doomed to die, and none of them noticing. In their company David felt that they would carry him along into the bright, cheap paradise reserved for them. In any crowd, the fear ebbed a little; he had reasoned that somewhere in the world there must exist a few people who believed what was necessary, and the larger the crowd, the greater the chance that he was near such a soul, within calling distance, if only he was not too ignorant, too ill-equipped, to spot him. The sight of clergymen cheered him; whatever they themselves thought, their collars were still a sign that somewhere, at some time, someone had recognized that we cannot, *cannot*, submit to death. The sermon topics posted outside churches, the flip, hurried pieties of disc jockeys, the cartoons in magazines showing angels or devils—on such scraps he kept alive the possibility of hope.

For the rest, he tried to drown his hopelessness in clatter and jostle. The pinball machine at the luncheonette was a merciful distraction; as he bent over its buzzing, flashing board of flippers and cushions, the weight and constriction in his chest lightened and loosened. He was grateful for all the time his father wasted in Olinger. Every delay postponed the moment when they must ride together down the dirt road into the heart of the dark farmland, where the only light was the kerosene lamp waiting on the dining-room table, a light that drowned their food in shadow and made it sinister.

He lost his appetite for reading. He was afraid of being ambushed again. In mystery novels people died like dolls being discarded; in science fiction enormities of space and time conspired to crush the humans; and even in P. G. Wodehouse he felt a hollowness, a turning away from reality that was implicitly bitter, and became explicit in the comic figures of futile clergymen. All gaity seemed minced out on the skin of a void. All quiet hours seemed invitations to dread.

Even on weekends, he and his father contrived to escape the farm; and when, some Saturdays, they did stay home, it was to do something destructive—tear down an old henhouse or set huge brush fires that threatened, while Mother shouted and flapped her arms, to spread to the woods. Whenever his father worked, it was with rapt violence; when he chopped kindling, fragments of the old henhouse boards flew like shrapnel and the ax-head was always within a quarter of an inch of flying off the handle. He was exhilarating to watch, sweating and swearing and sucking bits of saliva back into his lips.

School stopped. His father took the car in the opposite direction, to a highway construction job where he had been hired for the summer as a timekeeper, and David was stranded in the middle of acres of heat and greenery and blowing pollen and the strange, mechanical humming that lay invisibly in the weeds and alfalfa and dry orchard grass.

For his fifteenth birthday his parents gave him, with jokes about him being a hillbilly now, a Remington .22. It was somewhat like a pinball machine to take it out to the old kiln in the woods where they dumped their trash, and set up tin cans on the kiln's sandstone shoulder and shoot them off one by one. He'd take the puppy, who had grown long legs and a rich coat of reddish fur—he was part chow. Copper hated the gun but loved the boy enough to accompany him. When the flat acrid crack rang out, he would race in terrified circles that would tighten and tighten until they brought him, shivering, against David's legs. Depending upon his mood, David would shoot again or drop to his knees and comfort the dog. Giving this comfort to a degree returned comfort to him. The dog's ears, laid flat against his skull in fear, were folded so intricately, so—he groped for the concept—surely. Where the dull-studded collar made the fur stand up, each hair showed a root of soft white under the length, black-tipped, of the metal-colored that had lent the dog its name. In his agitation Copper panted through nostrils that were elegant slits, like two healed cuts, or like the keyholes of a dainty lock of black, grained wood. His whole whorling, knotted, jointed body was a wealth of such embellishments. And in the smell of the dog's hair David seemed to descend through many finely differentiated layers of earth: mulch, soil, sand, clay, and the glittering mineral base.

But when he returned to the house, and saw the books arranged on the low shelves, fear returned. The four adamant volumes of Wells like four thin bricks, the green Plato that had puzzled him with its queer softness and tangled purity, the dead Galsworthy and "Elizabeth," Grandpa's mammoth dictionary, Grandpa's Bible, the Bible that he himself had received on becoming a member of the Firetown Lutheran Church—at the sight of these, the memory of his fear reawakened and came around him. He had grown stiff and stupid in its embrace. His parents tried to think of ways to entertain him.

"David, I have a job for you to do," his mother said one evening at the table.

"What?"

"If you're going to take that tone perhaps we'd better not talk."

"What tone? I didn't take any tone."

"Your grandmother thinks there are too many pigeons in the barn."

"Why?" David turned to look at his grandmother, but she sat there staring at the burning lamp with her usual expression of bewilderment.

Mother shouted, "Mom, he wants to know why!"

Granmom made a jerky, irritable motion with her bad hand, as if generating the force for utterance, and said, "They foul the furniture."

"That's right,"Mother said. "She' afraid for that old Olinger furniture that we'll never use. David, she's been after me for a month about those poor pigeons. She wants you to shoot them."

"I don't want to kill anything especially," David said.

Daddy said, "The kid's like you are, Elsie. He's too good for this world. Kill or be killed, that's my motto."

His mother said loudly, "Mother, he doesn't want to do it."

"Not?" The old lady's eyes distended as if in horror, and her claw descended slowly to her lap.

"Oh, I'll do it, I'll do it tomorrow," David snapped, and a pleasant crisp taste entered his mouth with the decision.

"And I thought, when Boyer's men made the hay, it would be better if the barn doesn't look like a rookery," his mother added needlessly.

A barn, in day, is a small night. The splinters of light between the dry shingles pierce the high roof like stars, and the rafters and crossbeams and built-in ladders seem, until your eyes adjust, as mysterious as the branches of a haunted forest. David entered silently, the gun in one hand. Copper whined desperately at the door, too frightened to come in with the gun yet unwilling to leave the boy. David stealthily turned, said "Go away," shut the door on the dog, and slipped the bolt across. It was a door within a door; the double door for wagons and tractors was as high and wide as the face of the house.

The smell of old straw scratched his sinuses. The red sofa, half-hidden under its white-splotched tarpaulin, seemed assimilated into this smell, sunk in it, buried. The mouths of empty bins gaped like caves. Rusty oddments of farming—coils of baling wire, sole spare tines for a harrow, a handleless shovel—hung on nails driven here and there in the thick wood. He stood stock-still a minute; it took a while to separate the cooing of the pigeons from the rustling in his ears. When he had focused on the cooing, it flooded the vast interior with its throaty, bubbling outpour: there seemed no other sound. They were up behind the beams. What light there was leaked through the shingles and the dirty glass windows at the far end and the small round holes, about as big as basketballs, high on the opposite stone side walls, under the ridge of the roof.

A pigeon appeared in one of these holes, on the side toward the house. It flew in, with a battering of wings, from the outside, and waited there, silhouetted against its pinched bit of sky, preening and cooing in a throbbing, thrilled, tentative way. David tiptoed four steps to the side, rested his gun against the lowest rung of a ladder pegged between two upright beams, and lowered the gunsight into the bird's tiny, jauntily cocked head. The slap of the report seemed to come off the stone wall behind him, and the pigeon did not fall. Neither did it fly. Instead it stuck in the round hole, pirouetting, rapidly and nodding its head as if in frantic agreement. David shot the bolt back and forth and had aimed again before the spent cartridge had stopped jingling on the boards by his feet. He eased the tip of the sight a little lower, into the bird's breast, and took care to squeeze the trigger with perfect evenness. The slow contraction of his hand abruptly sprang the bullet; for a half-second there was doubt, and then the pigeon fell like a handful of rags, skimming down the barn wall into the layer of straw that coated the floor of the mow on this side.

Now others shook loose from the rafters, and whirled in the dim air with a great blurred hurtle of feathers and noise. They would go for the hole; he fixed his sight on the little moon of blue, and when a pigeon came to it, shot him as he was walking the ten inches of stone that would have carried him into the open air. This pigeon lay down in that tunnel of stone, unable to fall either one way or the other, although he was alive enough to lift one wing and cloud the light. It would sink back, and he would suddenly lift it again, the feathers flaring. His body blocked that exit. David raced to the other side of the barn's main aisle, where a similar ladder was symmetrically placed, and rested his gun on the same rung. Three birds came together to this hole; he got one, and two got through. The rest resettled in the rafters.

There was a shallow triangular space behind the cross beams supporting the roof. It was here they roosted and hid. But either the space was too small, or they were curious, for now that his eyes were at home in the dusty gloom David could see little dabs of gray popping in an out. The cooing was shriller now; its apprehensive tremolo made the whole volume of air seem liquid. He noticed one little smudge of a head that was especially persistent in peeking out; he marked the place, and fixed his gun on it, and when the head appeared again, had his finger tightened in advanced on the trigger. A parcel of fluff slipped off the beam and fell the barn's height onto a canvas covering some Olinger furniture, and where its head had peeked out there was a fresh prick of light in the shingles.

Standing in the center of the floor, fully master now, disdaining to steady the barrel with anything but his arms, he killed two more that way. He felt like a beautiful avenger. Out of the shadowy ragged infinity of the vast barn roof these impudent things dared to thrust their heads, presumed to dirty its starred silence with their filthy timorous life, and he cut them off, tucked them back neatly into the silence. He had the sensation of a creator; these little smudges and flickers that he was clever to see and even cleverer to hit in the dim recesses of the rafters—out of each of them he was making a full bird. A tiny peek, probe, dab of life, when he hit it, blossomed into a dead enemy, falling with good, final weight.

The imperfection of the second pigeon he had shot, who was still lifting his wing now and then up in the round hole, nagged him. He put a new slip into the stock. Hugging the gun against his body, he climbed the ladder. The barrel sight scratched his ear; he had a sharp, garish vision, like a color slide, of shooting himself and being found tumbled on the barn floor among his prey. He locked his arm around the top rung—a fragile, gnawed rod braced between uprights—and shot into the bird's body from a flat angle. The wing folded, but the impact did not, as he had hoped, push the bird out of the hole. He fired again, and again, and again, and still the little body, lighter than air when alive, was too heavy to budge from its high grave. From up here he could see green trees and a brown corner of the house through the hole. Clammy with the cobwebs that gathered between the rungs, he pumped a full clip of eight bullets into the stubborn shadow, with no success. He climbed down, and was struck by the silence in the barn. The remaining pigeons must have escaped out the other hole. That was all right; he was tired of it.

He stepped with his rifle into the light. His mother was coming to meet him, and it tickled him to see her shy away from the carelessly held gun. "You took a chip out of the house," she said. "What were those last shots about?"

"One of them died up in that little round hole and I was trying to shoot it down."

"Copper's hiding behind the piano and won't come out. I had to leave him."

"Well don't blame me. *I* didn't want to shoot the poor devils."

"Don't smirk. You look like your father. How many did you get?"

"Six."

She went into the barn, and he followed. She listened to the silence. Her hair was scraggly, perhaps from tussling with the dog. "I don't suppose the others will be back," she said wearily. "Indeed, I don't know why I let Mother talk me into it. Their cooing was such a comforting noise." She began to gather up the dead pigeons. Though he didn't want to touch them, David went into the mow and picked up by its tepid, horny, coral-colored feet the first bird he had killed. Its wings unfolded disconcertingly, as if the creature had been held together by threads that now were slit. It did not weigh much. He retrieved the one on the other side of the barn; his mother got the three in the middle and led the way across the road to the little southern slope of land that went down toward the foundations of the vanished tobacco shed. The ground was too steep to plant and mow; wild strawberries grew in the tangled grass. She put her burden down and said, "We'll have to bury them. The dog will go wild."

He put his two down on her three; the slick feathers let the bodies slide liquidly on one another. He asked, "Shall I get you a shovel?"

"Get it for yourself; *you* bury them. They're your kill. And be sure to make the hole deep enough so he won't dig them up." While he went to the tool shed for the shovel, she went into the house. Unlike her, she did not look up, either at the orchard to the right of her or at the meadow on her left, but instead held her rigidly, tilted a little, as if listening to the ground.

He dug the hole, in a spot where there were no strawberry plants, before he studied the pigeons. He had never seen a bird this close before. The feathers were more wonderful than dog's hair, for each filament was shaped within the shape of the feather, and the feathers in turn were trimmed to fit a pattern that flowed without error across the bird's body. He lost himself in the geometrical tides as the feathers now broadened and stiffened to make an edge for flight, now softened and constricted to cup warmth around the mute flesh. And across the surface of the infinitely adjusted yet somehow effortless mechanics of the feathers played idle designs of color, no two alike, designs executed, it seemed, in a controlled rapture, with a joy that hung level in the air above and behind him. Yet these birds bred in the millions and were exterminated as pests. Into the fragrant open earth he dropped one broadly banded in slate shades of blue, and on top of it another, mottled all over in rhythms of lilac and gray. The next was almost wholly white, but for a salmon glaze at its throat. As he fitted the last two, still pliant, on the top, and stood up, crusty coverings were lifted from him, and with a feminine, slipping sensation along his nerves that seemed to give the air hands, he was robed in this certainty:

that the God who had lavished such craft upon these worthless birds would not destroy His whole Creation by refusing to let David live forever.

Christian Perspectives

1. David's first encounter with anti-Christian views actually forced him to confront his own beliefs. To resolve his confusion, what does he want God to do for him? Give an example of someone in the Bible who had a similar request.
2. To David, "everything was all right, as long as it was clear." This statement typifies our wishes for answers that are always available. Describe a personal experience in which faith (in what you could not see) became real to you.
3. The story describes David as "being in a hole," which is how he seems to relate to his family, his peers, and his minister. What are his "observations" of the people around him, and why does he seem so detached?
4. The traditional ways to find God are not there for David. His minister betrays him; his mother offers philosophy; his peers seem indifferent. Ultimately he is alone in his search for God. Trace the biblical principles that support the idea that we are responsible for our own salvation.
5. How can David's father, a skeptical materialist in many ways, be presented as a Christian character, when his mother, so prone to spiritualizing, is not?
6. In at least three places in the story Updike shows David perceiving patterns, images of ordered color: imagining the hole in the earth where he will be buried, becoming part of the layers of the earth and chalk; the regular layers of color on Copper's hair; and the designs of color of the pigeons' wings. Can you find that this image motif reinforces the unfolding of David's resolution or insight?
7. David's grandfather seems to be the only one who was interested in finding the answers in the Bible, and yet David's mother says she never understood his grandfather. What could Updike be saying about the way others respond to those who seek a personal relationship with God?
8. The surrounding complacency toward Christianity seems to be a secret conspiracy to David. How is this realization an innocence-to-maturity experience?
9. David finds his answer in the unanticipated beauty of God's creation. Why do you think it was necessary for David to renew his faith in an ordinary occurrence rather than in a miraculous one?
10. St. Anselm said, "I believe in order that I might understand." While David's search in the story seems to be a search for faith, can it be read as a search for understanding by one who *has* faith? In that reading, can it be said that David's faith shapes his perceptions?
11. Trace the path of David's emotions as he shoots and then buries the pigeons. Ultimately he is reassured, but is it a reassurance we readers can take comfort in? What understanding of faith and hope does the story seem to present?

Spiritual Authenticity in the Community of God

TOWARD A CHRISTIAN ESTHETIC*
Dorothy L. Sayers

I have been asked to speak about the arts in [England]—their roots in Christianity, their present condition, and the means by which (if we find that they are not flourishing as they should) their mutilated limbs and withering branches may be restored by regrafting into the main trunk of Christian tradition.

This task is of quite peculiar difficulty, and I may not be able to carry it out in exactly the terms that have been proposed to me. And that for a rather strange reason. In such things as politics, finance, sociology, and so on, there really are a philosophy and a Christian tradition; we do know more or less what the Church has said and thought about them, how they are related to Christian dogma, and what they are supposed to do in a Christian country.

But oddly enough, we have no Christian esthetic—no Christian philosophy of the arts. The Church as a body has never made up her mind about the arts, and it is hardly too much to say that she has never tried. She has, of course, from time to time puritanically denounced the arts as irreligious and mischievous, or tried to exploit the arts as a means to the teaching of religion and morals—but I shall hope to show you that both these attitudes are false and degrading and are founded upon a completely mistaken idea of what art is supposed to be and do. And there have, of course, been plenty of writers on esthetics who happened to be Christians, but they seldom made any consistent attempt to relate their esthetic to the central Christian dogmas. Indeed, so far as European esthetic is concerned, one feels that it would probably have developed along precisely the same lines had there never been an Incarnation to reveal the nature of God—that is to say, the nature of all truth. But that is fantastic. If we commit ourselves to saying that the Christian revelation discovers to us the nature of all truth, then it must discover

---

* It will be immediately obvious how deeply this paper is indebted to R. G. Collingwood's <u>Principles of Art</u>, particularly as regards the disentangling of art proper (expression and imagination) from the pseudoarts of amusement and magic. The only contribution I have made of my own (exclusive of incidental errors) has been to suggest, however tentatively, a method of establishing the principles of art proper upon that Trinitarian doctrine of the nature of creative mind that does, I think, really underlie them. On this foundation it might perhaps be possible to develop a Christian aesthetic, which, finding its source and sanction in the theological center, would be at once more characteristically Christian and of more universal application than any aesthetic whose contact with Christianity is made only at the ethical circumference. —D.L.S.

to us the nature of the truth about art among other things. It is absurd to go placidly along explaining art in terms of a pagan esthetic and taking no notice whatever of the complete revolution of our ideas about the nature of things that occurred, or should have occurred, after the first Pentecost. I will go so far as to maintain that the extraordinary confusion of our minds about the nature and function of art is principally due to the fact that for nearly two thousand years we have been trying to reconcile a pagan, or at any rate a Unitarian, esthetic with a Christian—that is, a Trinitarian and Incarnational—theology. Even that makes us out too intelligent. We have not tried to reconcile them. We have merely allowed them to exist side by side in our minds; and where the conflict between them became too noisy to be overlooked, we have tried to silence the clamor by main force, either by brutally subjugating art to religion, or by shutting them up in separate prison cells and forbidding them to hold any communication with each other.

Now, before we go any further, I want to make it quite clear that what I am talking about now is esthetic (the philosophy of art) and not about art itself as practiced by the artists. The great artists carry on with their work on the lines God has laid down for them, quite unaffected by the esthetic worked out for them by philosophers. Sometimes, of course, artists themselves dabble in esthetic, and what they have to say is very interesting, but often very misleading. If they really are great and true artists, they make their poem (or whatever it is) first, and then set about reconciling it with the fashionable esthetic of their time; they do not produce their work to conform to their notions of esthetic—or, if they do, they are so much-the-less artists, and the work suffers. Secondly, what artists chatter about to the world and to one another is not as a rule their art but the technique of their art. They will tell you, as critics, how it is they produce certain effects (the poet will talk about assonance, alliteration, and meter; the painter about perspective, balance, and how he mixes his colors, etc.)—and from that we may get the misleading impression that the technique is the art, or that the aim of art is to produce some sort of effect. But this is not so. We cannot go for a march unless we have learned, through long practice, how to control the muscles of our legs; but it is not true to say that the muscular control is the march. And while it is a fact that certain tricks produce effects—such as Tennyson's use of vowels and consonants to produce the effect of a sleepy murmuring in "The moan of doves in immemorial elms," or of metallic clashing in "The bare black cliff clanged round him"—it is not true that the poem is merely a set of physical, or even of emotional, effects. What a work of art really is and does we shall come to later. For the moment I want only to stress the difference between esthetic and art and to make it clear that a great artist will produce great art, even though the esthetic of the time may be hopelessly inadequate to explain it.

For the origins of European esthetic we shall, of course, turn to Greece; and we are at once brought up against the two famous chapters in which Plato discusses the arts and decides that certain kinds of art, and in particular certain kinds of poetry, ought to be banished from the perfect state. Not all poetry—people often talk as though Plato had said this, but he did not; certain kinds he wished to keep, and this makes his attitude all the more puzzling because, though he tells us quite clearly why he disapproves of the rejected kinds, he never explains what it is that makes the other kinds valuable. He never gets down to considering, constructively, what true art is or what it does. He tells us only about what are (in his opinion) the bad results of certain kinds of art—nor does he ever tackle the question whether the bad moral results of which he complains may not be due to a falseness in the art, i.e., to the work's being pseudoart or inartistic art. He seems to say that certain forms of art are inherently evil in themselves. His whole handling of the thing seems to us very strange, confused, and contradictory; yet his esthetic has dominated all our critical thinking for many centuries and has influenced, in particular, the attitude of the Church more than the Church perhaps knows. So it is necessary that we should look at Plato's argument. Many of his conclusions are true—though often, I think, he reaches them from the wrong premises. Some of them are, I think, demonstrably false. But especially, his whole grasp of the subject is inadequate. That is not Plato's fault. He was one of the greatest thinkers of all time, but he was a pagan; and I am becoming convinced that no pagan philosopher could produce an adequate esthetic, simply for lack of a right theology. In this respect, the least in the kingdom of heaven is greater than John the Baptist.

What does Plato say?

He begins by talking about stories and myths, and after dismissing as beneath consideration the stories and poems that are obviously badly written, he goes on to reject those that are untrue, or that attribute evil and disgusting behavior to the gods, or that tend to inculcate bad and vulgar passions or antisocial behavior in the audience. After this (which sounds very much like what moralists and the clergy are always saying nowadays) he leaves the subject matter and goes on to certain forms of poetry and art—those forms that involve *mimesis*—the mimetic arts. Now *mimesis* can be translated as imitation or representation; and we can at once see that certain forms of art are more mimetic than others. Drama, painting, and sculpture are, on the whole mimetic—some natural object or action is represented or imitated (though we may find exceptions in modernist and surrealist paintings that seem to represent nothing in heaven or earth). Music, on the other hand, is not mimetic—nothing is imitated from the natural world, unless we count certain effects such as the noise of drums in a martial piece, or trills and arpeggios representing the song of birds or the falling of water, down to the squeaks, brayings, twitterings, and whistlings of cinema organs. In the third book of the *Republic,* Plato says he will allow the mimetic arts, provided that the imitation or representation is of something morally edifying, that sets a good example; but he would banish altogether the representation of unworthy objects, such as national heroes wallowing about in floods of tears, and people getting drunk, or using foul language. He thinks this kind of thing bad for the actors and also for the audience. Nor (which seems odd to us) are actors to imitate anything vulgar or base, such as artisans plying their trades, galley slaves or bos'ns; nor must there be any trivial nonsense about stage effects and farmyard imitations. Nothing is to be acted or shown except what is worthy to be imitated, the noble actions of wise men—a gallery of good examples.

We may feel that Plato's theater would be rather on the austere side. But in the tenth book he hardens his heart still further. He decides to banish all mimetic art, all representation of every kind—and that for two reasons.

The first reason is that imitation is a kind of cheat. An artist who knows nothing about carpentering may yet paint a carpenter, so that if the picture is set up at a distance, children and stupid people may be deceived into thinking that it really is a carpenter. Moreover, in any case, the realities of things exist only in heaven in an ideal and archetypal form; the visible world is only a pale reflection or bad imitation of the heavenly realities; and the work of art is only a cheating imitation of the visible world. Therefore, representational art is merely an imitation of an imitation—a deceptive trick that tickles and entertains while turning men's minds away from the contemplation of the eternal realities.

At this point some of you will begin to fidget and say, "Hi! Stop! Surely there is a difference between mimicry intended to deceive and representation. I admit that there are such things as tin biscuit boxes got up to look like the works of Charles Dickens, which may deceive the unwary, and that very simple-minded people in theaters have been known to hiss the villain or leap on the stage to rescue the heroine—but as a rule we know perfectly well that the imitation is only imitation and not meant to take anyone in. And surely there's a difference between farmyard imitations and John Gielgud playing Hamlet. And besides—even if you get an exact representation of something—say a documentary film about a war, or an exact verbal reproduction of a scene at the Old Bailey—that's not the same thing as *Coriolanus* or the trial scene in *The Merchant of Venice;* the work of art has something different, something more—poetry or a sort of a something . . ." and here you will begin to wave your hands about vaguely.

You are, of course, perfectly right. But let us for the moment just make a note of how Plato's conception of art is influenced by his theology—the visible world imitating, copying, reflecting a world of eternal changeless forms already existent elsewhere; and the artist, conceived of as a sort of craftsman or artisan engaged in copying or imitating something that exists already in the visible world.

Now let us take [Plato's] second reason for banishing all representational art. He says that even where the action represented is in itself good and noble, the effect on the audience is bad because it leads them to dissipate the emotions and energies that ought to be used for tackling the problems of life. The feelings of courage, resolution, pity, indignation, and so on are worked up in the spectators by the mimic passions on the stage (or in pictures or music) and then frittered away in a debauch of emotion over these unreal shadows, leaving the mind empty and slack, with no appetite except for fresh sensations of an equally artificial sort.

Now, that is a real indictment against a particular kind of art, which we ought to take seriously. In the jargon of modern psychology, Plato is saying that art of this kind leads to phantasy and daydreaming. Aristotle, coming about fifty years after Plato, defended this kind of art. He said that undesirable passions, such as pity and terror, were in this way sublimated—you worked them off in the theater, where they could do no harm. If, he means, you feel an inner urge to murder your wife, you go and see *Othello* or read a good, gory thriller, and satisfy your blood just that way, and if we had the last part of his *Poetics,* which dealt with comedy, we should probably find it suggested in the same way that an excess of sexual emotion can be worked off by going to a good, dirty farce or vulgar music hall and blowing the whole thing away in a loud, bawdy laugh.

Now, people still argue as to whether Plato or Aristotle was right about this. But there are one or two things I want you to notice. The first is that what Plato is really concerned with banishing from his perfect state is the kind of art that aims at mere entertainment—the art that dissipates energy instead of directing it into some useful channel. And though Aristotle defends art for entertainment, it is still the same kind of art he is thinking about.

The second thing is that both Plato and Aristotle—but especially Plato—are concerned with the moral effect of art. Plato would allow representational art so long as he thought that it had the effect of canalizing the energies and directing them to virtuous action. He banishes it, on further consideration, only because he has come to the conclusion that *no* representational art of any kind—not even the loftiest tragedy—is successful in bracing the moral constitution. He does not tell us very clearly what poetry he will keep, or why, except that it is to be what we should call a lyrical kind, and, presumably, bracing and tonic in sentiment, and directly inculcating the love of the good, the beautiful, and the true.

Thirdly: Plato lived at the beginning, and Aristotle in the middle, of the era that saw the collapse and corruption of the great Greek civilization. Plato sees the rot setting in and cries out like a prophet to his people to repent while there is yet time. He sees the theater audience is in fact looking to the theater for nothing but amusement and entertainment, that their energies are, in fact, frittering themselves away in spurious emotion—sob stuff and sensation, and senseless laughter, phantasy and daydreaming, and admiration for the merely smart and slick and clever and amusing. And there is an ominous likeness between his age and ours. We too have audiences and critics and newspapers assessing every play and book and novel in terms of its entertainment value, and a whole generation of young men and women who dream over novels and wallow in daydreaming at the cinema, and who seemed to be in a fair way of doping themselves into complete irresponsibility over the conduct of life until war came, as it did to Greece, to jerk them back to reality. Greek civilization was destroyed; ours is not yet destroyed. But it may be well to remember Plato's warning: "If you receive the pleasure-seasoned muse, pleasure and pain will be kings in your city instead of law and agreed principles."

And there is something else in Plato that seems to strike a familiar note. We seem to know the voice that urges artists to produce works of art with a high moral tone—propaganda works, directed to improving young people's minds and rousing them to a sense of their duties, doing them good, in fact. And at the same time, we find—among artists and critics alike—a tendency to repudiate representational art, in favor of something more austere, primitive, and symbolic, as though the trouble lay there.

It is as though, in the decline of Greece, and in what is known as the decline of the West, both Plato and we agreed in finding something wrong with the arts—a kind of mutual infection, by which the slick, sentimental, hedonistic art corrupts its audience, and the pleasure-loving, emotional audience in turn corrupts the arts by demanding of them nothing but entertainment value. And the same sort of remedy is proposed in both cases—first, to get rid of representationalism—which, it is hoped, will take away the pleasure and entertainment and so cure the audience's itch for amusement; secondly, to concentrate on works that provide a direct stimulus to right thinking and right action. What we have really got here is a sort of division of art into two kinds: entertainment art, which dissipates the energies of the audience and pours them down the drain; and another kind of art that canalizes energy into a sort of millstream to turn the wheel of action—and this we may perhaps call spellbinding art. But do these two functions comprise the whole of art? Or are they art at all? Are they perhaps only accidental effects of art, or false art—something masquerading under the name of art—or menial tasks to which we enslave art? Is the real nature and end of art something quite different from either? Is the real trouble something wrong with our esthetic, so that we do not know what we ought to look for in art, or how to recognize it when we see it, or how to distinguish the real thing from the spurious imitation?

Suppose we turn from Plato to the actual poets he was writing about—to Aeschylus, for instance, the great writer of tragedies. Drama, certainly, is a representational art, and therefore, according to Plato, pleasure art, entertainment art, emotional and relaxing art, sensational art. Let us read the *Agamemnon*. Certainly it is the representation by actors of something—and of something pretty sensational: the murder of a husband by an adulterous wife. But it is scarcely sensational entertainment in the sense that a thriller novel on the same subject is sensational entertainment. A daydreaming, pleasure-loving audience would hardly call it entertainment at all. It is certainly not relaxing. And I doubt whether it either dissipates our passions in Plato's sense or sublimates them in Aristotle's sense, any more than it canalizes them for any particular action, though it may trouble and stir us and plunge us into the mystery of things. We might extract some moral lessons from it; but if we ask ourselves whether the poet wrote that play in order to improve our minds, something inside us will, I think, say no. Aeschylus was trying to tell us something, but nothing quite so simple as that. He is saying something—something important—something enormous. And here we shall be suddenly struck with the inadequacy of the strictures against representational art.

"This," we shall say, "is not the copy or imitation of something bigger and more real than itself. It is bigger and more real than the real-life action that it represents. That a false wife should murder a husband—that might be a paragraph in the *News of the World* or a thriller to read in the train—but when it is shown to us like this, by a great poet, it is as though we went behind the triviality of the actual event to the cosmic significance behind it. And, what is more, this is not a representation of the actual event at all; if a BBC reporter had been present at the murder with a television set and microphone, what we heard and saw would have been nothing like this. This play is not anything that ever happened in this world—it is something happening in the mind of Aeschylus, and it had never happened before."

Now here, I believe, we are getting to something—something that Plato's heathen philosophy was not adequate to explain, but which we can begin to explain by the light of Christian theology. Very likely the heathen poet could not have explained it either. If he had made the attempt, he too would have been entangled in the terms of his philosophy. But we are concerned, not with what he might have said, but with what he did. Being a true poet, he was true in his work—that is, his art was that point of truth in him that was true to the external truth, and only to be interpreted in terms of eternal truth.

The true work of art, then, is something new; it is not primarily the copy or representation of anything. It may involve representation, but that is not what makes it a work of art. It is not manufactured to specification, as an engineer works to a plan—though it may involve compliance with the accepted rules for dramatic presentation and may also contain verbal "effects" that can be mechanically accounted for. We know very well, when we compare it with so-called works of art that are turned out to pattern, that in this connection neither circumcision availeth anything nor uncircumcision, but a new creature. Something has been created.

This word—this idea of art as creation—is, I believe, the one important contribution that Christianity has made to esthetics. Unfortunately, we are likely to use the words *creation* and *creativeness* very vaguely and loosely because we do not relate them properly to our theology. But it is significant that the Greeks did not have this word in their esthetic at all. They looked on a work of art as a kind of *techne*, a manufacture. Neither, for that matter, was the word in their theology—they did not look on history as the continual act of God fulfilling itself in creation.

How do we say that God creates, and how does this compare with the act of creation by an artist? To begin with, of course, we say that God created the universe "out of nothing"—he was bound by no conditions of any kind. Here there can be no comparison; the human artist is in the universe and bound by its conditions. He can create only within that framework and out of that material that the universe supplies. Admitting that, let us ask in what way God creates. Christian theology replies that God, who is a Trinity, creates by, or through, his Second Person, his Word or Son, who is continually begotten from the First person, the Father, in an eternal creative activity. And certain theologians have added this very significant comment: the Father, they say, is known only to himself by beholding his image in his Son.

Does that sound very mysterious? We will come back to the human artist and see what it means in terms of his activity. But first, let us take note of a new word that has crept into the argument by way of Christian theology—the word *image*. Suppose, having rejected the words *copy, imitation,* and *representation* as inadequate, we substitute the word *image* and say that what the artist is doing is imaging forth something or the other, and connect that with St. Paul's phrase: "God. . . hath spoken to us by his Son, the brightness of this glory and express image of his person." Something which, by being an image, expresses that which it images. Is that getting us a little nearer to something? There is something that is, in the deepest sense of the words, unimaginable, known to itself (and still more, to us) only by the image in which it expresses itself through creation; and, says Christian theology very emphatically, the Son, who is the express image, is not the copy, or imitation, or representation of the Father, nor yet inferior or subsequent to the Father in any way. In the last resort, in depths of their mysterious being, the unimaginable and the image are one and the same.

Now for our poet. We said, when we were talking of the *Agamemnon,* that this work of art seemed to be something happening in the mind of Aeschylus. We may now say, perhaps, more precisely, that the play is the expression of this interior happening. But what, exactly, was happening?

There is a school of criticism that is always trying to explain, or explain away, a man's works of art by trying to dig out the events of his life and his emotions outside the works themselves, and saying "these are the real Aeschylus, the real Shakespeare, of which the poems are only faint imitations." But any poet will tell you that this is the wrong way to go to work. It is the old, pagan esthetic that explains nothing—or that explains all sorts of things about the work except what makes it a work of art. The poet will say: "My poem is the expression of my experience." But if you then say, "What experience?" he will say, "I can't tell you anything about it except what I have said in the poem—the poem is the experience." The Son and the Father are *one;* the poet himself did not know what his experience was until he created the poem which revealed his own experience to himself.

To save confusion, let us distinguish between an event and an experience. An event is something that happens to one, but one does not necessarily experience it. To take an extreme instance: suppose you are hit on the head and get a concussion and, as often happens, when you come to, you cannot remember the blow. The blow on the head certainly happened to you, but you did not experience it; all you experience is the aftereffects. You only experience a thing when you can express it—however haltingly—to your own mind. You may remember the young man in T. S. Eliot's play, *The Family Reunion,* who says to his relatives:

> You are all people
> To whom nothing has happened, at most a continual
>   impact
> Of external events. . . .

He means that they have got through life without ever really experiencing anything because they have never tried to express to themselves the real nature of what has happened to them.

A poet is a man who not only suffers the impact of external events but also experiences them. He puts the experience into words in his own mind, and in so doing recognizes the experience for what it is. To the extent that we can do that, we are all poets. A poet so-called is simply a man like ourselves with an exceptional power of revealing his experience by expressing it, so that not only he, but we ourselves, recognize that experience as our own.

I want to stress the word *recognize.* A poet does not see something—say the full moon—and say: "This is a very beautiful sight; let me set about finding words for the appropriate expression of what people ought to feel about it." That is what the literary artisan does, and it means nothing. What happens is that then, or at some time after, he finds himself saying words in his head and says to himself: "Yes—that is right. That is the experience the full moon was to

77

me. I recognize it in expressing it, and now I know what it was." And so, when it is a case of mental or spiritual experience—sin, grief, joy, sorrow, worship—the thing reveals itself to him in words and so becomes fully experienced for the first time. By thus recognizing it in its expression, he makes it his own—integrates it into himself. He no longer feels himself battered passively by the impact of external events; it is no longer something happening to him, but something happening in him; the reality of the event is communicated to him in activity and power. So that the act of the poet in creation is seen to be threefold—a trinity—experience, expression, and recognition: the unknowable reality in the experience; the image of that reality known in its expression; and power in the recognition; the whole making up the single and indivisible act of a creative mind.

Now, what the poet does for himself, he can also do for us. When he has imaged forth his experience, he can incarnate it, so to speak, in a material body—words, music, painting—the thing we know as a work of art. And since he is a man like the rest of us, we shall expect that our experience will have something in common with his. In the image of his experience, we can recognize the image of some experience of our own—something that had happened to us, but which we had never understood, never formulated or expressed to ourselves, and therefore never known as a real experience. When we read the poem, or see the play or picture inside us. We say: "Ah! I recognize that! That is something that I obscurely felt to be going on in and about me, but I didn't know what it was and couldn't express it. But now that the artist has made its image—imaged it forth—for me, I can possess and take hold of it and make it my own and turn it into a source of knowledge and strength." This is the communication of the image in power, by which the third person of the poet's trinity brings us, through the incarnate image, into direct knowledge of the, in itself, unknowable and unimaginable reality. "No man cometh to the Father save by me," said the incarnate image; and he added, "but the spirit of power will lead you into all truth."

This recognition of the truth that we get in the artist's work comes to us as a revelation of new truth. I want to be clear about that. I am not referring to the sort of patronizing recognition we give to a writer by nodding our heads and observing: "Yes, yes, very good, very true—that's just what I'm always saying." I mean the recognition of a truth that tells us something about ourselves that we had not been always saying, something that puts a new knowledge of ourselves within our grasp. It is new, startling, and perhaps shattering, and yet it comes to us with a sense of familiarity. We did not know it before, but the moment the poet has shown it to us, we know that, somehow or other, we had always really known it.

Very well. But, frankly, is that the sort of thing the average British citizen gets, or expects to get, when he goes to the theater or reads a book? No, it is not. In the majority of cases, it is not in the least what he expects, or what he wants. What he looks for is not this creative and Christian kind of art at all. He does not expect or desire to be upset by sudden revelations about himself and the universe. Like the people of Plato's decadent Athens, he has forgotten or repudiated the religious origins of all art. He wants entertainment, or, if he is a little more serious-minded, he wants something with a moral, or to have some spell or incantation put on him to instigate him to virtuous action.

Now, entertainment and moral spellbinding have their uses, but they are not art in the proper sense. They may be the incidental effects of good art but they may also be the very aim and essence of false art. And if we continue to demand of the arts only these two things, we shall starve and silence the true artist and encourage instead the false artist, who may become a very sinister force indeed.

Let us take amusement art. What does that give us? Generally speaking, what we demand and get from it is the enjoyment of the emotions that usually accompany experience without having had the experience. It does not reveal us to ourselves; it merely projects on to a mental screen a picture of ourselves as we already fancy ourselves to be—only bigger and brighter. The manufacturer of this kind of entertainment is not by any means interpreting and revealing his own experience to himself and us—he is either indulging his own daydreams, or—still more falsely and venially—he is saying: "What is it the audience think they would like to have experienced? Let us show them that, so that they can wallow in emotion by pretending to have experienced it." This kind of pseudoart is "wish fulfillment" or "escape" literature in the worst sense. It is an escape, not from the "impact of external events" into the citadel of experienced reality, but an escape from reality and experience into a world of merely external events—the progressive externalization of consciousness. For occasional relaxation this is all right; but it can be carried to the point where, not merely art, but the whole universe of phenomena becomes a screen on which we see the magnified projection of our unreal selves as the object of equally unreal emotions. This brings about the complete corruption of the consciousness, which can no longer recognize reality in experience. When things come to this pass, we have a civilization that lives for amusement, a civilization without guts, without experience, and out of touch with reality.

Or take the spellbinding kind of art. This at first sight seems better because it spurs us to action, and it also has its uses. But it too is dangerous in excess because once again it does not reveal reality in experience, but only projects a lying picture of the self. As the amusement art seeks to produce the emotions without the experience, so this pseudoart seeks to produce the behavior without the experience. In the end it is directed to putting the behavior of the audience beneath the will of the spellbinder, and its true name is not art, but art magic. In its vulgarest form it becomes pure propaganda. It can (as we have reason to know) actually succeed in making its audience into the thing it desires to have them. It can really in the end corrupt the consciousness and destroy experience until the inner selves of its victims are wholly externalized and made the puppets and instruments of their own spurious passions. This is why it is dangerous for anybody—even for the Church—to urge artists to produce works of art for the express purpose of doing good to people. Let her by all means encourage artists to express their own Christian experience and communicate it to others. That is the true artist saying: "Look! Recognize your experience in my own." But "edifying art" may only too often be the pseudoartist corruptly saying: "This is what you are supposed to believe and feel and do—and I propose to work you into a state of mind in which you will believe and feel and do as you are told." This pseudoart does not really communicate power to us; it merely exerts power over us.

What is it, then, that these two pseudoarts—the entertaining and the spellbinding—have in common? And how are they related to true art? What they have in common is the falsification of consciousness; and they are to art as the idol is to the image. The Jews were forbidden to make any image for worship because before the revelation of the threefold unity in which image and unimaginable are one, it was only too fatally easy to substitute the idol for the image. The Christian revelation set free all the images by showing that the true image subsisted within the Godhead Itself. It was neither copy, nor imitation, nor representation, nor inferior, not subsequent, but the brightness of the glory, and the express image of the person—the very mirror in which reality knows itself and communicates itself in power.

But the danger still exists, and it always will recur whenever the Christian doctrine has never been fully used or understood, and in consequence our whole attitude to the artistic expression of reality has become confused, idolatrous, and pagan. We see the arts degenerating into mere entertainment that corrupts and relaxes our civilization, and we try in alarm to correct this by demanding a more moralizing and bracing kind of art. But this is only setting up one idol in place of the other. Or we see that art is becoming idolatrous, and we suppose that we can put matters right by getting rid of the representational element in it. But what is wrong is not the representation itself, but in fact that what we are looking at, and what we are looking for, are not the image but an idol. Little children, keep yourselves from idols.

It has become a commonplace to say that the arts are in a bad way. We are in fact largely given over to the entertainers and the spellbinders; and because we do not understand that these two functions do not represent the true nature of art, the true artists are, as it were, excommunicate and have no audience. But here there is not, I think, so much a relapse from a Christian esthetic as a failure ever to find and examine a real Christian esthetic based on dogma and not on ethics. This may not be a bad thing. We have at least a new line of country to explore that has not been trampled on and built over and fought over by countless generations of quarrelsome critics. What we have to start from is the Trinitarian doctrine of creative mind and the light that that doctrine throws on the true nature of images.

The great thing, I am sure, is not to be nervous about God—not to try and shut out the Lord Immanuel from any sphere of truth. Art is not he—we must not substitute art for God; yet this also is he for it is one of his images and therefore reveals his nature. Here we see in a mirror darkly—we behold only the images; elsewhere we shall see face to face, in the place where image and reality are one.

Christian Perspectives

1. According to Sayers, how was Plato's definition and model of art incomplete?
2. Compare the classical interpretation of art to Sayers' definition of art. Plato's ideal republic excludes representational art; Sayers' aesthetic does not. Why does Sayers defend representational art as legitimate?
3. Sayers discusses the mutual infection that has invaded art: a corrupted art and a corrupted audience. Obviously the connection between our art and our morality is not coincidental. The High Middle Ages and the Renaissance were times of great creative energy in art. What was the religious thinking of those periods? Do you see a connection?
4. Sayers' unique style employs a combination of humor and eloquence, often side by side. What is the effect of her style?
5. Sayers refers to the arts as having "mutilated limbs and withering branches" that need to be regrafted "into the main trunk of Christian tradition." How does her metaphor parallel the scriptures of the vine and the branches?

From THE EVERLASTING MAN
G. K. Chesterton

"Right in the middle of all these things stands up an enormous exception. . . . It is nothing less than the loud assertion that this mysterious maker of the world has visited his world in person. It declares that really and even recently, or right in the middle of historic times, there did walk into the world this original invisible being; about whom the thinkers make theories and the mythologists hand down myths; the Man Who Made the World. That such a higher personality exists behind all things had indeed always been implied by the best thinkers, as well as by all the most beautiful legends. But nothing of this sort had ever been implied in any of them. It is simply false to say that the other sages and heroes had claimed to be the mysterious master and maker, of whom the world had dreamed and disputed. Not one of them had ever claimed to be anything of the sort. The most that any religious prophet had said was that he was the true servant of such a being. The most that any primitive myth had ever suggested was that the Creator was present at the Creation. But that the Creator was present . . . in the daily life of the Roman Empire—that is something utterly unlike anything else in nature. It is the one great startling statement that man has made . . . it makes nothing but dust and nonsense of comparative religion."

C. S. Lewis refutes compromising attempts to mainstream Christianity into other ideologies and religions. He scoffs at the idea of accepting Jesus as just a good teacher. His premise leaves the reader with the choice to accept or reject the claims of Jesus Christ.

WHAT ARE WE TO MAKE OF JESUS CHRIST?
C. S. Lewis

What are we to make of Jesus Christ? This is a question which has, in a sense, a frantically comic side. For the real question is not what are we to make of Christ, but what is He to make of us? The picture of a fly sitting deciding what it is going to make of an elephant has comic elements about it. But perhaps the questioner meant what are we to make of Him in the sense of "How are we to solve the historical problem set us by the recorded sayings and acts of this Man?" This problem is to reconcile two things. On the one hand you have got the almost generally admitted depth and sanity of His moral teaching, which is not very seriously questioned, even by those who are opposed to Christianity. In fact, I find when I am arguing with very anti-God people that they rather make a point of saying, "I am entirely in favor of the moral teaching of Christianity"—and there seems to be a general agreement that in the teaching of this Man and of His immediate followers, moral truth is exhibited at its purest and best. It is not sloppy idealism, it is full of wisdom and shrewdness. The whole thing is realistic, fresh to the highest degree, the product of a sane mind. That is one phenomenon.

The other phenomenon is the quite appalling nature of this Man's theological remarks. You all know what I mean, and I want to stress the point that the appalling claim which this Man seems to be making is not merely made at one moment of His career. There is, of course, the one moment which led to His execution. The moment at which the High Priest said to Him, "Who are you?" "I am the Anointed, the Son of the uncreated God, and you shall see Me appearing at the end of all history as the judge of the Universe."

But that claim, in fact, does not rest on this one dramatic moment. When you look into his conversation, you will find this sort of claim running through the whole thing. For instance, He went about saying to people, "I forgive your sins." Now it is quite natural for a man to forgive something you do to him. Thus if somebody cheats me out of 5 pounds, it is quite possible and reasonable for me to say, "Well, I forgive him, we will say no more about it." What on earth would you say if somebody had done you out of 5 pounds and I said, "That is all right, I forgive him"?

Then there is a curious thing which seems to slip out almost by accident. On one occasion this Man is sitting looking down on Jerusalem from the hill above it and suddenly in comes an extraordinary remark—"I keep on sending you prophets and wise men." Nobody comments on it. And yet, quite suddenly, almost incidentally, He is claiming to be the power that all through the centuries is sending wise men and leaders into the world.

Here is another curious remark: in almost every religion there are unpleasant observances like fasting. This Man suddenly remarks one day, "No one need fast while I am here." Who is this Man who remarks that His mere presence suspends all normal rules? Who is the person who can suddenly tell the School they can have a half-holiday?

Sometimes the statements put forward the assumption that He, the Speaker, is completely without sin or fault. This is always the attitude. "You, to whom I am talking, are all sinners," and He never remotely suggests that this same reproach can be brought against Him. He says again, "I am begotten of the One God, before Abraham was, I am," and remember what the words "I am" were in Hebrew. They were the name of God, which must not be spoken by any human being, the name which it was death to utter.

Well, that is the other side. On the one side clear, definite moral teaching. On the other, claims which, if not true, are those of a megalomaniac, compared with whom Hitler was the most sane and humble of men. There is no halfway house and there is no parallel in other religions. If you had gone to Buddha and asked him, "Are you the son of Bramah?" he would have said, "My son, you are still in the vale of illusion." If you had gone to Socrates and asked, "Are you Zeus?" he would have laughed at you. If you had gone to Mohammed and asked, "Are you Allah?" he would first have rent his clothes and then cut your head off. If you had asked Confucius, "Are you Heaven?" I think he would probably have replied, "Remarks which are not in accordance with nature are in bad taste." The idea of a great moral teacher saying what Christ said is out of the question. In my opinion, the only person who can say that sort of thing is either God or a complete lunatic suffering from that form of delusion which undermines the whole mind of man. If you think you are a poached egg when you are looking for a piece of toast to suit you, you may be sane, but if you think you are God, there is no chance for you.

We may note in passing that He was never regarded as a mere moral teacher. He did not produce that effect on any of the people who actually met Him. He produced mainly three effects—Hatred—Terror—Adoration. There was no trace of people expressing mild approval.

82

THEOLOGY
C. S. Lewis

Everyone has warned me not to tell you what I am going to tell you. . . . They all say "the ordinary reader does not want Theology; give him plain practical religion." I have rejected their advice. I do not think the ordinary reader is such a fool. Theology means "the science of God," and I think any man who wants to think about God at all would like to have the clearest and most accurate ideas about Him which are available. You are not children: why should you be treated like children?

In a way I quite understand why some people are put off by Theology. I remember once when I had been giving a talk to the R.A.F., an old, hard-bitten officer got up and said, "I've no use for all that stuff. But, mind you, I'm a religious man too. I know there's a God. I've felt Him: out alone in the desert at night: the tremendous mystery. And that's just why I don't believe all your neat little dogmas and formulas about Him. To anyone who's met the real thing they all seem so petty and pedantic and unreal!"

Now in a sense I quite agreed with that man. I think he had probably a real experience of God in the desert. And when he turned from that experience to the Christian creeds, I think he really was turning from something real, to something less real. In the same way, if a man has once looked at the Atlantic from the beach, and then goes and looks at a map of the Atlantic, he also will be turning from something real to something less real: turning from real waves to a bit of colored paper. But here comes the point. The map is admittedly only colored paper, but there are two things you have to remember about it. In the first place, it is based on what hundreds and thousands of people have found out by sailing the real Atlantic. In that way it has behind it masses of experience just as real as the one you could have from the beach; only, while yours would be a single isolated glimpse, the map fits all those different experiences together. In the second place, if you want to go anywhere, the map is absolutely necessary. As long as you are content with walks on the beach, your own glimpses are far more fun than looking at a map. But the map is going to be more use than walks on the beach if you want to get to America.

Now Theology is like the map. Merely learning and thinking about the Christian doctrines, if you stop there, is less real and less exciting than the sort of thing my friend got in the desert. Doctrines are not God: they are only a kind of map. But the map is based on the experience of hundreds of people who really were in touch with God—experiences compared with which any thrills or pious feelings you or I are likely to get on our own way are very elementary and very confused. And secondly, if you want to get any further, you must use the map. You see, what happened to that man in the desert may have been real, and was certainly exciting, but nothing comes of it. It leads nowhere. There is nothing to do about it. In fact, that is just why a vague religion—all about feeling God in nature, and so on—is so attractive. It is all thrills and no work; like watching the waves from the beach. But you will not get to Newfoundland by studying the Atlantic that way, and you will not get eternal life by simply feeling the presence of God in flowers or music. Neither will you get anywhere by looking at maps without going to sea. Nor will you be very safe if you go to sea without a map.

In other words, Theology is practical: especially now. In the old days, where there was less education and discussion, perhaps it was possible to get on with a very few simple ideas about

God. But it is not so now. Everyone reads, everyone hears things discussed. Consequently if you do not listen to Theology, that will not mean that you have no ideas about God. It will mean that you have a lot of wrong ones—bad, muddled, out-of-date ideas. For a great many of the ideas about God which are trotted out as novelties today, are simply the ones which real Theologians tried centuries ago and rejected. To believe in the popular religion of modern England is retrogression—like believing the earth is flat.

For when you get down to it, is not the popular idea of Christianity simply this: that Jesus Christ was a great moral teacher and that if only we took his advice we might be able to establish a better social order and avoid another war? Now, mind you, that is quite true. But it tells you much less than the whole truth about Christianity and it has no practical importance at all.

It is quite true that if we took Christ's advice, we should soon be living in a happier world. You need not even go as far as Christ. If we did all that Plato or Aristotle or Confucius told us, we should get on a great deal better than we do. And so what? We have never followed the advice of the great teachers. Why are we likely to begin now? Why are we more likely to follow Christ than any others? Because He is the best moral teacher? But that makes it even less likely that we shall follow Him. If we cannot take the elementary lessons, is it likely we are going to take the most advanced one. If Christianity only means one more bit of good advice, then Christianity is of no importance. There has been no lack of good advice for the last four thousand years. A bit more makes no difference.

But as soon as you look at any real Christian writings, you find that they are talking about something quite different from this popular religion. They say that Christ is the Son of God (whatever that means). They say that those who give Him their confidence can also become Sons of God (whatever that means). They say that His death saved us from our sins (whatever that means).

There is no good complaining that these statements are difficult. Christianity claims to be telling us about another world, about something behind the world we can touch and hear and see. You may think the claim false; but if it were true, what it tells us would be bound to be difficult—at least as difficult as modern Physics, and for the same reason.

Now the point in Christianity which gives us the greatest shock is the statement that by attaching to Christ we can "become Sons of God." One asks "Aren't we Sons of God already? Surely the fatherhood of God is one of the main Christian ideas?" Well, in a certain sense, no doubt we are sons of God already. I mean, God brought us into existence and loves us and looks after us, and in that way is like a father. But when the Bible talks of our "becoming" Sons of God, obviously it must mean something different. And that brings us up against the very center of Theology.

Christian Perspectives

1. What *were* the responses to Jesus when He made the claims He did about Himself? (See Matthew 26:59-65.) Why are the responses often less hostile today?
2. Lewis acknowledges Christ's sound moral teaching, but he challenges us to look to all of His statements. Why does Christianity not parallel other religions?
3. We have all heard someone say, "It doesn't matter what your faith is in, as long as you believe in something?" Using Lewis' analogy of the map and territory, how would you respond to that statement?

4. Analogy is one pattern of writing that Lewis uses frequently. Identify some of these analogies.
5. Lewis was a master of the *dialectic* method of argument which is defined as "the art of arriving at truth by disclosing the contradictions in an opponent's argument and overcoming them." Identify his use of the dialectic by finding his thesis, his antithesis (opposition to thesis), and his conclusion.
6. Compare Lewis' conclusion about Jesus to Chesterton's conclusion in an excerpt from *The Everlasting Man*. Lewis often referred to Chesterton as one of his mentors; can you see Chesterton's influence in Lewis' writing?

PSALM 8

O Lord our Lord,
how excellent is thy name in all
    the earth!
who hast set thy glory above the heavens.
    Out of
the mouth of babes and
    sucklings
hast thou ordained strength
    because of thine enemies,
that thou mightest still the enemy and the avenger.
When I consider thy heavens, the
    work of thy fingers,
the moon and the stars, which thou
    hast ordained;
What is man, that thou art mindful of
    him?
and the son of man, that thou
    visitest him?
For thou hast made him a little lower
    than the angels,
and hast crowned him with glory
    and honour.
Thou madest him to have dominion over
    the works of thy hands;
thou hast put all things under his
    feet:
All sheep and oxen, yea,
    and the beasts of the field;
The fowl of the air, and the fish of
    the sea,
and whatsoever passeth through the paths of
    the seas.

O Lord our Lord,
how excellent is thy name in all
the earth!

Christian Perspective

1. The psalmist exhalts the majesty of the Lord and the works of His hands. What is man's role in God's creation?

GOD'S GRANDEUR

Gerald Manley Hopkins

The world is charged with the grandeur of God.
    It will flame out, like shining from shook foil;[1]
    It gathers to a greatness, like the ooze of oil
Crushed. Why do men then now not reck[2] his rod?
Generations have trod, have trod, have trod;
    And all is seared with trade; bleared, smeared with toil;
    And wears man's smudge and shares man's smell: the soil
Is bare now, nor can foot feel, being shod.

And for all this, nature is never spent;
    There lives the dearest freshness deep down things;
And though the last lights off the black West went
    Oh, morning, at the brown brink eastward, springs—
Because the Holy Ghost over the bent
World broods with warm breast and with ah! bright wings.

Christian Perspective

1. Both "Psalm 8" and "God's Grandeur" identify nature's role in God's redemptive plan for men. How does nature seem to "participate" with God?
2. Hopkins marvels at man's inability to recognize God's greatness when nature so clearly reflects it. Contrast man's indifference to nature's responsiveness.
3. Identify the poetic devices of personification and alliteration in the poems.

---

1. foil—metallic leaf, as gold or silver foil.
2. reck—to take heed of, or to change one's conduct on account of.

PIED[1] BEAUTY

Gerald Manley Hopkins

Glory be to God for dappled things —
    For skies of couple-color as a brindled[2] cow;
        For rose-moles all in stipple upon trout that swim;
Fresh-firecoal chesnut-falls; finches' wings;
    Landscapes plotted and pieced — fold, fallow, and plow;
        And all trades, their gear and tackle and trim.
All things counter, original, spare, strange;
    Whatever is fickle, freckled (who knows how?)
        With swift, slow; sweet, sour; adazzle, dim;
He fathers-forth whose beauty is past change:
    Praise Him.

Christian Perspectives

1. What does the poet mean by "dappled" things? using examples in the poem — "brinded cow," "trout," "finches' wings" — gives other examples of God's dappled creation.
2. What is the poet saying about the nature of God?
3. How does the rhythm of Hopkins' lines reflect their meaning? Contrast lines 4-9 with line 10. Does the different rhythm of line 10 help convey the differences between God and His creation?

EASTER WINGS

George Herbert

Lord, who createdst man in wealth and store,
Though foolishly he lost the same,
Decaying more and more,
Till he became
Most poore:
With thee
O let me rise
As larks, harmoniously,
And sing this day thy victories;
Then shall the fall further the flight in me.

1. pied — spotted, with two or more colors.
2. brindled — with dark streaks or flecks on a gray or tan background.

My tender age in sorrow did beginne:
And still with sicknesses and shame
Thou didst so punish sinne,
That I became
Most thinne.
With thee
Let me combine
And feel this day they victorie:
For, if I imp[1] my wing on thine,
Affliction shall advance the flight in me.

Christian Perspectives

1. This "shaped poem" mirrors its content in the form it takes on the page. Do you find that the form portrays an important Christian doctrine? Note the shortest lines of each stanza. How do they reflect the meeting of God and man?
2. Which stanza seems more personal to you?
3. How can Herbert say "Affliction shall advance the flight in me"? What does that idea, and, in fact, the idea of the whole poem, have to do with Easter?
4. Why are wings an effective symbol for an Easter poem?

THE PULLEY

George Herbert

God on one side trying to raise us towards Him

When God at first made man,
Having a glass of blessings standing by,
    "Let us," said he, "pour on him all we can,
Let the world's riches, which dispersed lie,
    Contract into a span."

pull together all of the worlds riches together

So strength first made a way;
Then beauty flowed, then wisdom, honor, pleasure.
    When almost all was out, God made a stay,
Perceiving that, alone of all his treasure,
    Rest in the bottom lay.

"For if I should," said he,
"Bestow this jewel also on my creature,
    He would adore my gifts instead of me,
And rest in Nature not the God of Nature;
    So both should losers be.

God-Man in all our blessings we would not look for God. Neither

Nature-Man believing yourself to be self sufficient as a mature being destroyed

1. imp—to graft or repair with a feather in order to improve a bird's flight.

88

"Yet let him keep the rest,
But keep them with repining[1] restlessness.
Let him be rich and weary, that at least,
If goodness lead him not, yet weariness
May toss him to my breast."

its not only in blessing that we turn to God. In fact, its in the time of restlessness that we run to him, longing for his careful arms to hold & embrace us through the hard times

Christian Perspective

1. In this poem, God wishes to bless man, but He knows that man will be tempted to worship the gifts instead of the giver. What does God do to keep man needing Him?
2. What is meant by the line, "So both should losers be"?

HOLY SONNET XIV
John Donne

Batter my heart, three-personed God; for you
As yet but knock, breathe, shine, and seek to mend;
That I may rise and stand, o'erthrow me, and bend
Your force, to break, blow, burn, and make me new.
I, like an usurped town, to another due,
Labor to admit you, but oh, to no end,
Reason, your viceroy[2] in me, me should defend,
But is captived, and proves weak or untrue.
Yet dearly I love you, and would be loved fain,
But am betrothed unto your enemy;
Divorce me, untie, or break that knot again,
Take me to you, imprison me, for I
Except you enthrall me, never shall be free,
Nor ever chaste, except you ravish me.

Christian Perspectives

1. What Christian doctrine is expressed in the metaphor of "an usurped town"? Does St. Paul's description of spiritual conflicts reflect what John Donne is speaking of? (See Romans 7:9-25.)
2. How is reason God's "viceroy" in the human soul? Why is it said to be "captived"?

1. repining—discontented, yearning.
2. viceroy—one placed in command by a greater authority; a governor.

3. Donne uses strong, almost violent imagery in referring to God: "batter, force, break, blow, burn, enthrall, ravish." What is the impact of these images on the poem?

THE WINDHOVER[1]

Gerard Manley Hopkins

To Christ our Lord

I caught this morning morning's minion[2], king-
   dom of daylight's dauphin[3], dapple-dawn-drawn Falcon, in
      his riding
Of the rolling level underneath him steady air, and striding
High there, how he rung upon the rein of a wimpling[4] wing
In his ecstasy! then off, off forth on swing,
   As a skate's heel sweeps smooth on a bow-bend: the hurl
      and gliding
Rebuffed the big wind. My heart in hiding
Stirred for a bird,—the achieve of, the mastery of the
      thing!

Brute[5] beauty and valor and act, oh, air[6], pride, plume, here
   Buckle[7] AND the fire that breaks from thee then, a billion
Times told lovelier, more dangerous, O my chevalier[8]!

   No wonder of it: sheer plod makes plow down sillion[9]
Shine, and blue-bleak embers, ah my dear,
Fall, gall[10] themselves, and gash gold-vermillion[11].

1. Windhover—a small falcon.
2. minion—darling
3. dauphin—a French prince, heir to the throne.
4. wimpling—rippling.
5. brute—natural creation, or animal.
6. air—demeanor or attitude, as in "air of courtliness.
7. Buckle—this word can be read here as imperative or indicative, and can mean either join or collapse.
8. chevalier—a cavalier or knight.
9. sillion—the ridge between plowed furrows in a field.
10. gall—break the surface
11. vermilion—a bright, rich red color.

90

Christian Perspectives

1. Why does the narrator say his heart is "in hiding"? Does the fact that the author was a priest help you understand this poem?
2. The poet suggests a relation between the natural world and the world of grace. Why does he use the word "AND" emphasizing it with capital letters, rather than the word "But"? Does this influence how you read the meaning of "Buckle!"? When does the focus of the poem change to Christ ("thee")?
3. How does the ending of the poem affirm the beauty and goodness of humble service to Christ?

GOD IS A DISTANT — STATELY LOVER — (357)

Emily Dickinson

God is a distant — stately Lover —
Woos, as He states us — by His Son —
Verily, a Vicarious Courtship —
"Miles[1]," and "Priscilla," were such an One —

But, lest the Soul — like fair "Priscilla"
Choose the Envoy — and spurn the Groom —
Vouches, with hyperbolic archness —
"Miles," and "John Alden" were Synonym —

Christian Perspectives

1. Does one metaphor seem to fit your view of God better than the others?
2. As a class activity you might each write a descriptive poem about God using an analogy or extended metaphor and compare your works.

---

1. Miles — Dickinson refers to the early American story of Captain Miles Standish, who was represented by John Alden in wooing Priscilla Mullens. She, perceiving that John loved her, even though he spoke for his friend, said, "Speak for thyself, John."

Making Connections

1. While Herberg observes modern American self-centeredness, Sayers confronts the mental laziness of modern Christians. Compare the descriptive statements of the typical Christian to the descriptive statements of Jesus Christ (i.e., natural bore, never bored a soul). If we are to be "little Christs," what is Sayers saying about the modern Christian?
2. Relate a childhood experience that made a lasting impression on your religious upbringing. (The experience may be positive or negative.) Has this experience affected your attitude toward God? the church? yourself? Write a personal essay in which you compare or contrast your experience with that which Hughes relates.
3. "Pigeon Feathers" is rich with patterns that appear over and over in the story. One pattern is the imagery of light and dark; another pattern is hands; still another pattern is color. Trace these patterns or find some of your own. Compose a brief analysis essay on one pattern of images found in the story.
4. Imagine David, from Updike's "Pigeon Feathers," asking his questions of someone described by Will Herberg. How satisfied do you think he would be by the answers of "religiosity"? How do you think you would answer David? How do you think Jesus would answer? Write a brief dialogue expressing one of these possible encounters.
5. Write a brief essay in which you synthesize Will Herberg's criticism of religiosity with O'Connor's treatment of Mrs. Turpin's self-righteousness in "Revelation." Remember to clarify a thesis for your essay.
6. C. S. Lewis writes that God uses pain to "plant the flag of truth within the rebel soul." How do some of the works in this section demonstrate God's severe mercy?
7. The essays in this unit have identified serious shortcomings we have in our culture, such as self-centeredness, lack of knowledge or mental laziness, and emphasis on external behavior. Identify the works that discuss these weaknesses, and use direct quotations from the authors.
8. Analogy is one pattern of writing that Lewis uses frequently. Identify some of these analogies. In a brief essay compare or contrast his use of analogies with those used by Anne Morrow Lindbergh in her essay "The Channelled Whelk."
9. Write an essay defining the various metaphors used to define God in the poetry from this unit.

PART II

The Search for a Moral Perspective

Introduction

The Christian faces a moral dilemma every day of his life. It may be the decision of whether to lie or tell the truth to a friend, to cheat or be honest on an exam, or to refrain from or participate in emotional cruelty to a classmate; but the dilemma is always the same. Yes or no. Act or react. Stop or go. We are all guilty of saying yes when we should have said no, or of saying nothing when we should have said something; yet to be aware of the choice is a beginning, and we can only discover our moral perspective through our experiences, whether they are positive or negative.

In the selection by C. S. Lewis we are told that every small decision we make will make us a more heavenly or hellish creature, and that the minor choices construct, bit by bit, our total character—making each decision crucial to the construction of the human spirit.

In this unit we will look at authors who have wrestled with decisions or faced moral dilemmas that have left a permanent mark on their lives or the lives of their fictional characters. In these works the authors communicate a moral perspective that resulted from viewing the atrocities of war, the helplessness of poverty, the cruelty of prejudice, or the depravity of the human character. As we live vicariously through these fictional and real characters in the works, we will be able to empathize with their suffering and to move toward the discovery of our own moral perspective.

Perhaps learning to filter literature through your Christian experience is natural for you. The editors of this anthology hope it is. Leland Ryken states in *Windows to the World,* "Every reader agrees or disagrees with the world view in works of literature on the basis of his or her own system of beliefs and values." Therefore, you will find literature that may not espouse Christianity but that may support Christianity's view of the human condition. Even literature that supports a repugnant view will help you in "clarifying" your defense and expanding your world view beyond personal experience. As you evaluate the opposition in light of your faith, you will find the courage to examine the quality of your own decision. As Socrates states, "The unexamined life is not worth living."

As Christians examining our own lives, we find in the Bible the appropriate perspective for our own crises or decisions. Ryken states, "Biblical Christianity is comprehensive. It has something to say on all the issues raised by works of literature." Literature, then, may not provide specific answers to life's questions; rather, it provides an extension of life by helping us learn to deal with imaginary issues before the real ones hit us head on. According to Ryken, "Literature is a catalyst to a person's thinking about the real issues of life."

Through literature, we expand personal experiences to universal experiences and discover for ourselves an effective and practical moral perspective based on conscientious examinations.

The Epistle of James tells us that our works give substance to faith. In fact, James admonishes us to use our faith for good works. Consequently, only through developing an understanding of the world around us can we fulfill our moral responsibilities and put that faith into practice.

Responsibility to Self

From HUCKLEBERRY FINN
Mark Twain

Once I said to myself it would be a thousand times better for Jim to be a slave at home where his family was, as long as he'd got to be a slave, and so I'd better write a letter to Tom Sawyer and tell him to tell Miss Watson where he was. But I soon give up that notion for two things: she'd be mad and disgusted at his rascality and ungratefulness for leaving her, and so she'd sell him straight down the river again; and if she didn't, everybody naturally despises an ungrateful nigger, and they'd make Jim feel it all the time, and so he'd feel ornery and disgraced. And then think of me! It would get all around that Huck Finn helped a nigger to get his freedom; and if I was ever to see anybody from that town again I'd be ready to get down and lick his boots for shame. That's just the way: a person does a low-down thing, and then he don't want to take no consequences of it. Thinks as long as he can hide, it ain't no disgrace. That was my fix exactly. The more I studied about this the more my conscience went to grinding me, and the more wicked and low-down and ornery I got to feeling. And at last, when it hit me all of a sudden that here was the plain hand of Providence slapping me in the face and letting me know my wickedness was being watched all the time from up there in heaven, whilst I was stealing a poor old woman's nigger that hadn't ever done me no harm, and now was showing me there's One that's always on the lookout, and ain't a-going to allow no such miserable doings to go only just so fur and no further, I most dropped in my tracks I was so scared. Well, I tried the best I could to kinder soften it up somehow for myself by saying I was brung up wicked, and so I warn't so much to blame; but something inside of me kept saying, "There was the Sunday-school, you could 'a' gone to it; and if you'd 'a' done it they'd 'a' learnt you there that people that acts as I'd been acting about that nigger goes to everlasting fire."

It made me shiver. And I about made up my mind to pray, and see if I couldn't try to quit being the kind of a boy I was and be better. So I kneeled down. But the words wouldn't come. Why wouldn't they? It warn't no use to try and hide it from Him. Nor from me, neither. I knowed very well why they wouldn't come. It was because my heart warn't right; it was because I warn't square; it was because I was playing double. I was letting on to give up sin, but away inside of me I was holding on to the biggest one of all. I was trying to make my mouth say I would do the right thing and the clean thing, and go and write to that nigger's owner and tell where he was; but deep down in me I knowed it was a lie, and He knowed it. You can't pray a lie—I found that out.

So I was full of trouble, full as I could be; and didn't know what to do. At last I had an idea; and I says, I'll go and write the letter — and then see if I can pray. Why, it was astonishing, the way I felt as light as a feather right straight off, and my troubles all gone. So I got a piece of paper and a pencil, all glad and excited, and set down and wrote:

> Miss Watson, your runaway nigger Jim is down here two mile below Pikesville, and Mr. Phelps has got him and he will give him up for the reward if you send.
>
> Huck   Finn.

I felt good and all washed clean of sin for the first time I had ever felt so in my life, and I knowed I could pray now. But I didn't do it straight off, but laid the paper down and set there thinking — thinking how good it was all this happened so, and how near I come to being lost and going to hell. And went on thinking. And got to thinking over our trip down the river; and I see Jim before me all the time: in the day and in the night-time; sometimes moonlight, sometimes storms, and we a-floating along, talking and singing and laughing. But somehow I couldn't seem to strike no places to harden me against him, but only the other kind. I'd see him standing my watch on top of his'n, 'stead of calling me, so I could go on sleeping; and see him how glad he was when I come back out of the fog; and when I come to him again in the swamp, up there where the feud was; and such-like times; and would always call me honey, and pet me, and do everything he could think of for me, and how good he always was; and at last I struck the time I saved him by telling the men we had smallpox aboard, and he was so grateful, and said I was the best friend old Jim ever had in the world, and the only one he's got now; and then I happened to look around and see that paper.

It was a close place. I took it up, and held it in my hand. I was a-trembling, because I'd got to decide, forever, betwixt two things, and I knowed it. I studied a minute, sort of holding my breath, and then says to myself:

"All right, then, I'll go to hell" — and tore it up.

It was awful thoughts and awful words, but they was said. And I let them stay said; and never thought no more about reforming. I shoved the whole thing out of my head, and said I would take up wickedness again, which was in my line, being brung up to it, and the other warn't. And for a starter I would go to work and steal Jim out of slavery again; and if I could think of anything worse, I would do that, too; because as long as I was in, and in for good, I might as well go the whole hog.

Christian Perspectives

1. Through Huck's innocent eyes, we see that his culture shaped his concept of God. Since the society of Huck's day presented a rigid interpretation of God, Huck viewed himself as unacceptable to that type of God. Why did Huck believe God would condemn him to hell?
2. Could our own culture misrepresent the true character of God? How?
3. Huck's decision was an ethical one. If he lied (a sin) to protect Jim, he was breaking the law. If he turned Jim in, he was breaking a trust. How did Huck reach his decision? How do you resolve conflicting ethical questions?
4. Although Huck sees himself as wicked and rebellious, you, as the reader, no doubt see another side of Huck. If you were with Huck, what would you say to him?

5. Twain narrates his story through Huck, using first person point of view. This technique *shows* rather than *tells* the reader all about Huck's character. What do you know about him? Would the story have been as effective if it were narrated in third person? Why or why not?

WHERE I LIVED, AND WHAT I LIVED FOR

Henry David Thoreau

An excerpt from *Walden*

When first I took up my abode in the woods, that is, began to spend my nights as well as my days there, which, by accident, was on Independence day, or the fourth of July, 1895, my house was not finished for winter, but was merely a defence against the rain, without plastering or chimney, the walls being of rough weather-stained boards, with wide chinks, which made it cool at night. The upright white hewn studs and freshly planed door and window casings gave it a clean and airy look, especially in the morning, when its timbers were saturated with dew, so that I fancied that by noon some sweet gum would exude from them. To my imagination it retained throughout the day more or less of this auroral character, reminding me of a certain house on a mountain which I had visited a year before. This was an airy and unplastered cabin, fit to entertain a traveling god, and where a goddess might trail her garments. The winds which passed over my dwelling were such as sweep over the ridges of mountains, bearing the broken strains, or celestial parts only, of terrestrial music. The morning wind forever blows, the poem of creation is uninterrupted; but few are the ears that hear it. Olympus is but the outside of the earth everywhere.

The only house I had been the owner of before, if I except a boat, was a tent, which I used occasionally when making excursions in the summer, and this is still rolled up in my garret; but the boat, after passing from hand to hand, has gone down the stream of time. With this more substantial shelter about me, I had made some progress toward settling in the world. This frame, so slightly clad, was a sort of crystallization around me, and reacted on the builder. It was suggestive somewhat as a picture in outlines. I did not need to go outdoors to take the air, for the atmosphere within had lost none of its freshness. It was not so much within doors as behind a door where I sat, even in the rainiest weather. The Harvamsa says, "An abode without birds is like a meat without seasoning." Such was not my abode, for I found myself suddenly neighbor to the birds; not having imprisoned one, but having caged myself near them. I was not only nearer to some of those which commonly frequent the garden and the orchard, but to those wilder and more thrilling songsters of the forest which never, or rarely, serenade a villager,—the wood-thrush, the veery, the scarlet tanager, the field-sparrow, the whippoorwill, and many others.

I was seated by the shore of a small pond, about a mile and a half south of the village of Concord and somewhat higher than it, in the midst of an extensive wood between that town and Lincoln, and about two miles south of that our only field known to fame, Concord Battle Ground; but I was so low in the woods that the opposite shore, half a mile off, like the rest, covered with wood, was my most distant horizon. For the first week, whenever I looked out on the pond it impressed me like a tarn high up on the side of a mountain, its bottom far above the surface of other lakes, and, as the sun arose, I saw it throwing off its nightly clothing of mist, and here and there, by degrees, its soft ripples or its smooth reflecting surface was revealed, while the mists, like ghosts, were stealthily withdrawing in every direction into the woods, as the breaking up of some nocturnal conventicle. The very dew seemed to hang upon the trees later into the day than usual, as on the sides of mountains. . . .

Every morning was a cheerful invitation to make my life equal simplicity, and I may say in-nocence, with Nature herself. I have been as sincere worshipper of Aurora as the Greeks. I got up early and bathed in the pond; that was a religious exercise, and one of the best things which I did. They say that characters were engraven on the bathing tub of king Tching-thang to this ef-fect: "Renew thyself completely each day; do it again and again and forever again." I can under-stand that. Morning brings back the heroic ages. I was as much affected by the faint hum of a mosquito making its invisible and unimaginable tour through my apartment at earliest dawn, when I was sitting with door and window open, as I could be by any trumpet that ever sang of fame. It was Homer's requiem; itself an Iliad and Odyssey in the air, singing its own wrath and wanderings. There was something cosmical about it; a standing advertisement, still forbidden, of everlasting vigor and fertility of the world. The morning, which is the most memorable season of the day, is the awakening hour. Then there is least somnolence in us; and for an hour, at least, some part of us awakes which slumbers all the rest of the day and night. Little is to be expected of that day and night. Little is to be expected of that day, if it can be called a day, to which we are not awakened by our genius, but by the mechanical nudging of some servitor, are not awakened by our own newly-acquainted force and aspirations from within, accompanied by the undulations of celestial music, instead of factory bells, and a fragrance filling the air—to a higher life than we fell asleep from; and thus the darkness bear its fruit, and prove itself to be good, no less than the light. That man who does not believe that each day contains an earlier, more sacred, and auroral hour than he has yet profaned, has despaired of life, and is pursuing a descending and darkening way. After a partial cessation of his sensuous life, the soul of man, or its organs rather, are reinvigorated each day, and his Genius tries again what noble life it can make. All memorable events, I should say, transpire in morning time and in a morning atmos-phere. The Vedas say, "All intelligences awake with the morning." Poetry and art, and the fairest and most memorable of the actions of men, date from such an hour. All poets and heroes, like Memmon, are the children of Aurora, and emit their music at sunrise. To him whose elastic and vigorous thought keeps pace with the sun, the day is a perpetual morning. It matters not what the clocks say or the attitudes and labors of men. Morning is when I am awake and there is a dawn in me. Moral reform is the effort to throw off sleep. Why is it that men give so poor an account of their day if they have not been slumbering? They are not such poor cal-culators. If they had not been overcome with drowsiness they would have performed something. The millions are awake enough for physical labor; but only one in a million is awake enough for effective intellectual exertion, only one in a hundred million to a poetic or divine life. To be awake is to be alive. I have never yet met a man who was quite awake. How could I have looked him in the face? . . .

I went to the woods because I wished to live deliberately, to front only the essential facts of life, and see if I could not learn what it had to teach, and not, when I came to die, discover that I had not lived. I did not wish to live what was not life, living is so dear; nor did I wish to practice resignation, unless it was quite necessary. I wanted to live deep and suck out all the marrow of life, to live so sturdily and Spartan-like as to put to rout all that was not life, to cut a broad swatch and shave close, to drive life into a corner, and reduce it to its lowest terms, and, if it proved to be mean, why then to get the whole and genuine meanness of it, and publish its meanness to the world; or if it were sublime, to know it by experience, and be able to give a true account of my excursion. For most men, it appears to me, are in a strange uncertainty about it, whether it is of the devil or of God, and have somewhat hastily concluded that it is the chief end of man here to "glorify God and enjoy him forever."

Still we live meanly, like ants; though the fable tells us that we were long ago changed into men; like pygmies we fight with cranes; it is error upon error, and clout upon clout, and our best virtue has for its occasion a superfluous and evitable wretchedness. Our life is frittered away by detail. An honest man has hardly need to count more than his ten fingers, or in extreme cases he may add his ten toes, and lump the rest. Simplicity, simplicity, simplicity! I say, let your affairs be as two or three and not hundreds or a thousand; instead of a million count half a dozen, and keep your accounts on your thumb nail. In the midst of this chopping sea of civilized life, such are the clouds and storms and quicksands and thousand-and-one items to be allowed for, that a man has to live, if he would not founder and go to the bottom and not make his port at all, by dead reckoning, and he must be a great calculator indeed who succeeds. Simplify, simplify. Instead of three meals a day, if it be necessary eat but one; instead of a hundred dishes, five; and reduce other things in proportion. Our life is like a German Confederacy, made up of petty states with its boundary forever fluctuating, so that even a German cannot tell you how it is bounded at any moment. The nation itself, with all its so-called internal improvements, which, by the way, are all external and superficial, is just such an unwieldy and overgrown establishment, cluttered with furniture and tripped up by its own traps, ruined by luxury and heedless expense, by want of calculation and a worthy aim, as the million households in the land; and the only cure for it is for them to be a rigid economy, a stern and more than Spartan simplicity of life and an elevation of purpose. It lives too fast. Men think that it is essential that the Nation have commerce, and export ice, and talk through a telegraph, and ride thirty miles an hour, without a doubt, whether they do or not; but whether we should live like baboons or like men, is a little uncertain. If we do not get out sleepers,[1] and forge rails, and devote days and nights to work, but go tinkering upon our lives to improve them, who will build railroads? And if railroads are not built, how shall we get to heaven in season? But if we stay at home and mind our business, who will want railroads? We do not ride on the railroad; it rides upon us. Did you ever think what those sleepers are that underlie the railroads? Each one is a man, an Irishman, or a Yankee man. The rails are laid on them, and they are covered with sand, and the cars run smoothly over them. They are sound sleepers, I assure you. And every few years a new lot is laid down and run over; so that, if some have the pleasure of riding on a rail, others have the misfortune to be ridden upon. And when they run over a man that is walking in his sleep, a supernumerary sleeper in the wrong position, and wake him up, they suddenly stop the cars, and make a hue and cry about it, as if this was an exception. I am glad to know that it takes a gang of men for every five miles to keep the sleepers down and level in their beds as it is, for this is a sign that they may sometimes get up again.

Why should we live with such hurry and waste of life? We are determined to be starved before we are hungry. Men say that a stitch in time saves nine, and so they take a thousand

1. railroad ties (Thoreau makes puns with this word in the next few sentences.)

99

stitches today to save nine tomorrow. As for work, we haven't any of any consequence. We have the Saint Vitus' dance, and cannot possibly keep our heads still. If I should only give a few pulls at the parish bell-rope, as for a fire, that is, without setting the bell, there is hardly a man on his farm in the outskirts of Concord, notwithstanding that press of engagements which was his excuse so many times this morning, nor a boy, nor a woman, I might almost say, but would forsake all and follow that sound, not mainly to save property from the flames, but, if we will confess the truth, much more to see it burn, since burn it must, and we, be it known, did not set it on fire, — or to see it put out, and have a hand in it, if that is done as handsomely; yes, even if it were the parish church itself. Hardly a man takes a half hour's nap after dinner, but when he wakes he holds up his head and asks, "What's the news?" as if the rest of mankind had stood his sentinels. Some give directions to be waked every half hour, doubtless for no other purpose; and then, to pay for it, they tell what they have dreamed. After a night's sleep the news is as indispensable as the breakfast. "Pray tell me anything new that has happened to a man anywhere on this globe," — and he reads it over his coffee and rolls, that a man has had his eyes gouged out this morning on the Wachito River, never dreaming the while he lives in the dark unfathomed mammoth cave of this world, and has but the rudiment of an eye himself.

For my part, I could easily do without the post-office. I think that there are very few important communications made through it. To speak critically, I never received more than one or two letters in my life — I wrote this some years ago — that were worth the postage. The penny-post is, commonly, an institution through which you seriously offer a man that penny for his thoughts which is so often safely offered in jest. And I am sure that I never read any memorable news in a newspaper. If we read of one man robbed, or murdered, or killed by an accident, or one house burned, or one vessel wrecked, or one steamboat blown up, or one cow run over on the Western Railroad, or one mad dog killed, or one lot of grasshoppers in the winter, — we never need of another. One is enough. If you are acquainted with the principle, what do you care for a myriad instances and applications? To a philosopher all news, as it is called, is gossip, and they who edit and read it are old women over their tea. Yet not a few are greedy after this gossip.

Christian Perspectives

1. Thoreau states that when it came time to die he did not want to discover that he had not really lived. What did he fear that "life" would do to him if he did not live in a drastically different manner? Doesn't the Bible make a similar claim? (See John 17:16–18.)
2. Thoreau's advice to simplify our lives can be compared to Jesus' teaching about the rich man who was burdened by his earthly goods. (See Matthew 19:24.) How can you simplify your life for spiritual purposes?
3. Jesus tells us not to spend so much time worrying about things. (See Matthew 6:25–32.) If worrying complicates lives, how would not worrying simplify them?

CHANNELLED WHELK

Anne Morrow Lindbergh

The shell in my hand is deserted. It once housed a whelk, a snail-like creature, and then temporarily, after the death of the first occupant, a little hermit crab, who has run away, leaving his tracks behind him like a delicate vine on the sand. He ran away, and left me his shell. It was once a protection to him. I turn the shell in my hand, gazing into the wide open door from which he made his exit. Had it become an encumbrance? Why did he run away? Did he hope to find a better home; a better mode of living? I too have run away, I realize, I have shed the shell of my life, for these few weeks of vacation.

But his shell—it is simple; it is bare, it is beautiful. Small, only the size of my thumb, its architecture is perfect, down to the finest detail. Its shape, swelling like a pear in the center, winds in a gentle spiral to the pointed apex. Its color, dull gold, is whitened by a wash of salt from the sea. Each whorl, each faint knob, each criss-cross vein in its egg-shell texture, is as clearly defined as on the day of creation. My eye follows with delight the outer circumference of that diminutive winding staircase up which this tenant used to travel.

My shell is not like this, I think. How untidy it has become! Blurred with moss, knobby with barnacles, its shape is hardly recognizable any more. Surely, it had a shape once. It has a shape still in my mind. What is the shape of my life?

The shape of my life today starts with a family. I have a husband, five children and a home just beyond the suburbs of New York. I have also a craft, writing, and therefore work I want to pursue. The shape of my life is, of course, determined by many other things; my background and childhood, my mind and its education, my conscience and its pressures, my heart and its desires. I want to give and take from my children and husband, to share with friends and community, to carry out my obligations to man and to the world as a woman, as an artist, as a citizen.

But I want first of all—in fact, as an end to these other desires—to be at peace with myself. I want a singleness of eye, a purity of intention, a central core to my life that will enable me to carry out these obligations and activities as well as I can. I want, in fact—to borrow from the language of the saints—to live "in grace" as much of the time as possible. I am not using this term in a strictly theological sense. By grace I mean an inner harmony, essentially spiritual, which can be translated into outward harmony. I am seeking perhaps what Socrates asked for in the prayer from the Phaedrus when he said, "May the outward and inward man be at one." I would like to achieve a state of inner spiritual grace from which I could function and give as I was meant to in the eye of God.

Vague as this definition may be, I believe most people are aware of periods in their lives when they seem to be "in grace" and other periods when they feel "out of grace," even though they may use different words to describe these states. In the first happy condition, one seems to carry all one's tasks before one lightly, as if borne along on a great tide; and in the opposite state one can hardly tie a shoe-string. It is true that a large part of life consists of learning a technique of tying the shoe-string, whether one is in grace or not. But there are techniques of living too; there are even techniques in the search for grace. And techniques can be cultivated. I have learned by some experience, by many examples, and by the writings of countless others before me, also occupied in the search, that certain environments, certain modes of life, certain rules of conduct are more conducive to inner and outer harmony than others. There are, in fact, certain roads that one may follow. Simplification of life is one of them.

I mean to lead a simple life, to choose a simple shell I can carry easily—like a hermit crab. But I do not. I find that my frame of life does not foster simplicity. My husband and five children must make their way in the world. The life I have chosen as wife and mother entrains a whole caravan of complications. It involves a house in the suburbs and either household drudgery or household help which wavers between scarcity and non-existence for most of us. It involves food and shelter, meals, planning, marketing, bills, and making the ends meet in a thousand ways. It involves not only the butcher, the baker, the candlestickmaker but countless other experts to keep my modern house with its modern "simplifications" (electricity, plumbing, refrigerator, gas-stove, oil-burner, dish-washer, radios, car, and numerous other labor-saving devices) functioning properly. It involves health; doctors, dentists, appointments, medicine, cod-liver oil, vitamins, trips to the drugstore. It involves education, spiritual, intellectual, physical; schools, school conferences, car-pools, extra trips for basket-ball or orchestra practice; tutoring; camps, camp equipment and transportation. It involves clothes, shopping, laundry, cleaning, mending, letting skirts down and sewing buttons on, or finding someone else to do it. It involves friends, my husband's, my children's, my own, and endless arrangements to get together; letters, invitations, telephone calls and transportation hither and yon.

For life today in America is based on the premise of ever-widening circles of contact and communication. It involves not only family demands, but community demands, national demands, inter-national demands on the good citizen, through social and cultural pressures, through newspapers, magazines, radio programs, political drives, charitable appeals, and so on. My mind reels with it. What a circus act we women perform every day of our lives. It puts the trapeze artist to shame. Look at us. We run a tight rope daily, balancing a pile of books on the head. Baby-carriage, parasol, kitchen chair, still under control. Steady now!

This is not the life of simplicity but the life of multiplicity that the wise men warn us of. It leads not to unification but to fragmentation. It does not bring grace; it destroys the soul. And this is not only true of my life, I am forced to conclude; it is the life of millions of women in America. I stress America, because today, the American woman more than any other has the privilege of choosing such a life. Women in large parts of the civilized world have been forced back by war, by poverty, by collapse, by the sheer struggle to survive, into a smaller circle of im-mediate time and space, immediate family life, immediate problems of existence. The American woman is still relatively free to choose the wider life. How long she will hold this enviable and precarious position no one knows. But her particular situation has a significance far above its apparent economic, national or even sex limitations.

For the problem of the multiplicity of life not only confronts the American woman, but also the American man. And it is not merely the concern of the American as such, but of our whole modern civilization, since life in America today is held up as the ideal of a large part of the rest of the world. And finally, it is not limited to our present civilization, though we are faced with it now in an exaggerated form. It has always been one of the pitfalls of mankind. Plotinus was preaching the dangers of multiplicity of the world back in the third century. Yet, the problem is particularly and essentially woman's. Distraction is, always has been, and probab-ly always will be, inherent in woman's life.

For to be a woman is to have interests and duties, raying out in all directions from the central mother-core, like spokes from the hub of a wheel. The pattern of our lives is essentially circular. We must be open to all points of the compass; husband, children, friends, home, community; stretched out, exposed, sensitive like a spider's web to each breeze that blows, to each call that comes. How difficult for us, then, to achieve a balance in the midst of these contradictory tensions, and yet how necessary for the proper functioning of our lives. How much we need, and how arduous of attainment is that steadiness preached in all rules for holy living. How desirable and how distant is the ideal of the contemplative, artist, or saint—the inner inviolable core, the single eye.

With a new awareness, both painful and humorous, I begin to understand why the saints were rarely married women. I am convinced it has nothing inherently to do, as I once supposed, with chastity or children. It has to do primarily with distractions. The bearing, rearing, feeding and educating of children; the running of a house with its thousand details; human relationships with their myriad pulls—woman's normal occupations in general run counter to creative life, or contemplative life, or saintly life. The problem is not merely one of Woman and Career, Woman and the Home, Woman and Independence. It is more basically: how to remain whole in the midst of the distractions of life; how to remain balanced no matter what centrifugal forces tend to pull one off center; how to remain strong, no matter what shocks come in at the periphery and tend to crack the hub of the wheel.

What is the answer? There is no easy answer, no complete answer. I have only clues, shells from the sea. The bare beauty of the channeled whelk tells me that one answer, and perhaps a first step, is in simplification of life, in cutting out some of the distractions. But how? Total retirement is not possible, I cannot shed my responsibilities. I cannot permanently inhabit a desert island. I cannot be a nun in the midst of family life. I would not want to be. The solution for me, surely, is neither in total renunciation of the world, nor in total acceptance of it. I must find a balance somewhere, or an alternating rhythm between these two extremes; a swinging of the pendulum between solitude and communion, between retreat and return. In my periods of retreat, perhaps I can learn something to carry back into my worldly life. I can at least practice for these two weeks the simplification of outward life, as a beginning. I can follow this superficial clue, and see where it leads. Here, in beach living, I can try.

One learns first of all in beach living the art of shedding; how little one can get along with, not how much. Physical shedding to begin with, which then mysteriously spreads into other fields. Clothes, first. Of course, one needs less in the sun. But one needs less anyway, one finds suddenly. One does not need a closet-full, only a small suitcase-full. And what a relief it is! Less taking up and down of hems, less mending, and—best of all—less worry about what to wear. One finds one is shedding not only clothes—but vanity.

Next, shelter. One does not need the airtight shelter one has in winter in the North. Here I live in a bare sea-shell of a cottage. No heat, no telephone, no plumbing to speak of, no hot water, a two-burner oil stove, no gadgets to go wrong. No rugs. There were some, but I rolled them up the first day; it is easier to sweep the sand off a bare floor. But I find I don't bustle about with unnecessary sweeping and cleaning here. I am no longer aware of the dust. I have shed my Puritan conscience about absolute tidiness and cleanliness. Is it possible that, too, is a material burden? No curtains. I do not need them for privacy; the pines around my house are enough protection. I want the windows open all the time, and I don't want to worry about rain. I begin to shed my Martha-like anxiety about many things. Washable slipcovers, faded and old—I hardly see them; I don't worry about the impression they make on other people. I am shedding pride. As little furniture as possible; I shall not need much. I shall ask into my shell only those friends with whom I can be completely honest. I find I am shedding hypocrisy in human relationships. What a rest that will be! The most exhausting thing in life, I have discovered, is being insincere. That is why so much of social life is exhausting; one is wearing a mask. I have shed my mask.

I find I live quite happily without those things I think necessary in winter in the North. And as I write these words, I remember, with some shock at the disparity of our lives, a similar statement made by a friend of mine in France who spent three years in a German prison camp. Of course, he said, qualifying his remark, they did not get enough to eat, they were sometimes atrociously treated, they had little physical freedom. And yet, prison life taught him how little one can get along with, and what extraordinary spiritual freedom and peace such simplification can bring. I remember again, ironically, that today more of us in America than anywhere else in the world have the luxury of choice between simplicity and complication of life. And for the most part, we, who could choose simplicity, choose complication. War, prison, survival periods, enforce a form of simplicity on man. The monk and the nun choose it of their own free will. But if one accidentally finds it, as I have for a few days, one finds also the serenity it brings.

Is it not rather ugly, one may ask? One collects material possessions not only for security, comfort or vanity, but for beauty as well. Is your sea-shell house not ugly and bare? No, it is beautiful, my house. It is bare, of course, but the wind, the sun, the smell of the pines blow through its bareness. The unfinished beams in the roof are veiled by cobwebs. They are lovely, I think, gazing up at them with new eyes; they soften the hard lines of the rafters as grey hairs soften the lines on a middle-aged face. I no longer pull out grey hairs or sweep down cobwebs. As for the walls, it is true they looked forbidding at first. I felt cramped and enclosed by their blank faces. I wanted to knock holes in them, to give them another dimension with pictures or windows. So I dragged home from the beach grey arms of driftwood, worn satin-smooth by wind and sand. I gathered trailing green vines with floppy red-tipped leaves. I picked up the whitened skeletons of conchshells, their curious hollowed-out shapes faintly reminiscent of abstract sculpture. With these tacked to walls and propped up in corners, I am satisfied. I have a periscope out to the world. I have a window, a view, a point of flight from my sedentary base.

I am content. I sit down at my desk, a bare kitchen table with a blotter, a bottle of ink, a sand dollar to weight down one corner, a clam shell for a pen tray, the broken tip of a conch, pink-tinged, to finger, and a row of shells to set my thoughts spinning.

I love my sea-shell of a house. I wish I could live in it always. I wish I could transport it home. But I cannot. It will not hold a husband, five children and the necessities and trappings of daily life. I can only carry back my little channelled whelk. It will sit on my desk in Connecticut, to remind me of the ideal of a simplified life, to encourage me in the game I played on the beach. To ask how little, not how much, can I get along with. To say—is it necessary?—when I am tempted to add one more accumulation to my life, when I am pulled toward one more centrifugal activity.

Simplification of outward life is not enough. It is merely the outside. But I am starting with the outside. I am looking at the outside of a shell, the outside of my life—the shell. The complete answer is not to be found on the outside, in an outward mode of living. This is only a technique, a road to grace. The final answer, I know, is always inside. But the outside can give a clue, can help one to find the inside answer. One is free, like the hermit crab, to change one's shell.

Channelled whelk, I put you down again, but you have set my mind on a journey, up an inwardly winding spiral staircase of thought.

Christian Perspectives

1. Contrast Lindbergh's observation of the simple life to Thoreau's. How do they differ? How does her view as a woman change her perspective?
2. Lindbergh identifies the "grace" periods of our lives as a harmony between the outer and inner life. What three choices does she suggest to achieve this harmony in our outer life?
3. Lindbergh's figures of speech create visual images, making her exposition almost like poetry. Find examples of two similes and two metaphors in her work. What visual images does she create?

THE WORLD IS TOO MUCH WITH US

William Wordsworth

The World is too much with us; late and soon,
Getting and spending, we lay waste our powers;
Little we see in Nature that is ours;
We have given our hearts away, a sordid boon[1]!
This Sea that bares her bosom to the moon,
The winds that will be howling at all hours,
And are up-gathered now like sleeping flowers,
For this, for everything, we are out of tune;
It moves us not. — Great God! I'd rather be
A Pagan suckled in a creed outworn;
So might I, standing on this pleasant lea,[2]
Have glimpses that would make me less forlorn;
Have sight of Proteus[3] rising from the sea;
Or hear old Triton[4] blow his wreathed horn.

Christian Perspectives

1. Mark 8:36 says, "For what shall it profit a man if he shall gain the whole world and lose his own soul?" Parallel the poem to this scripture.
2. Wordsworth uses an antithetical pair of words "sordid boon." Look up these words. Why did he use these words to express hopelessness?

---

1. boon — gift
2. lea — grassland or pasture.
3. Proteus — a god from Greek mythology who could change his form.
4. Triton — a demigod from Greek mythology, son of the sea god, Poseidon, and Amphitrite. He served as Poseidon's trumpeter, controlling the seas by his horn.

From MERE CHRISTIANITY

C. S. Lewis

Bad psychological material is not a sin but a disease. It does not need to be repented of, but to be cured. And by the way, that is very important. Human beings judge one another by their external actions. God judges them by their moral choices. When a neurotic who has a pathological horror of cats forces himself to pick up a cat for some good reason, it is quite possible that in God's eyes he has shown more courage than a healthy man may have shown in winning the V.C.[1] When a man who has been perverted from his youth and taught that cruelty is the right thing does some tiny kindness, or refrains from some cruelty he might have committed, and thereby, perhaps, risks being sneered at by his companions, he may, in God's eyes, be doing more than you and I would do if we gave up life itself for a friend.

It is as well to put this the other way round. Some of us who seem quite nice people may, in fact, have made so little use of a good heredity and good upbringing that we are really worse than those whom we regard as fiends. Can we be quite certain how we should have behaved if we had been saddled with the psychological outfit, and then with the bad upbringing, and then with the power, say, of Himmler?[2] That is why Christians are told not to judge. We see only the results which a man's choices make out of his raw material. But God does not judge him on the raw material at all, but on what he has done with it. Most of the man's psychological make-up is probably due to his body: when his body dies all that will fall off him, and the real central man, the thing that chose, that made the best or the worst of this material, will stand naked. All sorts of nice things which we thought were our own, but which were really due to good digestion, will fall off some of us: all sorts of nasty things which were due to complexes or bad health will fall off others. We shall then, for the first time, see every one as he really was. There will be surprises.

And that leads on to my second point. People often think of Christian morality as a kind of bargain in which God says, "If you keep a lot of rules I'll reward you, and if you don't I'll do the other thing." I do not think that is the best way of looking at it. I would much rather say that every time you make a choice you are turning the central part of you, the part of you that chooses, into something a little different from what it was before. And taking your life as a whole, with all your innumerable choices, all your life long you are slowly turning this central thing either into a heavenly creature or into a hellish creature: either into a creature that is in harmony with God, and with other creatures, and with itself, or else into one that is in a state of war and hatred with God, and with its fellow-creatures, and with itself. To be the one kind of creature is heaven: that is, it is joy and peace and knowledge and power. To be the other means madness, horror, idiocy, rage, impotence, and eternal loneliness. Each of us at each moment is progressing to the one state or the other.

That explains what always used to puzzle me about Christian writers; they seem to be so very strict at one moment and so very free and easy at another. They talk about mere sins of thought as if they were immensely important: and then they talk about the most frightful murders and treacheries as if you had only got to repent and all would be forgiven. But I have come

---

1. V.C. The Victoria Cross. Britain's highest military honor, equivalent to the American Medal of Honor.
2. Heinrich Himmler—a Nazi commander of Hitler's infamous SS troups.

to see that they are right. What they are always thinking of is the mark which the action leaves on that tiny central self which no one sees in this life but which each of us will have to endure — or enjoy — forever. One man may be so placed that his anger sheds the blood of thousands, and another so placed that however angry he gets he will only be laughed at. But the little mark on the soul may be much the same in both. Each has done something to himself which, unless he repents, will make it harder for him to keep out of the rage next time he is tempted, and will make the rage worse when he does fall into it. Each of them, if he seriously turns to God, can have that twist in the central man straightened out again: each is, in the long run, doomed if he will not. The bigness or smallness of the thing, seen from the outside, is not what really matters.

One last point. Remember that, as I said, the right direction leads not only to peace but to knowledge. When a man is getting better he understands more and more clearly the evil that is still left in him. When a man is getting worse, he understands his own badness less and less. A moderately bad man knows he is not very good; a thoroughly bad man thinks he is all right. This is common sense, really. You understand sleep when you are awake, not while you are sleeping. You can see mistakes in arithmetic when your mind is working properly: while you are making them you cannot see them. You can understand the nature of drunkenness when you are sober, not when you are drunk. Good people know about both good and evil: bad people do not know about either.

Christian Perspectives

1. With the realization that our choices are infinitely important, we see that our responsibility to ourselves is always an issue. Give some examples of relatively simple choices in your life that have had lasting effects.
2. Lewis states that "the right direction leads not only to peace but to knowledge." What scriptures affirm this? (See Proverbs 3:5,6.)
3. Identify a decision in your life that may have seemed insignificant at the time but that started you in a "right" direction — toward making other "right" decisions as well.

MAKING CONNECTIONS

1. Both Lindbergh and Thoreau use nature to contrast artificial lives to more natural selves. Lindbergh uses a beach house, a shell, and the ocean. Thoreau uses a log cabin, trees, and the woods. What biblical passages use nature to reveal the quality of life? (See John 15:1–5, romans 11:24, jeremiah 17:8, and job 14:2.)

2. Thoreau uses his experience with a piece of land to illustrate his ideas about an ideal simplicity of life. Write a brief essay in which you explain how one writer can use his life on the land as a positive move toward simplicity, while other writers use possessions as sources of negative, selfish concern.

3. Thoreau examines and revivifies old sayings, expressions from the Bible and other religious writings, and metaphors from everyday speech to make his point. Cite one example of this, and, in a paragraph, analyze how the author makes effective use of this expression.

4. Anne Morrow Lindbergh uses the shell of the channeled whelk as a metaphorical image for the desired simplicity. Think of some specific object which you could use to explain your life—or your life as you wish it to be—and write a paragraph developing the image, illustrating your life as you describe the object.

5. C. S. Lewis describes how moral choices shape the character or soul of a person. Using this idea, imagine two of your friends as they might become in old age. Write a brief description of their characters, using contrast as your method of development.

Responsibility to Others

THE TURBID EBB AND FLOW OF MISERY
Margaret Sanger

Every night and every morn
Some to misery are born.
Every morn and every night
Some are born to sweet delight.
Some are born to sweet delight.
Some are born to endless night.
— *William Blake*

During these years [about 1921] in New York trained nurses were in great demand. Few people wanted to enter hospitals; they were afraid they might be "practiced" upon, and consented to go only in desperate emergencies. Sentiment was especially vehement in the matter of having babies. A woman's own bedroom, no matter how inconveniently arranged, was the usual place for her lying-in. I was not sufficiently free from domestic duties to be a general nurse, but I could ordinarily manage obstetrical cases because I was notified far enough ahead to plan my schedule. And after serving my two weeks I could get home again.

Sometimes I was summoned to small apartments occupied by young clerks, insurance salesmen, or lawyers, just starting out, most of them under thirty and whose wives were having their first or second baby. They were always eager to know the best and latest method in infant care and feeding. In particular, Jewish patients, whose lives centered around the family, welcomed advice and followed it implicitly.

But more and more my calls began to come from the Lower East Side, as though I were being magnetically drawn there by some force outside my control. I hated the wretchedness and hopelessness of the poor, and never experienced that satisfaction in working among them that so many noble women have found. My concern for my patients was not quite different from my earlier hospital attitude. I could see that much was wrong with them which did not appear in the physiological or medical diagnosis. A woman in childbirth was not merely a woman in childbirth. My expanded outlook included a view of her background, her potentialities as a human being, the kind of children she was bearing, and what was going to happen to them.

The wives of small shopkeepers were my most frequent cases, but I had carpenters, truck drivers, dishwashers, and pushcart vendors. I admired intensely the consideration most of these people had for their own. Money to pay doctor and nurse had been carefully saved months in advance — parents-in-law, grandfathers, grandmothers, all contributing.

As soon as the neighbors learned that a nurse was in the building they came in a friendly way to visit, often carrying fruit, jellies, or gefilte fish made after a cherished recipe. It was infinitely pathetic to me that they, so poor themselves, should bring me food. Later they drifted in again with the excuse of getting the plate, and sat down for a nice talk; there was no hurry. Always back of the little gift was the question, "I am pregnant (or my daughter, or my sister is). Tell me something to keep from having another baby. We cannot afford another yet."

I tried to explain the only two methods I had ever heard of among the middle classes, both of which were invariably brushed aside as unacceptable. They were of no certain avail to the wife because they placed the burden of responsibility solely upon the husband — a burden which he seldom assumed. What she was seeking was self-protection she could herself use, and there was none.

Below this stratum of society was one in truly desperate circumstances. The men were sullen and unskilled, picking up odd jobs now and then, but more often unemployed, lounging in and out of the house at all hours of the day and night. The women seemed to slink on their way to market and were without neighborliness.

These submerged, untouched classes were beyond the scope of organized charity or religion. No labor union, no church, not even the Salvation Army reached them. They were apprehensive of everyone and rejected help of any kind, ordering all intruders to keep out; both birth and death they considered their own business. Social agents, who were just beginning to appear, were profoundly mistrusted because they pried into homes and lives, asking questions about wages, how many were in the family, had any of them ever been in jail. Often two or three had been there or were now under suspicion of prostitution, shoplifting, purse snatching, petty thievery, and, in consequence, passed furtively by the big blue uniforms on the corner.

The utmost depression came over me as I approached this surreptitious region. Below Fourteenth Street I seemed to be breathing a different air, to be in another world and country where the people had habits and customs alien to anything I had ever heard about.

There were then approximately ten thousand apartments in New York into which no sun ray penetrated directly; such windows as they had opened only on a narrow court from which rose fetid odors. It was seldom cleaned, though garbage and refuse often went down into it. All these dwellings were pervaded by the foul breath of poverty, that moldy, indefinable, indescribable smell which cannot be fumigated out, sickening to me but apparently unnoticed by those who lived there. When I set to work with antiseptics, their pungent sting, at least temporarily, obscured the stench. I remember one confinement case to which I was called by the doctor of an insurance company. I climbed up the five flights and entered the airless rooms, but the baby had come with too great speed. A boy of ten had been the only assistant. Five flights was a long way; he had wrapped the placenta in a piece of newspaper and dropped it out the window into the court.

Many families took in "boarders," as they were termed, whose small contributions paid the rent. These derelicts, wanderers, alternately working and drinking, were crowded in with the children; a single room sometimes held as many as six sleepers. Little girls were accustomed to dressing and undressing in front of the men, and were often violated, occasionally by their own fathers or brothers, before they reached the age of puberty.

Pregnancy was a chronic condition among the women of this class. Suggestions as to what to do for a girl who was "in trouble" or a married woman who was "caught" passed from mouth to mouth—herb teas, turpentine, steaming, rolling downstairs, inserting slippery elm, knitting needles, shoehooks. When they had word of a new remedy they hurried to the drugstore, and if the clerk were inclined to be friendly he might say, "Oh, that won't help you, but here's something that may." The younger druggists usually refused to give advice because, if it were to be known, they would come under the law; midwives were even more fearful. The doomed women implored to me to reveal the "secret" rich people had, offering to pay me extra to tell them; many really believed I was holding back information for money. They asked everybody and tried anything, but nothing did them any good. On Saturday nights I have seen groups of from fifty to one hundred with their shawls over their heads waiting outside the office of a five-dollar abortionist.

Each time I returned to this district, which was becoming a recurrent nightmare, I used to hear that Mrs. Cohen "had been carried to a hospital, but had never come back," or that Mrs. Kelly "had sent the children to a neighbor and had put her head into the gas oven." Day after day such tales were poured into my ears—a baby born dead, great relief—the death of an older child, sorrow but again relief of a sort—the story told a thousand times of death from abortion and children going into institutions. I shuddered with horror as I listened to the details and studied the reasons back of them—destitution linked with excessive childbearing. The waste of life seemed utterly senseless. One by one worried, and, pensive, and aging faces marshalled themselves before me in my dreams, sometimes appealingly, sometimes accusingly.

These were not merely "unfortunate conditions among the poor" such as we read about. I knew the women personally. They were living, breathing, human beings, with hopes, fears, and aspirations like my own, yet their weary, misshapen bodies, "always ailing, never failing," were destined to be thrown on the scrap heap before they were thirty-five. I could not escape from the facts of their wretchedness; neither was I able to see any way out. My own cozy and comfortable family existence was becoming a reproach to me.

Then one stifling mid-July day in 1912 I was summoned to a Grand Street tenement. My patient was a small, slight Russian Jewess, about twenty-eight years old, of the special cast of feature to which suffering lends a madonna-like expression. The cramped three-room apartment was in a sorry state of turmoil. Jake Sachs, a truck driver scarcely older than his wife, had come home to find the three children crying and her unconscious from the effects of a self-induced abortion. He had called the nearest doctor, who in turn had sent for me. Jake's earnings were trifling, and most of them had gone to keep the none-too-strong children clean and properly fed. But his wife's ingenuity had helped them to save a little, and this he was glad to spend on a nurse rather than have her go to a hospital.

The doctor and I settled ourselves to the task of fighting the septicemia. Never had I worked so fast, never so concentratedly. The sultry days and nights melted into a torpid inferno. It did not seem possible there could be such heat, and every bit of food, ice, and drugs had to be carried up three flights of stairs.

Jake was more kind and thoughtful than many of the husbands I had encountered. He loved his children, and had always helped his wife wash and dress them. He had brought water up and carried garbage down before he left in the morning, and did as much as he could for me while he anxiously watched her progress.

After a fortnight Mrs. Sachs' recovery was in sight. Neighbors, ordinarily fatalistic as to the results of abortion, were genuinely pleased that she had survived. She smiled wanly at all who came to see her and thanked them gently, but she could not respond to their hearty congratulations. She appeared to be more despondent and anxious than she should have been, and spent too much time in meditation.

At the end of three weeks, as I was preparing to leave the fragile patient to take up her difficult life once more, she finally voiced her fears, "Another baby will finish me, I suppose?"

"It's too early to talk about that," I temporized. But when the doctor came to make his last call, I drew him aside. "Mrs. Sachs is terribly worried about having another baby."

"She well may be," replied the doctor, and then he stood before her and said, "Any more such capers, young woman, and there'll be no need to send for me."

"I know, doctor," she replied timidly, "but," and she hesitated as though it took all her courage to say it, "what can I do to prevent it?"

The doctor was a kindly man, and he had worked hard to save her, but such incidents had become so familiar to him that he had long since lost whatever delicacy he might once have had. He laughed good-naturedly. "You want to have your cake and eat it too, do you? Well, it can't be done."

Then picking up his hat and bag to depart he said, "Tell Jake to sleep on the roof."

I glanced quickly at Mrs. Sachs. Even through my sudden tears I could see stamped on her face an expression of absolute despair. We simply looked at each other, saying no word until the door had closed behind the doctor. Then she lifted her thin, blue-veined hands and clasped them beseechingly. "He can't understand. He's only a man. But you do, don't you? Please tell me the secret, and I'll never breathe it to a soul. Please!"

What was I to do? I could not speak the conventionally comforting phrases which would be of no comfort. Instead, I made her as physically easy as I could and promised to come back in a few days to talk with her again. A little later, when she slept I tiptoed away.

Night after night the wistful image of Mrs. Sachs appeared before me. I made all sorts of excuses to myself for not going back. I was busy on other cases; I really did not know what to say to her or how to convince her of my own ignorance; I was helpless to avert such monstrous atrocities. Time rolled by and I did nothing.

The telephone rang one evening three months later, and Jake Sachs' agitated voice begged me to come at once; his wife was sick again and from the same cause. For a wild moment I thought of sending someone else, but actually, of course, I hurried into my uniform, caught up my bag, and started out. All the way I longed for a subway wreck, an explosion, anything to keep me from having to enter that home again. But nothing happened, even to delay me. I turned into a dingy doorway and climbed the familiar stairs once more. The children were there, young little things.

Mrs. Sachs was in a coma and died within ten minutes. I folded her still hands across her breast, remembering how they had pleaded with me, begging so humbly for the knowledge which was her right. I drew a sheet over her pallid face. Jake was sobbing, running his hands through his hair and pulling it out like an insane person. Over and over again he wailed, "My God! My God!"

I left him pacing desperately back and forth, and for hours I myself walked and walked and walked through the hushed streets. When I finally arrived home and let myself quietly in, all the household was sleeping. I looked out my window and down upon the dimly lighted city. Its pains and griefs crowded in upon me, a moving picture rolled before my eyes with photographic clearness: women writhing in travail to bring forth little babies; the babies themselves naked and hungry, wrapped in newspapers to keep them from the cold; six-year-old children with pinched, pale, wrinkled faces, old in concentrated wretchedness, pushed into gray and fetid cellars, crouching on stone floors, their small scrawny hands shuttling through rags, making lamp shades, artificial flowers; white coffins, black coffins, coffins, coffins, interminably passing in never-ending a succession. The scenes piled one upon another and on another. I could bear it no longer.

As I stood there the darkness faded. The sun came up and threw its reflection over the house tops. It was the dawn of a new day in my life also. The doubt and questioning, the experimenting and trying, were now to be put behind me. I knew I could not go back merely to keeping people alive.

I went to bed, knowing that no matter what it might cost, I was finished with palliatives and superficial cures; I was resolved to seek out the root of evil, to do something to change the destiny of mothers whose miseries were vast as the sky.

Christian Perspectives

1. Often a critical event like Sanger's will occur that makes an irreversible change in a person's life. Has an event like this occurred in your life or in the life of someone you know? Explain your answer.
2. Although Sanger writes from a historical experience that differs from our own, identify current problems that afflict the poor in our society.
3. Sanger's statement, "I knew [them] personally" adds impact to her experience. Have you had a personal experience with someone who is desperately poor? How did you respond to that person's need?

A MODEST PROPOSAL

Jonathan Swift

For preventing
the children of poor people
from being a burden
to their parents or country,
and for making them beneficial
to the public.

It is a melancholy object to those who walk through this great town, or travel in the country, when they see the streets, the roads, and cabin-doors crowded with beggars of the female sex, followed by three, four or six children, all in rage, and importuning every passenger for an alms. These mothers, instead of being able to work for their honest livelihood, are forced to employ all their time in strolling, to beg sustenance for their helpless infants, who, as they grow up, either turn thieves for want of work, or leave their dear Native Country to fight for the Pretender in Spain, or sell themselves to the Barbadoes.

I think it is agreed by all parties that this prodigious number of children in the arms, or on the backs, or at the heels of their mothers and frequently of their fathers, is in the present deplorable state of the kingdom a very great additional grievance; and therefore whoever could find out a fair, cheap, and easy method of making these children sound useful members of the commonwealth would deserve so well of the public as to have his statue set up for a preserver of the nation.

But my intention is very far from being confined to provide only for the children of professed beggars; it is of a much greater extent, and shall take in the whole number of infants at a certain age who are born of parents in effect as little able to support them as those who demand our charity in the streets.

As to my own part, having turned my thoughts, for many years, upon this important subject, and maturely weighed the several schemes of other projectors, I have always found them grossly mistaken in their computation. It is true a child, just dropped from its dam, may be supported by her milk for a solar year with little other nourishment, at most not above the value of two shillings, which the mother may certainly get, or the value in scraps, by her lawful occupation of begging, and it is exactly at one year old that I propose to provide for them, in such a manner as, instead of being a charge upon their parents, or the parish, or wanting food and rainment for the rest of their lives, they shall, on the contrary, contribute to the feeding and partly to the clothing of many thousands. . . .

The number of souls in this kingdom being usually reckoned one million and a half, of these I calculate there may be about two hundred thousand couples whose wives are breeders, from which number I subtract thirty thousand couples who are able to maintain their own children, although I apprehend there cannot be so many under the present distresses of the kingdom, but this being granted, there will remain an hundred and seventy thousand breeders. I again subtract fifty thousand for those women who miscarry, or whose children die by accident or disease within the year. There only remain an hundred and twenty thousand children of poor parents annually born: the question therefore is, how this number shall be reared, and provided for, which, as I have already said, under the present situation of affairs, is utterly impossible by all the methods hitherto proposed, for we can neither employ them in handicraft, or agriculture; they neither build houses (I mean in the country), nor cultivate land; they can very seldom pick up a livelihood by stealing till they arrive at six years old, except where they are of towardly parts, although, I confess they learn the rudiments much earlier, during which time they can however be properly looked upon only as probationers, as I have been informed by a principal gentleman in the County of Cavan, who protested to me that he never knew above one or two instances under the age of six, even in a part of the kingdom so renowned for the quickest proficiency in that art.

I am assured by our merchants that a boy or girl, before twelve years old, is no saleable commodity, and even when they come to this age, they will not yield above three pounds, or three pounds and half-a-crown at most on the Exchange, which cannot turn to account either to the parents or the kingdom, the charge of nutriment and rags having been at least four times that value.

I shall now therefore humbly propose my own thoughts, which I hope will not be liable to the least objection.

I have been assured by a very knowing American of my acquaintance in London, that a young healthy child well nursed is at a year old a most delicious, nourishing, and wholesome food, whether strewed, roasted, baked, or boiled, and I make no doubt that it will equally serve in a fricassee, or a ragout.

I do therefore humbly offer it to public consideration, that of the hundred and twenty thousand children already computed, twenty thousand may be reserved for breed, whereof only one fourth part to be males, which is more than we allow to sheep, black-cattle, or swine. . . . That the remaining hundred thousand may at a year old be offered in sale to the persons of quality, and fortune, through the kingdom, always advising the mother to let them feed plentifully in the last month, so as to render them plump, and fat for a good table. A child will make two dishes at an entertainment for friends, and when the family dines alone, the fore or hind quarter will make a reasonable dish, and seasoned with a little pepper or salt will be very good boiled on the fourth day, especially in winter.

I have reckoned upon a medium, that a child just born will weigh 12 pounds, and in a solar year if tolerably nursed increaseth to 28 pounds.

I grant this food will be somewhat dear, and therefore very proper for landlords, who, as they have already devoured most of the parents, seem to have the best title to the children. . . .

I have already computed the charge of nursing a beggar's child (in which list I reckon all cottagers, labourers, and four-fifths of the farmers) to be about two shillings per annum, rags included, and I believe no gentleman would repine to give ten shillings for the carcass of a good fat child, which, as I have said, will make four dishes of excellent nutritive meat, when he hath only some particular friend or his own family to dine with him. Thus the Squire will learn to be a good landlord, and grow popular among his tenants, the mother will have eight shillings net profit, and be fit for work till she produces another child.

Those who are more thrifty (as I must confess the times require) may flay the carcass; the skin of which, artificially dressed, will make admirable gloves for ladies, and summer boots for fine gentlemen.

As to our City of Dublin, shambles may be appointed for this purpose, in the most convenient parts of it, and butchers we may be assured will not be wanting, although I rather recommend buying the children alive, and dressing them hot from the knife, as we do roasting pigs.

A very worthy person, a true lover of this country, and whose virtues I highly esteem, was lately pleased, in discoursing on this matter, to offer a refinement upon my scheme. He said that many gentlemen of this kingdom, having of late destroyed their deer, be conceived that the want of venison might be well supplied by the bodies of young lads and maidens, not exceeding fourteen years of age, nor under twelve, so great a number of both sexes in every country being now ready to starve, for want of work and service: and these to be disposed of by their parents if alive, or otherwise by their nearest relations. But with due deference to so excellent a friend, and so deserving a patriot, I cannot be altogether in his sentiments; for as to the males, my American acquaintance assured me from frequent experience that their flesh was generally tough and lean, like that of our schoolboys, by continual exercise, and their taste disagreeable, and to fatten them would not answer the charge. Then as to the females, it would, I think with humble submission, be a loss to the public, because they soon would become breeders themselves: And besides, it is not improbable that some scrupulous people might be apt to censure such a practice (although indeed very injustly) as a little bordering upon cruelty, which, I confess, hath always been with me the strongest objection against any project, however so well intended.

But in order to justify my friend, he confessed that this expedient was put into his head by the famous Psalmanazar, a native of the island Formosa, who came from thence to London,

115

above twenty years ago, and in conversation told my friend that in his country when any young person happened to be put to death, the executioner sold the carcass to persons of quality, as a prime dainty, and that, in his time, the body of a plump girl of fifteen, who was crucified for an attempt to poison the emperor, was sold to his Imperial Majesty's Prime Minister of State, and other great Mandarins of the Court, in joints from the gibbet, at four hundred crowns. Neither indeed can I deny that if the same use were made of several plump young girls in this town, who, without one single groat to their fortunes, cannot stir abroad without a chair, and appear at the playhouse, and assemblies in foreign fineries, which they never will pay for, the kingdom would not be the worse.

Some persons of a desponding spirit are in great concern about that vast number of poor people, who are aged, diseased, or maimed, and I have been desired to employ my thoughts what course may be taken to ease the nation of so grievous an encumbrance. But I am not in the least pain upon that matter, because it is very well known that they are every day dying, and rotting, by cold, and famine, and filth, and vermin, as fast as can be reasonably expected. And as to the younger labourers they are now in almost as hopeful a condition. They cannot get work, and consequently pine away for want of nourishment, to a degree, that if at any time they are accidentally hired to common labour, they have not strength to perform it; and thus the country and themselves are happily delivered from the evils to come.

I have too long digressed, and therefore shall return to my subject. I think the advantages by the proposal which I have made are obvious and many, as well as of the highest importance.

For first, as I have already observed, it would greatly lessen the number of Papists, with whom we are yearly overrun, being the principal breeders of the nation, as well as our most dangerous enemies, and who stay at home on purpose with a design to deliver the kingdom to the Pretender, hoping to take their advantage by the absence of so many good Protestants, who have chosen rather to leave their country than stay at home, and pay tithes against their conscience to an Episcopal curate.

Secondly, The poorer tenants will have something valuable of their own, which by law be made liable to distress, and help to pay their landlord's rent, their corn and cattle being already seized, and money a thing unknown.

Thirdly, Whereas the maintenance of an hundred thousand children, from two years old, and upwards, cannot be computed at less than ten shillings a piece per annum, the nation's stock will be thereby increased fifty thousand pounds per annum, besides the profit of a new dish, introduced to the tables of all gentlemen of fortune in the kingdom, who have any refinement in taste, and the money will circulate among ourselves, the goods being entirely of our own growth and manufacture.

Fourthly, The constant breeders, besides the gain of eight shillings sterling per annum, by the sale of their children, will be rid of the charge of maintaining them after the first year.

Fifthly, This food would likewise bring great custom to taverns, where the vintners will certainly be so prudent as to procure the best receipts for dressing it to perfection, and consequently have their houses frequented by all the fine gentlemen, who justly value themselves upon their knowledge in good eating; and a skillful cook, who understands how to oblige his guests, will contrive to make it as expensive as they please.

Sixthly, This would be a great inducement to marriage, which all wise nations have either encouraged by rewards, or enforced by laws and penalties. It would increase the care and tenderness of mothers toward their children, when they were sure of a settlement for life, to the poor babes, provided in some sort by the public to their annual profit instead of expense. We

116

should see an honest emulation among the married women, which of them could bring the fattest child to the market, men would become as fond of their wives, during the time of their pregnancy, as they are now of their mares in foal, their cows in calf, or sows when they are ready to farrow, nor offer to beat or kick them (as it is too frequent a practice). . . .

Many other advantages might be enumerated: For instance, the addition of some thousand carcasses in our exportation of barrelled beef; the propagation of swine's flesh, and improvement in the art of making good bacon, so much wanted among us by the great destruction of pigs, too frequent at our tables, which are no way comparable in taste or magnificence to a well-grown, fat yearling child, which roasted whole will make a considerable figure at a Lord Mayor's feast, or any other public entertainment. But this and many others I omit, being studious of brevity.

Supposing that one thousand families in this city would be constant customers for infants' flesh, besides others who might have it at merry-meetings, particularly weddings and christenings, I compute that Dublin would take off annually about twenty thousand carcasses, and the rest of the kingdom (where probably they will be sold somewhat cheaper) the remaining eighty thousand.

I can think of no one objection that will possibly be raised against this proposal, unless it should be urged that the number of people will be thereby much lessened in the kingdom. This I freely own, and was indeed one principal design in offering it to the world. I desire the reader will observe, that I calculate my remedy for this one individual Kingdom of Ireland, and for no other that ever was, is, or, I think, ever can be upon earth. Therefore let no man talk to me of other expedients: Of taxing our absentees at five shillings a pound: Of using neither clothes, nor household furniture, except what is of our own growth and manufacture: Of utterly rejecting the materials and instruments that promote foreign luxury: Of curing the expensiveness of pride, vanity, idleness, and gaming in our women: Of introducing a vein of parsimony, prudence, and temperance: Of learning to love our Country, wherein we differ even from Laplanders, and the inhabitants of Topinamboo: Of quitting our animosities and factions, nor act any longer like the infidels, who were murdering one another at the very moment their city was taken: Of being a little cautious not to sell our country and consciences for nothing: Of teaching landlords to have at least, one degree of mercy toward their tenants. Lastly, of putting a spirit of honesty, industry, and skill into our shopkeepers, who, if a resolution could now be taken to buy only our native goods, would immediately unite to cheat and exact upon us in the price, the measure, and the goodness, nor could ever yet be brought to make one fair proposal of just dealing, though often and earnestly invited to it.

Therefore I repeat, let no man talk to me of these and the like expedients, till he hath at least some glimpse of hope that there will ever be some hearty and sincere attempt to put them in practice.

But as to myself, having been wearied out for many years with offering vain, idle, visionary thoughts, and at length utterly despairing of success, I fortunately fell upon this proposal, which as it is wholly new, so it hath something solid and real, of no expense and little trouble, full in our own power, and whereby we can incur no danger in disobliging England. For this kind of commodity will not bear exportation, the flesh being of too tender a consistence to admit a long continuance in salt, although perhaps I could name a country which would be glad to eat up our whole nation without it.

After all I am not so violently bent upon my own opinion as to reject any offer, proposed by wise men, which shall be found equally innocent, cheap, easy, and effectual. But before something of that kind shall be advanced in contradiction to my scheme, and offering a better, I desire the author, or authors, will be pleased maturely to consider two points. First, as things now stand, how they will be able to find food and raiment for an hundred thousand useless mouths and backs. And secondly, there being a round million of creatures in human figure, through this kingdom, whose whole subsistence put into a common stock would leave them in debt two millions of pounds sterling; adding those, who are beggars by profession, to the bulk of farmers, cottagers, and labourers with their wives and children, who are beggars in effect. I desire those politicians, who dislike my overture, and may perhaps be so bold to attempt an answer, that they will first ask the parents of these mortals whether they would not at this day think it a great happiness to have been sold for food at a year old, in the manner I prescribe, and thereby have avoided such a perpetual scene of misfortunes as they have since gone through, by the oppression of landlords, the impossibility of paying rent without money or trade, the want of common sustenance, with neither house nor clothes to cover them from the inclemencies of the weather, and the most inevitable prospect of entailing the like, or greater miseries upon their breed for ever.

I profess in the sincerity of my heart that I have not the least personal interest in endeavouring to promote this necessary work, having no other motive than the public good of my country, by advancing our trade, providing for infants, relieving the poor, and giving some pleasure to the rich. I have no children by which I can propose to get a single penny; the youngest being nine years old, and my wife past child-bearing.

Christian Perspective

1. Swift's feigned sincerity will probably create a mixed response as you read it, which is often the result of satire. Describe your immediate response to his suggestion. After reflecting on the work, did you change your view?
2. Emulating Swift's style or tone, write a satirical paragraph suggesting current options for dealing with poverty.
3. The blatant indifference to the poor is not a modern dilemma. Many works have been written on this same subject; yet Swift's work remains a classic. Why is this so?

MAKING CONNECTIONS

1. Margaret Sanger's essay is based on her intensely-felt experiences with the poor in New York during the first decade of this century. She communicates her own emotion to us by means of specific examples and concrete imagery. Pick out a sentence or two that you think are particularly effective and analyze how she involves the reader's senses as she describes a scene. Rewrite the sentences, replacing her images with contrasting ones; see what different effect you can create.

2. Authors usually speak directly to their readers in the essay genre. Is this true in Swift's "A Modest Proposal"? Write a brief analytical essay on this work, focusing on the narrative voice and the tone Swift achieves by employing this narrative technique.

3. Sanger and Swift seem to have a concern for the poor and share an anger at how society deals with them. Their literary methods differ, however. Write an essay contrasting the ways they narrate their works and the various effects they achieve.

4. Write an essay or a story that exposes some evil in society that upsets you. Think of the approach you want to take. Will your narrator be straightforward? Ironic? Humorous? Sarcastic? Be sure to include concrete imagery and specific example. Avoid direct preaching at your reader—make your story or your examples vivid enough to move the reader.

Commitment to a Cause

LETTER FROM BIRMINGHAM JAIL
Martin Luther King

An excerpt from *Why Can't We Wait*

April 16, 1963

My Dear Fellow Clergymen:

While confined here in the Birmingham city jail, I came across your recent statement calling my present activities "unwise and untimely." Seldom do I pause to answer criticism of my work and ideas. If I sought to answer all the criticisms that cross my desk, my secretaries would have little time for anything other than such correspondence in the course of the day, and I would have no time for constructive work. But since I feel that you are men of genuine good will and that your criticisms are sincerely set forth, I want to try to answer your statement in what I hope will be patient and reasonable terms.

I think I should indicate why I am here in Birmingham, since you have been influenced by the view which argues against "outsiders coming in." I have the honor of serving as president of the Southern Christian Leadership Conference, an organization operating in every southern state, with headquarters in Atlanta, Georgia. We have some eighty-five affiliated organizations across the South, and one of them is the Alabama Christian Movement for Human Rights. Frequently we share staff, educational and financial resources with our affiliates. Several months ago the affiliate here in Birmingham asked us to be on call to engage in a nonviolent direction action program if such were deemed necessary. We readily consented, and when the hour came we lived up to our promise. So I, along with several members of my staff, am here because I was invited here. I am here because I have organizational ties here.

But more basically, I am in Birmingham because injustice is here. Just as the prophets of the eight century B.C. left their villages and carried their "thus saith the Lord" far beyond the boundaries of their home towns, and just as the Apostle Paul left his village of Tarsus and carried the gospel of Jesus Christ to the far corners of the Greco-Roman world, so am I compelled to carry the gospel of freedom beyond my own home town. Like Paul, I must constantly respond to the Macedonian call for aid.

Moreover, I am cognizant of the interrelatedness of all communities and states. I cannot sit idly by in Atlanta and not be concerned about what happens in Birmingham. Injustice anywhere is a threat to justice everywhere. We are caught in an inescapable network of mutuality, tied in a single garment of destiny. Whatever affects one directly, affects all indirectly. Never again can we afford to live with the narrow, provincial "outside agitator" idea. Anyone who lives inside the United States can never be considered an outsider anywhere within its bounds.

You deplore the demonstrations taking place in Birmingham. But your statement, I am sorry to say, fails to express a similar concern for the conditions that brought about the demonstrations. I am sure that none of you would want to rest content with the superficial kind of social analysis that deals merely with effects and does not grapple with underlying causes. It is unfortunate that demonstrations are taking place in Birmingham, but it is even more unfortunate that the city's white power structure left the Negro community with no alternative.

In any nonviolent campaign there are four basic steps: collection of the facts to determine whether injustice exists; negotiation; self-purification; and direct action. We have gone through all these steps in Birmingham. There can be no gainsaying the fact that racial injustice engulfs this community. Birmingham is probably the most thoroughly segregated city in the United States. Its ugly record of brutality is widely known. Negroes have experienced grossly unjust treatment in the courts. There have been more unsolved bombings of Negro homes and churches in Birmingham than in any other city in the nation. These are the hard, brutal facts of case. On the basis of these conditions, Negro leaders sought to negotiate with the city fathers. But the latter consistently refused to engage in good-faith negotiation.

Then, last September, came the opportunity to talk with leaders of Birmingham's economic community. In the course of the negotiations, certain promises were made by the merchants—for example, to remove the stores' humiliating racial signs. On the basis of these promises, the Reverend Fred Shuttlesworth and the leaders of the Alabama Christian Movement for Human Rights agreed to a moratorium on all demonstrations. As the weeks and months went by, we realized that we were the victims of a broken promise. A few signs, briefly removed, returned; the others remained.

As in so many past experiences, our hopes had been blasted, and the shadow of deep disappointment settled upon us. We had no alternative except to prepare for direct action, whereby we would present our very bodies as a means of laying our case before the conscience of the local and national community. Mindful of the difficulties involved, we decided to undertake a process of self-purification. We began a series of workshops on nonviolence, and we repeatedly asked ourselves: "Are you able to accept blows without retaliating?" "Are you able to endure the ordeal of jail?" We decided to schedule our direct-action program for the Easter season, realizing that except for Christmas, this is the main shopping period of the year. Knowing that a strong economic-withdrawal program would be the by-product of direct action, we felt that this would be the best time to bring pressure to bear on the merchants for the needed change.

Then it occurred to us that Birmingham's mayoral election was coming up in March, and we speedily decided to postpone action until after election day. When we discovered that the Commissioner of Public Safety, Eugene "Bull" Connor, had piled up enough votes to be in the run-off, we decided again to postpone action until the day after the run-off so that the demonstrations could not be used to cloud the issues. Like many others, we waited to see Mr. Connor defeated, and to this end we endured postponement after postponement. Having aided in this community need, we felt that our direct-action program could be delayed no longer.

You may well ask: "Why direct action? Why sit-ins, marches and so forth? Isn't negotiation a better path?" You are quite right in calling for negotiation. Indeed, this is the very purpose of direct action. Nonviolent direct action seeks to create such a crisis and foster such a tension that a community which has constantly refused to negotiate is forced to confront the issue. It seeks so to dramatize the issue that it can no longer be ignored. My citing the creation of tension as part of the work of nonviolent-resister may sound rather shocking. But I must confess that I am not afraid of the word "tension." I have earnestly opposed violent tension, but there is a type of constructive, nonviolent tension in the mind so that individuals could rise from the bondage of myths and half-truths to the unfettered realm of creative analysis and objective appraisal, so must we see the need for nonviolent gadflies to create the kind of tension in society that will help men rise from the dark depths of prejudice and racism to the majestic heights of understanding and brotherhood.

The purpose of our direct-action program is to create a situation so crisis-packed that it will inevitably open the door to negotiation. I therefore concur with you in your call for negotiation. Too long has our beloved Southland been bogged down in a tragic effort to live in monologue rather than dialogue.

One of the basic points in your statement is that the action that I and my associates have taken in Birmingham is untimely. Some have asked: "Why didn't you give the new city administration time to act?" The only answer that I can give to this query is that the new Birmingham administration must be prodded about as much as the outgoing one, before it will act. We are sadly mistaken if we feel that the election of Albert Boutwell as mayor will bring the millennium to Birmingham. While Mr. Boutwell is a much more gentle person than Mr. Connor, they are both segregationists, dedicated to maintenance of the status quo. I hope that Mr. Boutwell will be reasonable enough to see the futility of massive resistance to desegregation. But he will not see this without pressure from devotees of civil rights. My friends, I must say to you that we have not made a single gain in civil rights without determined legal and nonviolent pressure. Lamentably, it is an historical fact that privileged groups seldom give up their privileges voluntarily. Individuals may see the moral light and voluntarily give up their unjust posture; but, as Reinhold Niebuhr has reminded us, groups tend to be more immoral than individuals.

We know through painful experience that freedom is never voluntarily given by the oppressor; it must be demanded by the oppressed. Frankly, I have yet to engage in a direct-action campaign that was "well timed" in the view of those who have not suffered unduly from the disease of segregation. For years now I have heard the word "Wait!" It rings in the ear of every Negro with piercing familiarity. This "Wait" has almost always meant "Never." We must come to see, with one of our distinguished jurists, that "justice too long delayed is justice denied."

We have waited for more than 340 years for our constitutional and God-given rights. The nations of Asia and Africa are moving with jetlike speed toward gaining political independence, but we still creep at horse-and-buggy pace toward gaining a cup of coffee at a lunch counter. Perhaps it is easy for those who have never felt the stinging darts of segregation to say, "Wait." But when you have seen vicious mobs lynch your mothers and fathers at will and drown your sisters and brothers at whim; when you have seen hate-filled policemen curse, kick and even kill your black brothers and sisters; when you see the vast majority of twenty million negro brothers smothering in an airtight cage of poverty in the midst of an affluent society; when you suddenly find your tongue twisted and your speech stammering as you seek to explain to your six-year-old daughter why she can't go to the public amusement park that has just been advertised on television, and see tears welling up in her eyes when she is told that Funtown is closed to colored children, and see ominous clouds of inferiority beginning to form in her little mental sky, and see her beginning to distort her personality by developing an unconscious bitterness

123

toward white people; when you have to concoct an answer for a five-year-old son who is asking: "Daddy, why do white people treat colored people so mean?"; when you take a cross-country drive and find it necessary to sleep night after night in the uncomfortable corners of your automobile because no motel will accept you; when you are humiliated day in and day out by nagging signs reading "white" and "colored"; when your first name becomes "nigger," your middle names becomes "boy" (however old you are) and your last name becomes "John," and your wife and mother are never given the respected title "Mrs." when you are harried by day and haunted by night by the fact that you are a Negro, living constantly at tiptoe stance, never quite knowing what to expect next, and are plagued with inner fears and outer resentments; when you are forever fighting a degenerating sense of "nobodiness"—then you will understand why we find it difficult to wait. There comes a time when a cup of endurance runs over, and men are no longer willing to be plunged into the abyss of despair. I hope, sirs, you can understand our legitimate and unavoidable impatience.

You express a great deal of anxiety over our willingness to break laws. This is certainly a legitimate concern. Since we so diligently urge people to obey the Supreme Court's decision of 1954 outlawing segregation in the public schools, at first glance it may seem rather paradoxical for us consciously to break laws. One may well ask: "How can you advocate breaking some laws and obeying others?" The answer lies in the fact that there are two types of laws: just and unjust. I would be the first to advocate obeying just laws. One has not only a legal but a moral responsibility to obey just laws. Conversely, one has a moral responsibility to disobey unjust laws. I would agree with St. Augustine that "an unjust law is no law at all."

Now, what is the difference between the two? How does one determine whether a law is just or unjust? A just law is a man-made code that squares with the moral law or the law of God. An unjust law is a code that is out of harmony with the moral law. To put it in the terms of St. Thomas of Aquinas: An unjust law is a human law that is not rooted in eternal law and natural law. Any law that uplifts human personality is just. Any law that degrades human personality is unjust. All segregation statutes are unjust because segregation distorts the soul and damages the personality. It gives the segregator a false sense of superiority and the segregated a false sense of inferiority. Segregation, to use the terminology of the Jewish philosopher Martin Buber, substitutes an "I-it" relationship for an "I-thou" relationship and ends up relegating persons to the status of things. Hence segregation is not only politically, economically and sociologically unsound, it is morally wrong and sinful. Paul Tillich has said that sin is separation. Is not segregation an existential expression of man's tragic separation, his awful estrangement, his terrible sinfulness? Thus it is that I can urge men to obey the 1954 decision of the Supreme Court, for it is morally right; and I can urge them to disobey segregation ordinances, for they are morally wrong.

Let us consider a more concrete example of just and unjust laws. An unjust law is a code that a numerical or power majority group compels a minority group to obey but does not make binding on itself. This is difference made legal. By the same token, a just law is a code that a majority compels a minority to follow and that it is willing to follow itself. This is sameness made legal.

Let me give another explanation. A law is unjust if it is inflicted on a minority that, as a result of being denied the right to vote, had no part in enacting or devising the law. Who can say that the legislature of Alabama which set up that state's segregation laws was democratically elected? Throughout Alabama all sorts of devious methods are used to prevent Negroes from becoming registered voters, and there are some counties in which, even though Negroes constitute a majority of the population, not a single Negro is registered. Can any law enacted under such circumstances be considered democratically structured?

Sometimes a law is just on its face and unjust in its application. For instance, I have been arrested on a charge of parading without a permit. Now, there is nothing wrong in having an ordinance which requires a permit for a parade. But such an ordinance becomes unjust when it is used to maintain segregation and to deny citizens the First-Amendment privilege of peaceful assembly and protest.

I hope you are able to see the distinction I am trying to point out. In no sense do I advocate evading or defying the law, as would the rabid segregationist. That would lead to anarchy. One who breaks an unjust law must do so openly, lovingly, and with a willingness to accept the penalty. I submit that an individual who breaks a law that conscience tells him is unjust, and who willingly accepts the penalty of imprisonment in order to arouse the conscience of the community over its injustice, is in reality expressing the highest respect for law.

Of course, there is nothing new about this kind of civil disobedience. It was evidenced sublimely in the refusal of Shadrach, Meshach and Abednego to obey the laws of Nebuchadnezzar, on the ground that a higher moral law was at stake. It was practiced superbly by the early Christians, who were willing to face hungry lions and the excruciating pain of chopping blocks rather than submit to certain unjust laws of the Roman Empire. To a degree, academic freedom is a reality today because Socrates practiced civil disobedience. In our own nation, the Boston Tea Party represented a massive act of civil disobedience.

We should never forget that everything Adolf Hitler did in Germany was "legal" and everything the Hungarian freedom fighters did in Hungary was "illegal." It was "illegal" to aid and comfort a Jew in Hitler's Germany. Even so, I am sure that, had I lived in Germany at the time, I would have aided and comforted my Jewish brothers. If today I lived in a Communist country where certain principles dear to the Christian faith are suppressed, I would openly advocate disobeying that country's antireligious laws.

I must make two honest confessions to you, my Christian and Jewish brothers. First, I must confess that over the past few years I have been gravely disappointed with the white moderate. I have almost reached the regrettable conclusion that the Negro's great stumbling block in his stride toward freedom is not the White Citizen's Councilor or the Ku Klux Klanner, but the white moderate who is more devoted to "order" than to justice; who prefers a negative peace which is the absence of tension to a positive peace which is the presence of justice; who constantly says: "I agree with you in the goal you seek, but I cannot agree with your methods of direct action: who paternalistically believes he can set the timetable for another man's freedom; who lives by a mythical concept of time and who constantly advises the Negro to wait for a "more convenient season." Shallow understanding from people of good will is more frustrating than absolute misunderstanding from people of ill will. Lukewarm acceptance is much more bewildering than outright rejection.

I had hoped that the white moderate would understand that law and order exist for the purpose of establishing justice and that when they fail in this purpose they become the dangerously structured dams that block the flow of social progress. I had hoped that the white moderate would understand that the present tension in the South is a necessary phase of the transition from an obnoxious negative peace, in which the Negro passively accepted his unjust plight, to a substantive and positive peace, in which all men will respect the dignity and worth of human personality. Actually, we who engage in nonviolent direct action are not the creators of tension. We merely bring to the surface the hidden tension that is already alive. We bring it out in the open, where it can be seen and dealt with. Like a boil that can never be cured so long as it is covered up but must be opened with all its ugliness to the natural medicines of air and light, injustice must be exposed, with all the tension its exposure creates, to the light of human conscience and the air of national opinion before it can be cured.

In your statement you assert that our actions, even though peaceful, must be condemned because they precipitate violence. But is this a logical assertion? Isn't this like condemning a robbed man because his possession of money precipitated the evil act of robbery? Isn't this like condemning Socrates because his unswerving commitment to truth and his philosophical inquiries precipitated the act by the misguided populace in which they made him drink hemlock? Isn't this lie condemning Jesus because his unique God-consciousness and never-ceasing devotion to God's will precipitated the evil act of crucifixion? We must come to see that, as the federal courts have consistently affirmed, it is wrong to urge an individual to cease his efforts to gain his basic constitutional rights because the quest may precipitate violence. Society must protect the robbed and punish the robber.

I had also hoped that the white moderate would reject the myth concerning time in relation to the struggle for freedom. I have just received a letter from a white brother in Texas. He writes: "All Christians know that the colored people will receive equal rights eventually, but it is possible that you are in too great a religious hurry. It has taken Christianity almost two thousand years to accomplish what it has. The teachings of Christ take time to come to earth." Such an attitude stems from a tragic misconception of time, from the strangely irrational notion that there is something in the very flow of time that will inevitably cure all ills. Actually, time itself is neutral; it can be used either destructively or constructively. More and more I feel that the people of ill will have used time much more effectively than have the people of good will. We will have to repent in this generation not really for the hateful words and actions of the bad people but for the appalling silence of the good people. Human progress never rolls in on wheels of inevitability; it comes through the tireless efforts of men willing to be co-workers with God, and without this hard work, time itself becomes an ally of the forces of social stagnation. We must use time creatively, in the knowledge that the time is always ripe to do right. Now is the time to make real the promise of democracy and transform our pending national elegy into a creative psalm of brotherhood. Now is the time to lift our national policy from the quicksand of racial injustice to the solid rock of human dignity.

You speak of our activity in Birmingham as extreme. At first I was rather disappointed that fellow clergymen would see my nonviolent efforts as those of an extremist. I began thinking about the fact that I stand in the middle of two opposing forces in the Negro community. One is a force of complacency, made up in part of Negroes who, as a result of long years of oppression, are so drained of self-respect and a sense of "somebodiness" that they have adjusted to segregation; and in part of a few middle-class Negroes who, because of a degree of academic and economic security and because in some ways they profit by segregation, have become insensitive to the problems of the masses. The other force is one of bitterness and hatred, and it comes perilously close to advocating violence. It is expressed in the various black nationalist groups that are springing up across the nation, the largest and best-known being Elijah Muhammad's Muslim movement. Nourished by the Negros' frustration over the continued existence of racial discrimination, this movement is made up of people who have lost faith in America, who have absolutely repudiated Christianity, and who have concluded that the white man is an incorrigible "devil."

I have tried to stand between these two forces, saying that we need emulate neither the "do-nothingism" of the complacent nor the hatred and despair of the black nationalist. For there is the more excellent way of love and nonviolent protest. I am grateful to God that, through the influence of the Negro church, the way of nonviolence became an integral part of our struggle.

If this philosophy had not emerged, by now many streets of the South would, I am convinced, be flowing with blood. And I am further convinced that if our white brothers dismiss as "rabble-rousers" and "outside agitators" those of us who employ nonviolent direct action, and if they refuse to support our nonviolent efforts, millions of Negroes will, out of frustration and despair, seek solace and security in black-nationalist ideologies—a development that would inevitably lead to a frightening racial nightmare.

Oppressed people cannot remain oppressed forever. The yearning for freedom eventually manifests itself, and that is what has happened to the American Negro. Something within has reminded him of his birthright of freedom, and something without has reminded him that it can be gained. Consciously or unconsciously, he has been caught up by the *Zeitgeist,* and with his black brothers of Africa and his brown and yellow brothers of Asia, South America and the Caribbean, the United States Negro is moving with a sense of great urgency toward the promised land of racial justice. If one recognizes this vital urge that has engulfed the Negro community, one should readily understand why public demonstrations are taking place. The Negro has many pent-up resentments and latent frustrations, and he must release them. So let him march; let him make prayer pilgrimages to the city hall; let him go on freedom rides—and try to understand why he must do so. If his repressed emotions are not released in nonviolent ways, they will seek expression through violence; this is not a threat but a fact of history. So I have not said to my people: "Get rid of your discontent." Rather, I have tried to say that this normal and healthy discontent can be channeled into the creative outlet of nonviolent direct action. And now this approach is being termed extremist.

But though I was initially disappointed at being categorized as an extremist, as I continued to think about the matter I gradually gained a measure of satisfaction from the label. Was not Jesus an extremist for love: "Love your enemies, bless them that curse you, do good to them that hate you, and pray for them which despitefully use you, and persecute you." Was not Amos an extremist for justice: "Let justice roll down like waters and righteousness like an ever-flowing stream." Was not Paul an extremist for the Christian gospel: "I bear in my body the marks of the Lord Jesus." Was not Martin Luther an extremist. "Here I stand; I cannot do otherwise, so help me God." And John Bunyan, "I will stay in jail to the end of my days before I make a butchery of my conscience." And Abraham Lincoln: "This nation cannot survive half slave and half free." And Thomas Jefferson: "We hold these truths to be self-evident, that all men are created equal. . . ." So the question is not whether we will be extremists, but what kind of extremists we will be. Will we be extremists for hate or for love? Will we be extremists for the preservation of injustice or for the extension of justice? In that dramatic scene on Calvary's hill three men were crucified. We must never forget that all three were crucified for the same crime—the crime of extremism. Two were extremists for immorality, and thus fell below their environment. The other, Jesus Christ, was an extremist for love, truth and goodness, and thereby rose above his environment. Perhaps the South, the nation and the world are in dire need of creative extremists.

I had hoped that the white moderate would see this need. Perhaps I was too optimistic; perhaps I expected too much. I suppose I should have realized that few members of the oppressor race can understand the deep groans and passionate yearnings of the oppressed race, and still fewer have the vision to see that injustice must be rooted out by strong, persistent and determined action. I am thankful, however, that some of our white brothers in the South have grasped the meaning of this social revolution and committed themselves to it. They are still too few in quantity, but they are big in quality. some—such as Ralph McGill, Lillian Smith, Harry Golden, James McBride Dabbs, Ann Braden and Sara Patton Boyle—have written about our struggle in eloquent and prophetic terms. Others have marched with us down nameless streets of the South. They have languished in filthy, roach-infested jails, suffering the abuse and brutality of policemen who view them as "dirty-nigger-lovers." Unlike so many of their moderate brothers and sisters, they have recognized the urgency of the moment and sensed the need for powerful "action" antidotes to combat the disease of segregation.

Let me take note of my other major disappointment. I have been so greatly disappointed with the white church and its leadership. Of course, there are some noble exceptions. I am not unmindful of the fact that each of you has taken some significant stands on this issue. I commend you, Reverent Stallings, for your Christian stand on this past Sunday, in welcoming Negroes to your worship service on a nonsegregated basis. I commend the Catholic leaders of this state for integrating Spring Hill College several years ago.

But despite these notable exceptions, I must honestly reiterate that I have been disappointed with the church. I do not say this as one of those negative critics who can always find something wrong with the church. I say this as a minister of the gospel, who loves the church; who was nurtured in its bosom; who has been sustained by its spiritual blessings and who will remain true to it as long as the cord of life shall lengthen.

When I was suddenly catapulted into the leadership of the bus protest in Montgomery, Alabama, a few years ago, I felt we would be supported by the white church. I felt that the white ministers, priests and rabbis of the South would be among our strongest allies. Instead, some have been outright opponents, refusing to understand the freedom movement and misrepresenting its leaders; all too many others have been more cautious than courageous and have remained silent behind the anesthetizing security of stained-glass windows.

 In spite of my shattered dreams, I came to Birmingham with the hope that the white religious leadership of this community would see the justice of our cause and, with deep and moral concern, would serve as the channel through which our just grievances could reach the power structure. I had hoped that each of you would understand. But again I have been disappointed.

I have heard numerous southern religious leaders admonish their worshipers to comply with a desegregation decision because it is the law, but I have longed to hear white ministers declare: "Follow this decree because integration is morally right and because the Negro is your brother." In the midst of blatant injustices inflicted upon the Negro, I have watched white churchmen stand on the sideline and mouth pious irrelevancies and sanctimonious trivialities. In the midst of a mighty struggle to rid our nation of racial and economic injustice, I have heard many ministers say, "Those are social issues, with which the gospel has no real concern." And I have watched many churches commit themselves to a completely other worldly religion which makes a strange, un-Biblical distinction between body and soul, between the sacred and the secular.

I have traveled the length and breadth of Alabama, Mississippi and all the other southern states. On sweltering summer days and crisp autumn mornings I have looked at the South's beautiful churches with their lofty spires pointing heavenward. I have beheld the impressive outlines of her massive religious-education buildings. Over and over I have found myself asking: "What kind of people worship here? Who is their God? Where were their voices when the lips of Governor Barnett dripped with words of interposition and nullification? Where were they when Governor Wallace gave a clarion call for defiance and hatred? Where were their voices of support when bruised and weary Negro men and women decided to rise from the dark dungeons of complacency to the bright hills of creative protest?"

Yes, these questions are still in my mind. In deep disappointment I have wept over the laxity of the church. But be assured that my tears have been tears of love. There can be no deep disappointment where there is not deep love. Yes, I love the church. How could I do otherwise? I am in the rather unique position of being the son, the grandson and the great-grandson of preachers. Yes, I see the church as the body of Christ. But, oh! How we have blemished and scarred that body through social neglect and through fear of being nonconformists.

There was a time when the church was very powerful—in the time when the Early Christians rejoiced at being deemed worthy to suffer for what they believed. In those days the church was not merely a thermometer that recorded the ideas and principles of popular opinion; it was a thermostat that transformed the mores of society. Whenever the early Christians entered a town, the people in power became disturbed and immediately sought to convict the Christians for being "disturbers of the peace" and "outside agitators." But the Christians pressed on, in the conviction that they were a "colony of heaven" called to obey God rather than man. Small in number, they were big in commitment. They were too God-intoxicated to be "astronomically intimidated." By their effort and example they brought an end to such ancient evils as infanticide and gladiatorial contests.

Things are different now. So often the contemporary church is a weak ineffectual voice with an uncertain sound. So often it is an archdefender of the status quo. Far from being disturbed by the presence of the church, the power structure of the average community is consoled by the church's silence—and often even vocal—sanction of things as they are.

But the judgment of God is upon the church as never before. If today's church does not recapture the sacrificial spirit of the early church, it will lose its authenticity, forfeit the loyalty of millions, and be dismissed as an irrelevant social club with no meaning for the twentieth century. Every day I meet young people whose disappointment with the church has turned into outright disgust.

Perhaps I have once again been too optimistic. Is organized religion too inextricably bound to the status quo to save our nation and the world? Perhaps I must turn my faith to the inner spiritual church, the church within the church as the true *ekklesia* and the hope of the world. But again I am thankful to God that some noble souls from the ranks of organized religion have broken loose from the paralyzing chains of conformity and joined us as active partners in the struggle for freedom. They have left their secure congregations and walked the streets of Albany, Georgia, with us. They have gone down the highways of the South on torturous rides for freedom. Yes, they have gone to jail with us. Some have been dismissed from their churches, have lost the support of their bishops and fellow ministers. But they have acted in the faith that right defeated is stronger than evil triumphant. Their witness has been the spiritual salt that has preserved the true meaning of the gospel in these troubled times. They have carved a tunnel of hope through the dark mountain of disappointment.

I hope the church as a whole will meet the challenge of this decisive hour. But even if the church does not come to the aid of justice, I have no despair about the future. I have no fear about the outcome of our struggle in Birmingham, even if our motives are at present misunderstood. We will reach the goal of freedom in Birmingham and all over the nation, because the goal of America is freedom. Abused and scorned though we may be, our destiny is tied up with America's destiny. Before the pilgrims landed at Plymouth, we were here. Before the pen of Jefferson etched the majestic words of the Declaration of Independence across the pages of history, we were here. For more than two centuries our forebears labored in this country without wages; they made cotton king; they built the homes of their masters while suffering gross injustice and shameful humiliation—and yet out of a bottomless vitality they continued to thrive and develop. If the inexpressible cruelties of slavery could not stop us, the oppression we now face will surely fail. We will win our freedom because the sacred heritage of our nation and the eternal will of God are embodied in our echoing demands.

Before closing I feel impelled to mention one other point in your statement that has troubled me profoundly. You warmly commended the Birmingham police force for keeping "order" and "preventing violence." I doubt that you would have so warmly commended the police force if you had seen its dogs sinking their teeth into unarmed, nonviolent Negroes. I doubt that you would have so quickly commended the policemen if you were to observe their ugly and inhuman treatment of Negroes here in the city jail; if you were to watch them push and curse old Negro women and young Negro girls; if you were to see them slap and kick old Negro men and young boys; if you were to observe them, as they did on two occasions, refuse to give us food because we wanted to sing our grace together. I cannot join you in your praise of the Birmingham police department.

It is true that the police have exercised a degree of discipline in handling the demonstrators. In this sense they have conducted themselves rather "nonviolently" in public. But for what purpose? To preserve the evil system of segregation. Over the past few years I have consistently preached that nonviolence demands that the means we use must be as pure as the ends we seek. I have tried to make clear that it is wrong to use immoral means to attain moral ends. But now I must affirm that it is just as wrong, or perhaps even more so, to use moral means to preserve immoral ends. Perhaps Mr. Connor and his policemen have been rather nonviolent in public, as was Chief Pritchett in Albany, Georgia, but they have used the moral means of nonviolence to maintain the immoral end of racial injustice. As T.S. Eliot has said: "The last temptation is the greatest treason: To do the right deed for the wrong reason."

I wish you had commended the Negro sit-ins and demonstrators of Birmingham for their sublime courage, their willingness to suffer and their amazing discipline in the midst of provocation. One day the South will recognize the real heroes. They will be the James Merediths, with the noble sense of purpose that enables them to face jeering and hostile mobs, and with the agonizing loneliness that characterizes the life of the pioneer. They will be old, oppressed, battered Negro women, symbolized in a seventy-two-year-old woman in Montgomery, Alabama, who rose up with a sense of dignity and with her people decided not to ride segregated buses, and who responded with ungrammatical profundity to one who inquired about her weariness: "My feet's tired, but my soul is at rest." They will be the young high school and college students, the young ministers of the gospel and a host of their elders, courageously and nonviolently sitting in at lunch counters and willingly going to jail for conscience sake. One day the South will know that when these disinherited children of God sat down at lunch counters, they were in reality standing up for what is best in the American dream and for the most sacred values in our Judaeo-Christian heritage, thereby bringing our nation back to those great wells of democracy which were dug deep by the founding fathers in their formulation of the Constitution and the Declaration of Independence.

Never before have I written so long a letter. I'm afraid it is much too long to take your precious time. I can assure you that it would have been shorter if I had been writing from a comfortable desk, but what else can one do when he is alone in a narrow jail cell, other than write long letters, think long thoughts and pray long prayers?

If I have said anything in this letter that overstates the truth and indicates an unreasonable impatience, I beg you to forgive me. If I have said anything that understates the truth and indicates my having a patience that allows me to settle for anything less than brotherhood, I beg God to forgive me.

I hope this letter finds you strong in the faith. I also hope that circumstances will soon make it possible for me to meet each of you, not as an integrationist or a civil-rights leader but as a fellow clergyman and a Christian brother. Let us all hope that dark clouds of racial prejudice will soon pass away and the deep fog of misunderstanding will be lifted from our fear-drenched communities, and in some not too distant tomorrow the radiant stars of love and brotherhood will shine over our great nation with all their scintillating beauty.

Yours for the cause of Peace and Brotherhood

Martin Luther King, Jr.

Christian Perspectives

1. Since Martin Luther King, Jr., is writing to clergymen he assumes a common agreement of scriptural premises. identify one of these premises which is based on the teaching of Jesus. (It may be implicitly or explicitly expressed.)
2. Do you agree with King's statement about just and unjust laws? King's interpretation of the law caused a stir similar to Jesus' response to the Jewish laws. How should we respond to the law?
3. According to King, what constitutes the greatest stumbling block against freedom? Read Revelation 3:16 and explain this scripture in light of King's statement, "lukewarm acceptance is much more bewildering than outright rejection."
4. King's disappointment with the church's separation of the sacred from the secular identifies a dilemma that still plagues us today. King observes that as "an arch defender of the status quo," the church has lost its effectiveness as a major influence in the world. Is he correct in his suggestion of the alternative to a dying church? Does this alternative exist today?
5. Many of us are only aware of the black man's struggles through reading books or watching television, but we see that King's dream in many ways has been realized. What hope did King have that Blacks would reach their goal? Is there a movement or cause today that, according to "world's standards," seems impossible?
6. Discuss the strategy of King's writing. How do his historical and literary allusions appeal to his audience and their values? Are the Southern clergymen the only audience he seems to have in mind?

DULCE ET DECORUM EST[1]

Wilfred Owen

Bent double, like old beggars under sacks,
Knock-kneed, coughing like hags, we cursed through sludge,
Till on the haunting flares we turned our backs
And towards our distant rest began to trudge.
Men marched asleep. Many had lost their boots
But limped on, blood-shod. All went lame; all blind;
Drunk with fatigue; deaf even to the hoots
Of disappointed shells that dropped behind.[2]

Gas! Gas! Quick, boys! — An ecstasy of fumbling,
Fitting the clumsy helmets just in time;
But someone still was yelling out and stumbling
And floundering like a man in fire or lime. —
Dim, through the misty panes[3] and thick green light
As under a green sea, I saw him drowning.

In all my dreams, before my helpless sight,
He plunges at me, guttering, choking, drowning.
If in some smothering dreams you too could pace
Behind the wagon that we flung him in,
And watch the white eyes writhing in his face,
His hanging face, like a devil's sick of sin;
If you could hear, at every jolt, the blood
Come gargling from the froth-corrupted lungs,
Obscene as cancer, bitter as the cud
Of vile, incurable sores on innocent tongues, —
My friend,[4] you would not tell with such high zest
To children ardent for some desperate glory,
The old Lie: Dulce et decorum est
Pro patria mori.

---

1. The title refers to the Latin motto, <u>dulce et decorum est pro patria mori</u>, which means, "it is sweet and fitting to die for one's country."
2. Line eight has variant readings. One version reads, "Of tired, outstripped Five-Nines that dropped behind," Five-Nines being a type of mortar shell. Another version reads, "Of disappointed shells that dropped behind."
3. panes—celluloid windows in gas masks.
4. friend—Jessie Pope, the friend for whom the poem was written.

Christian Perspectives

1. The war Owen writes of was the First World War. The Latin motto he quotes means "It is sweet and fitting to die for one's country." How does this treatment of war differ from that of the other poets in this section?
2. Owen's view reflects contemporary thinking about war. Do you agree with him? Why or why not?

TO LUCASTA, GOING TO THE WARS

Richard Lovelace

Tell me not, sweet, I am unkind
    That from the nunnery
Of thy chaste breast and quiet mind,
    To war and arms I fly.

True, a new mistress now I chase,
    The first foe in the field;
And with a stronger faith embrace
    A sword, a horse, a shield.

Yet this inconstancy is such
    As you too shall adore;
I could not love thee, dear, so much,
    Loved I not Honor more.

Christian Perspective

1. In this poem, the persona proclaims that by loving honor (in this case his self respect) he also loves Lucasta. We cannot love others if we aren't able to love ourselves; in fact, the Bible makes several references to loving ourselves as a prerequisite to loving others. (See Matthew 22:39, Galatians 5:14, Romans 13:9,10, and Luke 10:27,28.) What importance does honor play in our society today?
2. Lovelace wrote this poem in 17th century England. How does his view contrast with that of Cummings? with that of Owen?

A VALEDICTION: FORBIDDING MOURNING

John Donne

This poem is a valediction which forbids mourning or farewells. It was written by John Donne for his wife and emphasizes the spiritual nature of their love for each other. This poem contains several famous metaphors. The first two stanzas compare the author's leaving his wife to the way a virtuous man would die.

As virtuous men pass mildly away,
    And whisper to their souls to go,
Whilst some of their sad friends do say
    The breath goes now, and some say, No;

So let us melt, and make no noise,
    No tear-floods, nor sigh-tempests move,
'Twere profanation of our joys
    To tell the laity our love.

Moving of th' earth brings harms and fears,
    Men reckon what it did and meant;
But trepidation of the spheres,
    Though greater far, is innocent.

Dull sublunary lovers' love
    (Whose soul is sense) cannot admit
Absence, because it doth remove
    Those things which elemented it.

But we by a love so much refined
    That ourselves know not what it is,
Inter-assured of the mind,
    Careless, eyes, lips, and hands to miss.

Our two souls therefore, which are one,
    Though I must go, endure not yet
A breach, but an expansion,
    Like gold to airy thinness beat.

If they be two, they are two so
    As stiff twin compasses are two;
Thy soul, the fixed foot, makes no show
    To move, but doth, if th' other do.

And though it in the center sit,
    Yet when the other far doth roam,
It leans and hearkens after it,
    And grows erect, as that comes home.

Such wilt thou be to me, who must
    Like th' other foot, obliquely run;
Thy firmness makes my circle just,
    And makes me end where I begun.

Christian Perspectives

1. How would a virtuous man's death differ from that of one who is not so virtuous?
2. In stanzas four through six, Donne begins a comparison of sublunary (under the moon, i.e., physical) lovers and spiritual lovers. Notice that he uses words which we associate with the refining of metals. How is spiritual love like true gold while merely physical love is like base metal?
3. The last three stanzas compare Donne's love to a drawing compass (such as you would use to draw circles in mathematics). Explain how he and his love are like the parts of a compass.
4. The biblical idea for marriage is that husband and wife become "one flesh." What are the spiritual dimensions of being "one flesh"? (See Ephesians 5:31-33).
5. Christ describes His love for His church as being like that of a bridegroom for his bride. In light of "A Valediction: Forbidding Mourning," why is that metaphor appropriate? (See Mark 2:19.)

NEXT TO OF COURSE GOD AMERICA I

e. e. cummings

"next to of course god america i
love you land of the pilgrims' and so forth oh
say can you see by the dawn's early my
country 'tis of centuries come and go
and are no more what of it we should worry
in every language even deafanddumb
thy sons acclaim your glorious name by gorry
by jingo by gee by gosh by gum
why talk of beauty what could be more beautiful than these heroic happy dead
who rushed like lions to the roaring slaughter
they did not stop to think they died instead
then shall the voice of liberty be mute?"

He spoke. And drank rapidly a glass of water

Christian Perspectives

1. What tone does cummings achieve in this poem? How does his technique differ from that of Owen? Which seems more effective to you?
2. Analyze how cummings uses ordinary language and cliches for satiric effect.

From ECCLESIASTICUS[1]

Trades and crafts

Leisure is what gives the scribe the opportunity to acquire wisdom;
  the man with few business affairs grows wise.
How can the ploughman become wise,
  whose sole ambition is to wield the goad;
driving his oxen, engrossed in their work,
  his conversation is of nothing but cattle?
His mind is fixed on the furrows he traces,
  and his evenings pass in fattening his heifers.
So it is with every workman and craftsman,
  toiling day and night;
those who engrave seals,
  always trying to think of new designs:
they set their heart on producing a good likeness,
  and stay up perfecting the work.
So it is with the blacksmith sitting by his anvil;
  he considers what to do with the pig-iron,
the breath of the fire scorches his skin,
  as he contends with the heat of the furnace;
he batters his ear with the din of the hammer,
  his eyes are fixed on the pattern;
he sets his heart on completing his work,
  and stays up putting the finishing touches,
So it is with the potter, sitting at his work,
  turning the wheel with his feet;
constantly on the alert over his work,
  each flick of the finger premeditated;
he pummels the clay with his arm,
  and puddles it with his feet;
he sets his heart on perfecting the glaze,
  and stays up cleaning the kiln.
All these put their trust in their hands,
  and each is skilled at his own craft,

1. an apochraphal book accepted by some Christians as canonical.

A town could not be built without them,
  there would be no settling, no travelling,
But they are not required at the council,
  they do not hold high rank in the assembly.
They do not sit on the judicial bench,
  and have no grasp of the law.
They are not remarkable for culture or sound judgement,
  and are not found among the inventors of maxims.
But they give solidity to the created world,
  while their prayer is concerned with what pertains to their trade.

The scholar

It is otherwise with the man who devotes his soul
  to reflecting on the Law of the Most High.
He researches into the wisdom of all the Ancients,
  he occupies his time with the prophecies.
He preserves the discourses of famous men,
  he is at home with the niceties of parables.
He researches into the hidden sense of proverbs,
  he ponders the obscurities of parables.
He enters the service of princes,
  he is seen in the presence of rulers.
He travels in foreign countries,
  he has experienced human good and human evil.
At dawn and with all his heart
  he resorts to the Lord who made him;
he pleads in the presence of the Most High,
  he opens his mouth in prayer
  and makes entreaty for his sins.
If it is the will of the great Lord,
  he will be filled with the spirit of understanding,
he will shower forth words of wisdom,
  and in prayer give thanks to the Lord.
He will grow upright in purpose and learning,
  he will ponder the Lord's hidden mysteries.
He will display the instruction he has received,
  taking his pride in the Law of the Lord's covenant.
Many will praise his understanding,
  and it will never be forgotten.
His memory will not disappear,
  generation after generation his name will live.

Christian Perspectives

1. In this piece, the writer observes that our work also requires our heart. Notice the repetition of "They set their hearts on. . . ." What is the opportunity here? (See Colossians 3:23.)
2. How does the author give honor to craftsmen—manual laborers? Do we tend to value such workers and artists in this way? What do you think is meant by the phrase "they give solidity to the created world"?
3. Do you agree that leisure gives us the opportunity to acquire wisdom?
4. What do we use leisure time for now? Why do you think we have changed?

MAKING CONNECTIONS

1. Write a brief essay in which you analyze Martin Luther King's sense of the audience for his "Letter from Birmingham Jail." Be sure to note if he has in mind more than the clergymen he directly addresses, and note how the moral authorities he appeals to are likely to affect his audience.
2. Briefly describe the methods King uses to make his argument. Write an evaluation of his use of moral authority figures, of his logic, and of his emotional appeals. Which of his methods do you find most persuasive?
3. The poems by Lovelace, Owen, and cummings illustrate contrasting views on war and patriotism. Write an essay in which you describe what going to war might mean to a seventeenth century English nobleman and what it means to you as a twentieth century young person.
4. Compose a poem using cummings' "next to god of course america i" as a model. Use cliches or jargon to make your point satirically.
5. Write a descriptive essay on a specific work or craft, showing how it can provide meaning for a person by uniting "avocation" and "vocation." You may use ideas from Hopkin's "The Windhover" or the excerpt from Ecclesiasticus.

PART III

The Search for Individuality

Introduction

Who am I? So much human creativity begins from an attempt to answer this question. A young artist paints a picture, a musician composes a song, a poet writes a poem. The need to define, establish, and express individuality is strongly felt by young people in our modern Western society.

You have probably questioned your own sense of who you are. Perhaps you have suffered a trauma that left you shaken out of your comfortable and secure hold on your identity. Perhaps you are caught in situations which cause you to react badly to your past experiences; or, on the other hand, you may find yourself in conflicts with new friends or teachers who make you unduly defensive of your values. Such occasions cause fresh questions and require renewed self-affirmation.

Human life is always a *becoming* process; and, in some form, we are always establishing who we are by taking positions on issues, by telling our experiences, by expressing ideas, and by the many other ways we *speak ourselves* into the present moment, saying who we are to God, to others, and to ourselves.

This last unit offers works that explore several writers' attempts to define and express their individuality. Garrison Keillor uses humor to tell readers of his childhood and of the pain he felt at being considered "different." Malcolm X tells his story to challenge readers to grasp every opportunity to learn and develop all their potential.

In this literature you see the writers not merely expressing a self, but making connections between the self and the outer world. Flannery O'Connor writes, "Art requires a delicate adjustment of the outer and inner worlds in such a way that without changing their nature, they can be seen through each other." Literature helps us make that connection through others' experiences and then helps us cope with our own.

Through our experiences, both real and vicarious, our impressions of the world continually change. Plato, Milton, and Blake demonstrate that the awareness of both good and evil forces us to respond by choosing between them.

Christians understand that they must always be adapting to the world without from their world within. Jesus' words about the presence of the kingdom of God have been translated in at least two ways: "The kingdom is *within* you," and "The kingdom of God is *among* you." Both assertions emphasize a truth of faith. Relationship with God is highly personal, yet must be enacted in society, as God's prophets remind the faithful community again and again, to create justice, to love kindness, and to walk humbly before God.

The final section explores the possibilities open to those who are willing to risk themselves to gain the greater life of the kingdom of God. Jesus said, "The greatest commandment is this: "Thou shalt love the Lord thy God with all thy heart, and with all thy soul, and with all thy mind. . . . And the second is like unto it, "Thou shalt love thy neighbor as thyself" (Matthew 22:37,38). By knowing and loving God, by extending ourselves to others, and by understanding and accepting ourselves, we are fulfilling this commandment.

Defining Individuality

From LAKE WOBEGON DAYS

Garrison Keillor

In a town where everyone was either Lutheran or Catholic, our family was not and never has been. We were Sanctified Brethren, a sect so tiny that nobody but us and God knew about it. So when kids asked what I was, I just said Protestant. It was too much to explain, like having six toes. You would rather keep your shoes on.

Grandpa Cotten was once tempted toward Lutheranism by a preacher who gave a rousing sermon on grace that Grandpa heard as a young man while taking Aunt Esther's dog home who had chased a Model T across town. He sat down on the church steps and listened to the voice boom out of the open windows until he made up his mind to go in and unite with the truth, but he took one look from the vestibule and left. "He was dressed up like the Pope of Rome," said Grandpa, "and the altar and the paintings and the gold candlesticks — my gosh, it was just a big show. And he was reading the whole darn thing off a page, like an actor."

Jesus said, "Where two or three are gathered together in my name, there am I in the midst of them," and the Brethren believed that was enough. We met in Uncle Al and Aunt Flo's bare living room, with plain folding chairs arranged facing in toward the middle. No clergyman in a black smock. No organ or piano, for that would make one person too prominent. No upholstery — it would lead to complacence. No picture of Jesus — He was in our hearts.

The faithful sat down at the appointed hour and waited for the Spirit to move one of them to speak or to pray or to give out a hymn from our Little Flock Hymnal. No musical notation, for music must come from the heart and not off a page. We sang the texts to a tune that fit the meter of the many tunes we all knew. The idea of reading a prayer was sacrilege to us — "If a man can't remember what he wants to say to God, let him sit down and think a little harder," Grandpa said.

"There's the Lord's Prayer," said Aunt Esther meekly. We were all sitting on the porch after Sunday dinner. Esther and Harvey were visiting from Minneapolis and had attended Lake Wobegon Lutheran, she having turned Lutheran when she married him, a subject that was never brought up in our family.

"You call that prayer? Sitting and reciting like a bunch of schoolchildren?"

Harvey cleared his throat and turned to me and smiled. "Speaking of school, how are you doing?" he asked.

There was a lovely silence in the Brethren assembled on Sunday morning as we waited for the Spirit. Either the Spirit was moving someone to speak who was taking his sweet time or else the Spirit was playing a wonderful joke on us and letting us sit, or perhaps silence was the point of it. We sat listening to rain on the roof, distant traffic, a radio playing from across the street, kids whizzing by on bikes, dogs barking, as we waited for the Spirit to inspire us. It was like sitting on the porch with your family, when nobody feels that they have to make talk. So quiet in church. Minutes drifted by in silence that was sweet to us. The old Regulator clock ticked, the rain stopped, and the room changed light as the sun broke through—shafts of brilliant sun through the windows and motes of dust falling through it—the smell of clean clothes and floor wax and wine and the fresh bread of Aunt Flo, which was Christ's body given for us. Jesus in our midst, who loved us. So peaceful; and we loved each other, too. I thought perhaps the Spirit was leading me to say that, but I was just a boy, and children were supposed to keep still.

And my affections were not pure. They were tainted with a sneaking admiration of Catholics—Catholic Christmas, Easter, the Living Rosary, and the Blessing of the Animals, all magnificent. Everything we did was so plain, but they were regal—especially the Feast Day of Saint Francis, which they did right out in the open, a feast for the eyes. Cows, horses, some pets, right on the church lawn. The turmoil, animals bellowing and barking and clucking and a cat scheming how to escape and suddenly leaping out of the girl's arms who was holding on tight, the cat dashing through the crowd, dogs straining at the leash, and the ocarina band of third graders playing a song, and the great calm of the sisters, and the flags, and the Knights of Columbus decked out in their handsome black suits—the whole thing was gorgeous. I stared at it until my eyes almost fell out, and then I wished it would go on much longer.

"Christians," my Uncle Al used to say, "do not go in for show," referring to the Catholics. We were sanctified by the blood of the Lord, therefore we were saints, like Saint Francis, but we didn't go in for feasts or ceremonies, involving animals or not. We went in for sitting, all nineteen of us, in Uncle Al and Aunt Flo's living room on Sunday morning and having a plain meeting and singing hymns in our poor thin voices, while not far away the Catholics were whooping it up. I wasn't allowed inside Our Lady, of course, but if the Blessing of Animals on the Feast Day of Saint Francis was any indication, Lord, I didn't know but what they had elephants in there or acrobats. I sat in our little group and envied them for the splendor and gorgeousness, as we tried to sing without even so much as a harmonica to give us the pitch. Hymns, Uncle Al said, didn't have to be sung perfect, because God looks on the heart, and if you are In The Spirit, then all praise is good.

The Brethren, also known as The Saints Gathered in the Name of Christ Jesus, who met in the living room were all related to each other and raised in the Faith from infancy except Brother Mel, who was rescued from a life of drunkenness, saved as a brand from the burning, a drowning sailor, a sheep on the hillside, whose immense red nose testified of his previous condition. I envied his amazing story of how he came to be with us. Born to godly parents, Mel left home at fifteen and joined the Navy. He sailed to distant lands in a submarine and had exciting experiences while traveling the downward path, which led him finally to the Union Gospel Mission in Minneapolis, where he heard God's voice "as clear as my voice speaking to you." He was twenty-six, he slept under bridges and in abandoned buildings, he drank two quarts of white muscatel every day, and then God told him that he must be born again, and so he was, and became the new Mel, except for his nose.

Except for his nose, Mel Burgess looked like any forty-five-year Brethren man: sober, preferring dark suits, soft-spoken, tending toward girth. His nose was what made you look twice: battered, swollen, very red with tiny purplish lines, it looked ancient and dead on his otherwise fairly handsome face, the souvenir of what he had been saved from, the "Before" of his "Before . . . and After" advertisement for being born again.

For me, there was nothing before. I was born among the born-again. This living room so hushed, the Brethren in their customary places on folding chairs (the comfortable ones were put away on Sunday morning) around the end table draped with a white cloth and the glass of wine and loaf of bread (unsliced), was as familiar to me as my mother and father, before whom there was nobody. I had always been here.

I never saw the "before" until the Sunday we drove to St. Cloud for dinner and traipsed into a restaurant that a friend of Dad's had recommended, Phil's House of Good Food. The waitress pushed two tables together and we sat down and studied the menu. My mother blanched at the prices. A chicken dinner went for $2.50, the roast beef for $3.75. "It's a nice place," Dad said, multiplying the five of us times $2.50. "I'm not so hungry, I guess," he said. "Maybe I'll just have soup." We weren't restaurantgoers—"Why pay good money for food you can make better at home?" was Mother's philosophy—so we weren't at all sure about restaurant customs. For example, could a person who had been seated in a restaurant simply get up and walk out? Would it be proper? Would it be *legal?*

The waitress came and stood by Dad. "Can I get you something from the bar?" she said. Dad blushed a deep red. The question seemed to imply that he looked like a drinker.

"No," he whispered, as if he were turning down her offer to take off her clothes and dance on the table.

Then another waitress brought a tray of glasses to a table of four couples next to us. "Martini," she said, setting the drink down, "whiskey sour, whiskey sour, Manhattan, whiskey sour, gin and tonic, martini, whiskey sour."

"Ma'am? Something from the bar?" Mother looked at her in disbelief.

Suddenly the room changed for us. Our waitress looked hardened, rough, cheap; across the room a woman laughed obscenely, "Haw, haw, haw"; the man with her lit a cigarette and blew a cloud of smoke; a swearword drifted out from the kitchen like a whiff of urine; even the soft lighting seemed suggestive, diabolical. To be seen in such a place on the Lord's Day—*what had we done?*

"Ed," my mother said, rising.

"We can't stay. I'm sorry," Dad told the waitress. We all got up and put on our coats. Everyone in the restaurant had a good long look at us. A bald little man in a filthy white shirt emerged from the kitchen, wiping his hands. "Folks? Something wrong?" he said.

"We're in the wrong place," Mother told him. Mother always told the truth, or something close to it.

"This is *humiliating.*" I said out on the sidewalk. "I feel like a *leper* or something. Why do we always have to make such a big production out of everything? Why can't we be like regular people?"

She put her hands on my shoulder. 'Be not conformed to this world," she said. I knew the rest by heart: ". . . but be ye transformed by the renewing of your mind, that ye may prove what is that good and acceptable and perfect will of God."

"Where we gonna eat?" Phyllis asked.

"We'll find someplace reasonable," said Mother, and we walked six blocks across the river and found a lunch counter and ate sloppy joes (called Maid-Rites) for fifteen cents apiece.

They did not agree with us, and we were aware of them all afternoon through prayer meeting and Young People's.

Christian Perspectives

1. The writer gives us a humorous, yet realistic view of his family that formed his religious foundation. Describe your own religious upbringing. Did you feel "different"?
2. As a child, the writer was fascinated with the "fancy" Catholics that contrasted with the plain religion of the Sanctified Brethren. A Catholic child might have a similar fascination with Protestants. Discuss your early impressions about denominations that were foreign to you.
3. Keillor's colloquial style makes him a popular writer and speaker. One technique in this selection is his intentional use of jargon which creates a rapport with his audience. Identify some of these familiar phrases and explain their significance to you.

FREEDOM THROUGH LEARNING TO READ
Malcolm X

From *The Autobiography of Malcolm X*

It was because of my letters that I happened to stumble upon starting to acquire some kind of a homemade education.

I became increasingly frustrated at not being able to express what I wanted to convey in letters that I wrote, especially those to Mr. Elijah Muhammad. In the street, I had been the most articulate hustler out there—I had commanded attention when I said something. But now, trying to write simple English, I not only wasn't articulate, I wasn't even functional. How would I sound writing in slang, the way I would say it, something such as, "Look, daddy, let me pull your coat about a cat, Elijah Muhammad—"

Many who today hear me somewhere in person, or on television, or those who read something I've said, will think I went to school far beyond the eighth grade. This impression is due entirely to my prison studies.

It had really begun back in the Charlestown Prison, when Bimbi first made me feel envy of his stock of knowledge. Bimbi had always taken charge of any conversations he was in, and I had tried to emulate him. But every book I picked up had few sentences which didn't contain anywhere from one to nearly all of the words that might as well have been in Chinese. When I just skipped those words, of course, I really ended up with little idea of what the book said. So I had come to the Norfolk Prison Colony still going through only book-reading motions. Pretty soon, I would have quit even these motions, unless I had received the motivation that I did.

I saw that the best thing I could do was get hold of a dictionary—to study, to learn some words. I was lucky enough to reason also that I should try to improve my penmanship. It was sad. I couldn't even write in a straight line. It was both ideas together that moved me to request a dictionary along with some tablets and pencils from the Norfolk Prison Colony school.

I spent two days just riffling uncertainly through the dictionary's pages. I'd never realized so many words existed! I didn't know *which* words I needed to learn. Finally, just to start some kind of action, I began copying.

In my slow, painstaking, ragged handwriting, I copied into my tablet everything printed on that first page, down to the punctuation marks.

I believe it took me a day. Then, aloud, I read back, to myself, everything I'd written on the tablet. Over and over, aloud, to myself, I read my own handwriting.

I woke up the next morning, thinking about those words—immensely proud to realize that not only had I written so much at one time, but I'd written words that I never knew were in the world. Moreover, with a little effort, I also could remember what many of these words meant. I reviewed the words whose meanings I didn't remember. Funny thing, from the dictionary first page right now, that "aardvark" springs to my mind. The dictionary had a picture of it, a long-tailed, long-eared, burrowing African mammal, which lives off termites caught by sticking out its tongue as an anteater does for ants.

I was so fascinated that I went on—I copied the dictionary's next page, and the same experience came when I studied that. With every succeeding page, I also learned of people and places and events from history. Actually the dictionary is like a miniature encyclopedia. Finally the dictionary's A section had filled a whole tablet—and I went on into the B's. That was the way I started copying what eventually became the entire dictionary. It went a lot faster after so much practice helped me pick up handwriting speed. Between what I wrote in my tablet, and writing letters, during the rest of my time in prison I would guess I wrote a million words.

I suppose it was inevitable that as my word-base broadened, I could for the first time pick up a book and read and now begin to understand what the book was saying. Anyone who has read a great deal can imagine the new world that opened. Let me tell you something: from then until I left that prison, in every free moment I had, if I was not reading in the library, I was reading on my bunk. You couldn't have gotten me out of books with a wedge. Between Mr. Muhammad's teachings, my correspondence, my visitors—usually Ella and Reginald—and my reading of books, months passed without my even thinking about being imprisoned. In fact, up to then, I never had been so truly free in my life.

The Norfolk Prison Colony's library was in the school building. A variety of classes was taught there by instructors who came from such places as Harvard and Boston universities. The weekly debates between inmate teams were also held in the school building. You would be astonished to know how worked up convict debaters and audiences would get over subjects like "Should Babies Be Fed Milk?"

Available on the prison library's shelves were books on just about every general subject. Much of the big private collection that Parkhurst had willed to the prison was still in crates and boxes in the back of the library—thousands of old books. Some of them looked ancient: covers faded, old-time parchment-looking binding. Parkhurst, I've mentioned, seemed to have been principally interested in history and religion. He had the money and the special interest to have a lot of books that you wouldn't have in general circulation. Any college library would have been lucky to get that collection.

As you can imagine, especially in a prison where there was heavy emphasis on rehabilitation, an inmate was smiled upon if he demonstrated an unusually intense interest in books. There was a sizable number of well-read inmates, especially the popular debaters. Some were said by many to be practically walking encyclopedias. They were almost celebrities. No university would ask any student to devour literature as I did when this new world opened to me, of being able to read and *understand*.

I read more in my room than in the library itself. An inmate who was known to read a lot could check out more than the permitted maximum number of books. I preferred reading in the total isolation of my own room.

When I progressed to really serious reading, every night at about ten P.M. I would be outraged with the "lights out." It always seemed to catch me right in the middle of something engrossing.

Fortunately, right outside my door was a corridor light that cast a glow into my room. The glow was enough to read by, once my eyes adjusted to it. So when "lights out" came, I would sit on the floor where I could continue reading in that glow.

At one-hour intervals the night guards paced past every room. Each time I heard the approaching footsteps, I jumped into bed and feigned sleep. And as soon as the guard passed, I got back out of bed onto the floor area of that light glow, where I would read for another fifty-eight minutes until the guard approached again. That went on until three or four every morning. Three or four hours of sleep a night was enough for me. Often in the years in the streets I had slept less than that.

The teachings of Mr. Muhammad stressed how history had been "whitened"—when white men had written history books, the black man simply had been left out. Mr. Muhammad couldn't have said anything that would have struck me much harder. I had never forgotten how when my class, me and all of those whites, had studied seventh-grade United States history back in Mason, the history of the Negro had been covered in one paragraph, and the teacher had gotten a big laugh with his joke, "Negroes' feet are so big that when they walk, they leave a hole in the ground."

This is one reason why Mr. Muhammad's teachings spread so swiftly all over the United States, among *all* Negroes, whether or not they become followers of Mr. Muhammad. The teachings ring true—to every Negro. You can hardly show me a black adult in America—or a white one, for that matter—who knows from the history books anything like the truth about the black man's role. In my own case, once I heard of the "glorious history of the black man," I took special pains to hunt in the library for books that would inform me on details about black history.

I can remember accurately the very first set of books that really impressed me. I have since bought that set of books and I have it at home for my children to read as they grow up. It's called *Wonders of the World*. It's full of pictures of archeological finds, statues that depict, usually, non-European people.

I found books like Will Durant's *Story of Civilization*. I read H. G. Wells' *Outline of History*. *Souls of Black Folk* by W. E. B. Du Bois gave me a glimpse into the black people's history before they came to this country. Carter G. Woodson's *Negro History* opened my eyes about black empires before the black slave was brought to the United States, and the early Negro struggles for freedom.

J. A. Rogers' three volumes of *Sex and Race* told about race-mixing before Christ's time; about Aesop being a black man who told fables; about Egypt's Pharoahs; about the Coptic Christian Empires; about Ethiopia, the earth's oldest continuous black civilization, as China is the oldest continuous civilization.

Mr. Muhammad's teachings about how the white man had been created led me to *Findings in Genetics* by Gregor Mendel. (The dictionary's G section was where I had learned what

"Genetics" meant.) I really studied this book by the Austrian monk. Reading it over and over, especially certain sections, helped me to understand that if you started with a black man, a white man could be produced; but starting with a white man man, you could never produce a black man—because the white chromosome is recessive. And since no one disputes that there was but one Original Man, the conclusion is clear.

During the last year or so, in the *New York Times,* Arnold Toynbee used the word "bleached" in describing the white man. (His words were: "White i.e., bleached) human beings of North European origin. . . ." Toynbee also referred to the European geographic area as only a peninsula of Asia. He said there is no such thing as Europe. And if you look at the globe, you will see for yourself that America is only an extension of Asia. (But at the same time Toynbee is among those who have helped to bleach history. He has written that Africa was the only continent that produced no history. He won't write that again. Every day now, the truth is coming to light.)

I never will forget how shocked I was when I began reading about slavery's total horror. It made such an impact upon me that it later became one of my favorite subjects when I became a minister of Mr. Muhammad's. The World's most monstrous crime, the sin and the blood on the white man's hands, are almost impossible to believe. Books like the one by Frederick Olmstead opened my eyes to the horrors suffered when the slave was landed in the United States. The European woman, Fannie Kimball, who had married a Southern white slaveowner, described how human beings were degraded. Of course I read *Uncle Tom's Cabin.* In fact I believe that's the only novel I have ever read since I started serious reading.

Parkhurst's collection also contained some bound pamphlets of the Abolitionist Anti-Slavery Society of New England. I read descriptions of atrocities, saw those illustrations of black slave women tied up and flogged with whips; of black mothers watching their babies being dragged off, never to be seen by their mothers again; of dogs after slaves, and of the fugitive slave catchers, evil white men with whips and clubs and chains and guns. I read about the slave preacher Nat Turner, who put the fear of God into the white slavemaster. Nat Turner wasn't going around preaching pie-in-the-sky and "non-violent" freedom for the black man. There in Virginia one night in 1831, Nat and seven other slaves started out at his master's home and through the night they went from one plantation "big house" to the next, killing, until the next morning 57 white people were dead and Nat had about 70 slaves following him. White people, terrified for their lives, fled from their homes, locked themselves up in public buildings, hid in the woods, and some even left the state. A small army of soldiers took two months to catch and hang Nat Turner. Somewhere I have read where Nat Turner's example is said to have inspired John Brown to invade Virginia and attack Harper's Ferry nearly thirty years later, with thirteen white men and five Negroes.

I read Herodotus, "the father of History," or, rather, I read about him. And I read the histories of various nations, which opened my eyes gradually, then wider and wider, to how the whole world's white men had indeed acted like devils, pillaging and raping and bleeding and draining the whole world's non-white people. I remember, for instance, books such as Will Durant's *The Story of Oriental Civilization,* and Mahatma Gandhi's accounts of the struggle to drive the British out of India.

Book after book showed me how the white man had brought upon the world's black, brown, red, and yellow peoples every variety of the sufferings of exploitation. I saw how since the sixteenth century, the so-called "Christian trader" white man began to ply the seas in his lust for Asian and African empires, and plunder, and power. I read, I saw, how the white man never has gone among the non-white peoples bearing the Cross in the true manner and spirit of Christ's teaching—meek, humble, and Christlike.

I perceived, as I read, how the collective white man had been actually nothing but a piratical opportunist who used Faustian machinations to make his own Christianity his initial wedge in criminal conquests. First, always "religiously," he branded "heathen" and "pagan" labels upon the ancient non-white cultures and civilizations. The stage thus set, he then turned upon his non-white victims his weapons of war.

I read now, entering India—half a *billion* deeply religious brown people—the British white man, by 1759, through promises, trickery and manipulations, controlled much of India through Great Britain's East India Company. The parasitical British administration kept tenacling out to half of the sub-continent. In 1857, some of the desperate people of India finally mutinied—and, excepting for the African slave trade, nowhere has history recorded any more unnecessary bestial and ruthless human carnage than the British suppression of the non-white Indian people.

Over 115 million African blacks—close to the 1930's population of the United States—were murdered or enslaved during the slave trade. And I read how when the slave market was glutted, the cannibalistic white powers of Europe next carved up, as their colonies, the richest areas of the black continent. And Europe's chancelleries for the next century played a chess game of naked exploitation and power from Cape Horn to Cairo.

Ten guards and the warden couldn't have torn me out of those books. Not even Elijah Muhammad could have been more eloquent than those books were in providing indisputable proof that the collective white man had acted like a devil in virtually every contact he had with the world's collective non-white man. I listen today to the radio, and watch television, and read the headlines about the collective white man's fear and tension concerning China. When the white man professes ignorance about why the Chinese hate him so, my mind can't help flashing back to what I read, there is prison, about how the blood forebears of this same white man raped China at a time when China was trusting and helpless. These original white "Christian traders" sent into China millions of pounds of opium. By 1839, so many of the Chinese were addicts that China's desperate government destroyed twenty thousand chests of opium. The first Opium War was promptly declared by the white man. Imagine! Declaring war upon someone who objects to being narcotized! The Chinese were severely beaten, with Chinese-invented gunpowder.

The treaty of Nanking made China pay the British white man for the destroyed opium; forced open China's major ports to British trade; forced China to abandon Hong King; fixed China's import tariffs so low that cheap British articles soon flooded in, maiming China's industrial development.

After a second Opium War, the Tientsin Treaties legalized the ravaging opium trade, legalized a British-French-American control of China's customs. China tried delaying that Treaty's ratification; Peking was looted and burned.

"Kill the foreign white devils!" was the 1901 Chinese war cry in the Boxer Rebellion. Losing again, this time the Chinese were driven from Peking's choicest area. The vicious, arrogant white man put up the famous signs, "Chinese and dogs are not allowed."

Red China after World War II closed its doors to the Western white world. Massive Chinese agricultural, scientific, and industrial efforts are described in a book that *Life* magazine recently published. Some observers inside Red China have reported that the world never has known such a hate-white campaign as is now going on in this non-white country where, present birth-rates continuing, in fifty more years Chinese will be half the earth's population. And it seems that some Chinese chickens will soon come home to roost, with China's recent successful nuclear tests.

Let us face reality. We can see in the United Nations a new world order being shaped, along color lines—an alliance among the non-white nations. American's U.N. Ambassador Adlai Stevenson complained not long ago that in the United Nations "a skin game" was being played. He was right. He was facing reality. A "skin game" *is* being played. But Ambassador Stevenson sounded like Jesse James accusing the marshall of carrying a gun. Because who in the world's history has ever played a worse "skin game" than the white man?

Mr. Muhammad, to whom I was writing daily, had no idea of what a new world had opened to me through my efforts to document his teachings in books.

When I discovered philosophy, I tried to touch all the landmarks of philosophical development. Gradually, I read most of the old philosophers, Occidental and Oriental. The Oriental philosophers were the ones I came to prefer; finally, my impression was that most Occidental philosophy had largely been borrowed from the Oriental thinkers. Socrates, for instance, traveled in Egypt. Some sources even say that Socrates was initiated into some of the Egyptian mysteries. Obviously Socrates got some of his wisdom among the East's wise men.

I have often reflected upon the new vistas that reading opened to me. I knew right there in prison that reading had changed forever the course of my life. As I see it today, the ability to read awoke inside me some long dormant craving to be mentally alive. I certainly wasn't seeking any degree, the way a college confers a status symbol upon its students. My homemade education gave me, with every additional book that I read, a little bit more sensitivity to the deafness, dumbness, and blindness that was afflicting the black race in America. Not long ago, an English writer telephoned me from London, asking questions. One was, "What's your alma mater?" I told him, "Books." You will never catch me with a free fifteen minutes in which I'm not studying something I feel might be able to help the black man.

Yesterday I spoke in London, and both ways on the plane across the Atlantic I was studying a document about how the United Nations proposes to insure the human rights of the oppressed minorities of the world. The American black man is the world's most shameful case of minority oppression. What makes the black man think of himself as only an internal United States issue in just a catch-phrase, two words, "civil-rights." How is the black man going to get "'civil rights" before first he wins him *human* rights? If the American black man will start thinking about *human* rights, and then start thinking of himself as part of one of the world's great peoples, he will see he has a case for the United Nations.

I can't think of a better case! Four hundred years of black blood and sweat invested here in America, and the white man still has the black man begging for what every immigrant fresh off the ship can take for granted the minutes he walks down the gangplank.

But I'm digressing. I told the Englishman that my alma mater was books, a good library. Every time I catch a plane, I have with me a book that I want to read—and that's a lot of books these days. If I weren't out here every day battling the white man, I could spend the rest of my life reading, just satisfying my curiosity—because you can hardly mention anything I'm not curious about. I don't think anybody ever got more out of going to prison that I did. In fact, prison enabled me to study far more intensively than I would have if my life had gone differently and I had attended some college. I imagine that one of the biggest troubles with colleges is there are too many distractions, too much panty-raiding, fraternities, and boola-boola and all of that. Where else but in a prison could I have attacked my ignorance by being able to study intensely sometimes as much as fifteen hours a day?

Christian Perspectives

1. Malcolm X states that reading forever changed the course of his life. For him, to be mentally alive was to be an effective leader for his people. Describe the term *mentally alive* and its significance for you as a Christian and to the community of believers. Do you have a similar responsibility?
2. Attempt a serious discussion with someone about the historical development of Christianity since the first century. If you are unable to do so, why? Is our understanding of Christianity's historical development significant? Why or why not?
3. Certainly God wants us to educate ourselves. The Bible tells us that we are "destroyed for lack of knowledge" (Hosea 4:6). How could lack of knowledge destroy us? What is the difference between valuable knowledge and knowledge that is "puffed up"?
4. Identify Malcolm X's use of ethos, pathos, and logos as strategies to develop his argument.

I'M NOBODY

Emily Dickinson

I'm Nobody! Who are you?
Are you—Nobody—Too?
Then there's a pair of us!
Don't tell! they'd banish us—you know!

How dreary—to be—Somebody!
How public—like a Frog—
To tell your name—the livelong June—
To an admiring Bog!

Christian Perspectives

1. The same feeling of anonymity Dickinson conveys exists today among many people. What are some of the factors in our society that contribute to the feeling of anonymity in the business world? in our neighborhood?
2. Striving for importance seemed "dreary" to Emily Dickinson, and her point is a good one, but the Christian can see himself in a different perspective from the one presented in "I'm Nobody." What do Matthew 10:28-31, Psalm 139, and Psalm 8:4-6 reveal about our importance?

150

3. Is it possible to be a nobody externally and yet be somebody internally? Describe a person in the Bible who was like this. (See Hebrews 11:37, Proverbs 13:7, Luke 21:1-4, and Luke 21:12-19.)

THE UNKNOWN CITIZEN
JS/07/M/378
This Marble Monument Is Erected by the State
W. H. Auden

He was found by the Bureau of Statistics to be
One against whom there was no official complaint,
And all the reports on his conduct agree
That, in the modern sense of an old-fashioned word, he was a saint,
For in everything he did he served the Greater Community.
Except for the war till the day he retired
He worked in the factory and never got fired,
But satisfied his employers, Fudge Motors Inc.
Yet he wasn't a scab or odd in his views,
For his Union reports that he paid his dues,
(Our report on his Union shows it was sound)
And our Social Psychology workers found
That he was popular with his mates and liked a drink.
The Press are convinced that he bought a paper every day
And that his reactions to poetry were normal in every way.
Policies taken out in his name prove that he was fully insured,
And his Health Card shows he was once in a hospital but left it cured.
Both Producers Research and High-Grade Living declare
He was fully sensible to the advantages of the Installment Plan
And had everything necessary to the Modern Man,
A gramophone, a radio, a car, and a frigidaire.
Our researchers into public opinion are content
That he held the proper opinions for the time of year.
When there was peace, he was for peace; when there was war, he went.
He was married and added five children to the population,
Which our Eugenists say was the right number for a parent of his generation,
And our teachers report that he never interfered with their education.
Was he free? Was he happy? The question is absurd:
Had anything been wrong, we certainly should have heard.

Christian Perspectives

1. Is this poem an indictment against the individual or the society? Explain your answer.
2. Jesus says that we are the salt of the earth. How would a person who fits Jesus' description be different from the unknown citizen?

THE COLLAR

George Herbert

I struck the board and cried, "No more:
  I will abroad!
What? shall I ever sigh and pine?
My lines and life are free, free as the road,
  Loose as the wind, as large as store.
   Shall I be still in suit?
  Have I no harvest but a thorn
  To let me blood, and not restore
What I have lost with cordial fruit?
   Sure there was wine
  Before my sighs did dry it; there was corn
   Before my tears did drown it.
  Is the year only lost to me?
   Have I no bays to crown it,
  No flowers, no garlands gay? All blasted?
    All wasted?
   Not so, my heart; but there is fruit,
    And thou hast hands.
   Recover all thy sigh-blown age
  On double pleasures: leave thy cold dispute
  Of what is fit and not. Forsake thy cage,
    Thy rope of sands,
  Which petty thoughts have made, and made to thee
   Good cable, to enforce and draw,
    And be thy law,
  While thou didst wink and wouldst not see.
    Away! take heed;
    I will abroad.
Call in thy death's-head there; tie up thy fears.
    He that forbears
   To suit and serve his need,
    Deserves his load."
But as I raved and grew more fierce and wild

At every word,
Methought I heard one calling, *Child!*,
And I replied *My Lord.*

Christian Perspectives

1. What is the significance of the title "The Collar"?
2. Compare the use of the *collar* to the scriptural reference to the *yoke*. Are they similar?
3. Do you find the action of the poem convincing? How can one word from God so change a person's direction and attitude?

Defining a Personal Philosophy

THE ALLEGORY OF THE CAVE
Plato

Next, said I, here is a parable to illustrate the degrees in which our nature may be enlightened or unenlightened. Imagine the condition of men living in a sort of cavernous chamber underground, with an entrance open to the light and a long passage all down the cave. Here they have been from childhood, chained by the leg and also by the neck, so that they cannot move and can see only what is in front of them, because the chains will not let them turn their heads. At some distance higher up is the light of a fire burning behind them; and between the prisoners and the fire is a track with a parapet built along it, like the screen at a puppet-show, which hides the performers while they show their puppets over the top.

I see, said he.

Now behind this parapet imagine persons carrying along various artificial objects, including figures of men and animals in wood or stone or other materials, which project above the parapet. Naturally, some of these persons will be talking, others silent.

It is a strange picture, he said, and a strange sort of prisoners.

Like ourselves, I replied; for in the first place prisoners so confined would have seen nothing of themselves or of one another, except the shadows thrown by the fire-light on the wall of the Cave facing them, would they?

Not if all their lives they had been prevented from moving their heads.

And they would have seen as little of the objects carried past.

Of course.

Now, if they could talk to one another, would they not suppose that their words referred only to those passing shadows which they saw?

Necessarily.

And suppose their prisoner had an echo from the wall facing them? When one of the people crossing behind them spoke, they could only suppose that the sound came from the shadow passing before their eyes.

No doubt.

In every way, then, such prisoners would recognize as reality nothing but the shadows of those artificial objects.

Inevitably.

Now consider what would happen if their release from the chains and the healing of their unwisdom should come about in this way. Suppose one of them set free and forced suddenly to stand up, turn his head, and walk with eyes lifted to the light; all these movements would be painful, and he would be too dazzled to make out the objects whose shadows he had been used to seeing. What do you think he would say, if someone told him that what he had formerly seen was meaningless illusion, but now, being somewhat nearer to reality and turned towards more real objects, he was getting a truer view? Suppose further that he were shown the various objects being carried by and were made to say, in reply to questions, what each of them was. Would he not be perplexed and believe the objects now shown him to be not so real as what he formerly saw?

Yes, not nearly so real.

And if he were forced to look at the fire-light itself, would not his eyes ache, so that he would try to escape and turn back to the things which he could see distinctly, convinced that they really were clearer than these other objects now being shown to him?

Yes.

And suppose someone were to drag him away forcibly up the steep and rugged ascent and not let him go until he had hauled him out into the sunlight, would he not suffer pain and vexation at such treatment, and, when he had come out into the light, find his eyes so full of its radiance that he could not see a single one of the things that he was now told were real?

Certainly he would not see them all at once.

He would need, then, to grow accustomed before he could see things in that upper world. At first it would be easiest to make out shadows, and then the images of men and things reflected in water, and later on the things themselves. After that, it would be easier to watch the heavenly bodies and the sky itself by night, looking at the light of the moon and stars rather than the Sun and the sun's light in the daytime.

Yes, surely.

Last of all, he would be able to look at the Sun and contemplate its nature, not as it appears when reflected in water or any alien medium, but as it is in itself in its own domain.

No doubt.

And now he would begin to draw the conclusion that it is the Sun that produces the seasons and the course of the year and controls everything in the visible world, and moreover is in a way the cause of all that he and his companions used to see.

Clearly he would come at last to that conclusion.

Then if he called to mind his fellow prisoners and what passed for wisdom in his former dwelling-place, he would surely think himself happy in the change and be sorry for them. They may have had a practice of honouring and commending one another, with prizes for the man who had the keenest eye for the passing shadows and the best memory for the order in which they followed or accompanied one another, so that he could make a good guess as to which was going to come next. Would our released prisoner be likely to covet those prizes or to envy the men exalted to honour and power in the Cave? Would he not feel like Homer's Achilles, that he would far sooner be on earth as a hired servant in the house of a landless man or endure anything rather than go back to his old beliefs and live in the old way?

Yes, he would prefer any fate to such a life.

Now imagine what would happen if he went down again to take his former seat in the Cave. Coming suddenly out of the sunlight, his eyes would be filled with darkness. He might be

156

required once more to deliver his opinion on those shadows, in competition with the prisoners who had never been released, while his eyesight was still dim and unsteady; and it might take some time to become used to the darkness. They would laugh at him and say that he had gone up only to come back with his sight ruined; it was worth no one's while even to attempt the ascent. If they could lay hands on the man who was trying to set them free and lead them up, they would kill him.

Yes, they would.

Every feature in this parable, my dear Glaucon, is meant to fit our earlier analysis. The prison dwelling corresponds to the region revealed to us through the sense of sight, and the fire-light within it to the power of the Sun. The ascent to see the things in the upper world you may take as standing for the upward journey of the soul into the region of the intelligible; then you will be in possession of what I surmise, since that is what you wish to be told. Heaven knows whether it is true; but this, at any rate, is how it appears to me. In the world of knowledge, the last thing to be perceived and only with great difficulty is the essential Form of Goodness. Once it perceived, the conclusion must follow that, for all things, this is the cause of whatever is right and good; in the visible world it gives birth to light and to the lord of light, while it is itself sovereign in the intelligible world and the parent of intelligence and truth. Without having had a vision of this Form no one can act with wisdom, either in his own life or in the matter of state.

Christian Perspectives

1. Compare what Plato says about the prisoner who returns to the cave to what Jesus says about the prophets in the Old Testament. (See Matthew 5:12.) What happened to them? What happens to bearers of truth when their message contradicts the common belief of the day?
2. Write an emulation, an imitative essay, using a different allegory to depict the cave's representation of ignorance and spiritual darkness and the light's representation of knowledge and spiritual awareness.
3. Would the prisoner have been better off never going to the light? When developing our personal philosophy, the challenge of changing often makes us want to retreat to our old ways of thinking. Give an example of an idea that has been painful, and even isolating, for you to change.

From AREOPAGITICA[1]

John Milton

Not to insist upon the examples of Moses, Daniel, and Paul, who were skilful [sic] in all the learning of the Egyptians, Chaldeans, and Greeks, which could not probably be without reading their books of all sorts; in Paul especially, who thought it no defilement to insert into holy scripture the sentences of three Greek poets, and one of them a tragedian; the question was not withstanding sometimes controverted among the primitive doctors, but with great odds

1. See notes on page 161.

on that side which affirmed it both lawful and profitable, as was then evidently perceived when Julian the Apostate[1] and subtlest enemy to our faith, made a decree forbidding Christians the study of heathen learning; for, said he, they wound us with our own weapons, and with our own arts and sciences they overcome us. And indeed the Christians were put so to their shifts by this crafty means, and so much in danger to decline into all ignorance, that the two Apollinarii[2] were fain, as a man may say, to coin all the seven liberal sciences out of the Bible, reducing it into divers forms of orations, poems, dialogue, even to the calculating of a new Christian grammar. But, saith the historian Socrates, the providence of God provided better than the industry of Apollinarius and his son by taking away that illiterate law with the life of him who devised it.

So great an injury they then held it to be deprived of Hellenic learning; and thought it a persecution more undermining, and secretly decaying the church, than the open cruelty of Decius or Diocletian.[3] And perhaps it was the same politic drift that the devil whipped St. Jerome in a Lenten dream, for reading Cicero[4]; or else it was a phantasm bred by the fever which had then seized him. For had an angel been his discipliner, unless it were for dwelling too much upon Ciceronianisms, and had chastised the reading, not the vanity, it had been plainly partial; first to correct him for grave Cicero, and not for scurril Plautus[5], whom he confesses to have been reading not long before; next to correct him only, and let so many more ancient fathers wax old in those pleasant and florid studies without the lack of such a tutoring apparition; insomuch that Basil teaches how some good use may be made of *Margites*,[6] a sportful poem not now extant writ by Homer; and why not then of *Morgante*,[7] an Italian romance much to the same purpose?

But if it be agreed we shall be tried by visions, there is a vision recorded by Eusebius, far ancienter than this tale of Jerome to the nun Eustochium, and, besides, has nothing of a fever in it. Dionysius Alexandrinus was, about the year 240, a person of great name in the church for piety and learning, who had wont to avail himself much against heretics by being conversant in their books; until a certain presbyter laid it scrupulously to his conscience, how he durst venture himself among those defiling volumes. The worthy man, loth to give offense, fell into a new debate with himself what was to be thought; when suddenly a vision sent from God (it is his own *Epistle* that so avers it) confirmed him in these words: "Read any books whatever comes to thy hands, for thou art sufficient both to judge aright and to examine each matter." To this revelation he assented the sooner, as he confesses, because it was answerable to that of the apostle to the Thessalonians: "Prove all things, hold fast that which is good."[8]

And he might have added another remarkable saying of the same author: "To the pure, all things are pure"[9]; not only meats and drinks, but all kinds of knowledge whether of good or

---

1. Julian the Apostate (331-363 A.D.). Roman Emperor from 361 to 363, when he was killed by the Persians. He denied his early Christian faith, and when he became Emperor, he decreed that Christians could not teach any of the pagan writers.

2. Apollinarii A father and son who countered Julian's decree by translating and paraphrasing Biblical books into forms familiar to classical scholars.

3. Decius and Diocletian. Roman Emperors who severely persecuted Christians. Decius reigned from 249-251, Diocletian from 284-305.

4. Cicero. Respected Roman orator.

5. Planus Roman. Roman comic playwright.

6. Margites. A legendary work by Homer, traditionally thought to be the first great comic poem.

7. Morgante. A rather coarse mock-heroic romance by Luigi Pulci (1431-1487).

8. 1 Thessalonians 5:21..

9. Titus 1:15.

158

evil; the knowledge cannot defile, nor consequently the books, if the will and conscience be not defiled. For books are as meats and viands[10] are—some of good, some of evil substance, and yet God in that unapocryphal vision said without exception, "Rise, Peter, kill and eat," leaving the choice to each man's discretion. Wholesome meats to a vitiated stomach differ little or nothing from unwholesome, and best books to a naughty mind are not unapplicable to occasions of evil. Bad meats will scarce breed good nourishment in the healthiest concoction; but herein the difference is of bad books, that they to a discreet and judicious reader serve in many respects to discover, to confute, to forewarn, and to illustrate.

Whereof what better witness can ye expect I should produce than one of your own now sitting in parliament, the chief of learned men reputed in this land, Mr. Selden, whose volume of natural and national laws proves, not only by great authorities brought together, but by exquisite reasons and theorems almost mathematically demonstrative, that all opinions, yea errors, known, read, and collated, are of main service and assistance toward the speedy attainment of what is truest.

I conceive, therefore, that when God did enlarge the universal diet of man's body, saving ever the rules of temperance, he then also, as before, left arbitrary the dieting and repasting of our minds; as wherein every mature man might have to exercise his own leading capacity. How great a virtue is temperance, how much of a moment through the whole life of man! Yet God commits the managing so great a trust, without particular law or prescription, wholly to the demeanor of every grown man. And therefore, when he himself tabled the Jews from heaven, that omer[11] which every man's daily portion of manna, is computed to have been more than might have well sufficed the heartiest feeder thrice as many meals. For those actions which enter into a man, rather than issue out of him, and therefore defile not, God uses not to captivate under a perpetual childhood of prescription, but trusts him with the gift of reason to be his own chooser; there were but little work left for preaching, if law and compulsion should grow so fast upon those things which heretofore were governed only by exhortation. Solomon informs us that much reading is a weariness to the flesh; but neither he nor other inspired authors tell us that such or such reading is unlawful; yet certainly had God thought good to limit us herein, it had been much more expedient to have told us what was unlawful than what was wearisome.

As for the burning of those Ephesian books by St. Paul's converts; 'tis replied the books were magic, the Syriac so renders them. It was a private act, a voluntary act, and leaves us to a voluntary imitation: the men in remorse burnt those books which were their own; the magistrate by this example is not appointed; these men practised the books, another might perhaps have read them in some sort usefully.

Good and evil we know in the field of this world grow up together almost inseparably; and the knowledge of good is so involved and interwoven with the knowledge of evil, and in so many cunning resemblances hardly to be discerned, that those confused seeds which were imposed on Psyche[12] as an incessant labor to cull out and sort asunder, were not more intermixed. It was from out the rind of one apple tasted, that the knowledge of good and evil, as two twins cleav-

10. Viands. Food.
11. Omer. The measure of manna rationed out daily to the Israelites. Milton is emphasizing the abundance of God's gift, which man must respond to with temperance.
12. Psyche. In the Greek story, venus imposes upon Psyche the task of sorting out seeds from a pile of mixed grain, for Psyche had won the love of Cupid, Venus' son.

ing together, leaped forth into the world. And perhaps this is that doom which Adam fell into of knowing good and evil, that is to say, of knowing good by evil.

As therefore the state of man now is, what wisdom can there be to choose, what continence to forbear without the knowledge of evil? He that can apprehend and consider vice with all her baits and seeming pleasures, and yet abstain, and yet distinguish, and yet prefer that which is truly better, he is the true warfaring Christian. I cannot praise a fugitive and cloistered virtue, unexercised and unbreathed, that never sallies out and sees her adversary, but slinks out of the race where the immortal garland is to be run for, not without dust and heat. Assuredly we bring not innocence into the world, we bring impurity much rather: that which purifies us is trial and trial is by what is contrary. That virtue therefore which is but a youngling in the contemplation of evil, and knows not the uttermost that vice promises to her followers, and rejects it, is but a blank virtue, not a pure; her whiteness is but an excremental[13] whiteness; which was the reason why our sage and serious poet Spenser, whom I dare be known to think a better teacher than Scotus[14] or Aquinas[15], describing true temperance under the person of Guyon, brings him in with his palmer through the cave of Mammon and the bower of earthly bliss, that he might see and know, and yet abstain.

Since therefore, the knowledge and survey of vice is in this world so necessary to the constituting of human virtue, and the scanning of error to the confirmation of truth, how can we more safely and with less danger scout into the regions of sin and falsity than by reading all manner of tractates and hearing all manner of reason? And this is the benefit which may be had of books promiscuously[16] read.

To sequester out of the world into Atlantic and Utopian[17] polities, which never can be drawn into use, will not mend our condition; but to ordain wisely as in this world of evil, in the midst whereof God hath placed us unavoidably. Nor is it Plato's licensing of books will do this, which necessarily pulls along with it so many other kinds of licensing as will make us all both ridiculous and weary, and yet frustrate; but those unwritten, or at least unconstraining, laws of virtuous education, religious and civil nurture, which Plato there mentions as the bonds and ligaments of the commonwealth, the pillars and the sustainers of every written statute; these they be which will bear chief sway in such matters as these, when all licensing will be easily eluded. Impunity and remissness, for certain, are the bane of a commonwealth; but here the great art lies, to discern in what the law is to bid restraint and punishment, and in what things persuasion only is to work. If every action which is good or evil in man at ripe years were to be under pittance[18] and prescription and compulsion, what were virtue but a name, what praise could be then due to well-doing, what gramercy[19] to be sober, just, or continent?

Many there be that complain of divine providence for suffering Adam to transgress. Foolish tongues! When God gave him reason he gave him freedom to choose, for reason is but choosing; he had been else a mere artificial Adam, such an Adam as he is in the motions. We ourselves esteem not of that obedience, or love, or gift, which is of force. God therefore left him free, set before him a provoking object, ever almost in his eyes; herein considered his merit,

13. excremental. external

14. Scotus. John Duns Scotus (1865-1308). A theological thinker in the scholastic tradition.

15. Aquinas. St. Thomas Aquinas (1225-1274) considered the greatest Christian thinker of the scholastic tradition.

16. promiscuously. In Milton's time the word meant "randomly" or "without order."

17. Atlantic and Utopian. Milton alludes here to the unrealistic notions of states made "bure" by laws and political institutions, as portrayed in St. Francis Bacon's New Atlantis and Sir Thomas More's Utopia.

18. to be put under pittance. To be given an allowance.

herein the right of his reward, the praise of abstinence. Wherefore did he create passions within us, pleasures round about us, but that these rightly tempered are the very ingredients of virtue? They are not skilful considerers of human things who imagine to remove sin by removing the mater of sin. For, besides that it is a huge heap increasing under the very act of diminishing, though some part of it may for a time be withdrawn from some persons, it cannot from all, in such a universal thing as books are; and when this is done, yet the sin remains entire. Though ye take from a covetous man all his treasure, he has yet one jewel left—ye cannot bereave him of his covetousness. Banish all objects of lust, shut up all youth into the severest discipline that can be exercised in any hermitage, ye cannot make them chaste that came not thither so: such great care and wisdom is required to the right managing of this point.

Suppose we could expel sin by this means; look how much we thus expel of sin, so much we expel of virtue: for the matter of them both is the same; remove that, and ye remove them both alike. This justifies the high providence of God, who, though he command us temperance, justice, continence, yet pours out before us, even to a profuseness, all desirable things and gives us minds that we can wander beyond all limit and satiety. Why should we then affect a rigor contrary to the manner of God and of nature, by abridging or scanting those means which books freely permitted are, both to the trial of virtue and the exercise of truth?

The title *Areopagitica* refers to the court in ancient Athens which had traditionally met on the hill of Ares, the Areopagus. St. Paul preached before this group of Athenian philosophers in his "Mar's Hill" sermon recorded in Acts 17.

Milton writes this famous defense of Christian liberty in response to the English Parliament's laws requiring licensing of all works prior to publication. Parliament's intention, as Milton understood it, was to bring writings on political and religious subjects under the authority of officials of the English Church. Current controversies in the United States about censorship usually center on material that is offensive because of sexual exploitation. Milton was not talking about that kind of literature, but about state control over religious and political writing.

Christian Perspectives

1. What view is Milton refuting? How does he defend his premise?
2. What should the Christian community do with the "evil that is alongside the good"?
3. Defending his view scripturally, Milton quotes the apostle Paul. What does he want the church to endorse?
4. How does the reader profit from reading both kinds of literature?
5. What did the Christian community at that time fear would happen if "secular" literature were read by the public?

THE TIGER

William Blake

Tiger, Tiger, burning bright
In the forests of the night,
What immortal hand or eye
Could frame thy fearful symmetry?

In what distant deeps or skies
Burnt the fire of thine eyes?
On what wings dare he aspire?
What the hand dare seize the fire?

And what shoulder and what art,
Could twist the sinews of thy heart?
And when thy heart began to beat,
What dread hand, and what dread feet?

What the hammer? What the chain?
In what furnace was thy brain?
What the anvil? What dread grasp
Dare it deadly terrors clasp?

When the stars threw down their spears
And watered heaven with their tears,
Did he smile his work to see?
Did he who made the Lamb make thee?

Tiger, Tiger, burning bright
In the forests of the night,
What immortal hand or eye
Dare frame thy fearful symmetry?

Christian Perspectives

1. The first stanza creates a mental image of a tiger moving through "the forests of the night." List the connotations *night* has for you. Decide which of these seem to apply also to the tiger. (Notice that night has both positive connotations, for example, romance, and negative ones such as crime.)
2. How is the tiger's symmetry fearful?
3. Although the first and last stanzas of the poem are about the tiger, the middle four stanzas ask questions about its creation and its creator. Why does the writer question whether the fire for the tiger's eyes came from "deeps or skies"? Traditionally, heaven is above the skies, and hell is beneath the earth. Does the writer question whether the tiger comes from heaven or hell? (Support your answer with other thoughts from the poem.)
4. If the tiger was formed by "an immortal hand," who could be its creator? Why does the author wonder if the creator of the lamb created the tiger? (See Blake's companion poem, "The Lamb.")
5. Stanza four compares the tiger's creator to a blacksmith. Why is this metaphor appropriate?
6. The poem, like the tiger, is symmetrical, but one word of the last line is different from the word used in the last line of stanza one. Why?
7. What does the tiger symbolize in the poem?
8. What is the relationship between good and evil? Are they exact opposites, or could they be different uses of the same force?
9. Why would a good God create deadly creatures or terrible natural phenomena such as tornados? (See Romans 8:22, 23.)

THE LAMB

William Blake

Little Lamb, who made thee?
Dost thou know who made thee?
Gave thee life, and bid thee feed
By the stream and o'er the mead;
Gave thee clothing of delight,
Softest clothing wooly bright;
Gave thee such a tender voice,
Making all the vales rejoice?
Little Lamb, who made thee?
Dost thou know who made thee?

Little Lamb, I'll tell thee!
Little Lamb, I'll tell thee!
He is called by thy name,
For he calls himself a lamb,
He is meek and he is mild;
He became a little child.
I a child and thou a lamb,
We are called by his name.
Little Lamb, God bless thee!
Little Lamb, God bless thee!

Christian Perspective

1. Contrast the diction of this poem with that of "The Tiger."
2. In what sense is this poem a "song of innocence" while "the Tiger" is a "song of experience?"

THE BET

Anton P. Checkhov

I

It was a dark autumn night. The old banker was pacing from corner to corner of his study, recalling to his mind the party he gave in the autumn fifteen years before. There were many clever people at the party and much interesting conversation. They talked among other things of capital punishment. The guests, among them not a few scholars and journalists, for the most part disapproved of capital punishment. They found it obsolete as a means of punishment, unfitted to a Christian State and immoral. Some of them thought that capital punishment should be replaced universally by life-imprisonment.

"I don't agree with you," said the host. "I myself have experienced neither capital punishment nor life-imprisonment, but if one may judge *a priori*, then in my opinion capital punishment is more moral and more humane than imprisonment. Execution kills instantly, life-imprisonment kills by degrees. Who is the more humane executioner, one who kills you in a few seconds or one who draws the life out of you incessantly, for years?"

"They're both equally immoral," remarked one of the guests, "because their purpose is the same, to take away life. The State is not God. It has no right to take away that which it cannot give back, if it should so desire."

Among the company was a lawyer, a young man of about twenty-five. On being asked his opinion, he said:

"Capital punishment and life-imprisonment are equally immoral; but if I were offered the choice between them, I would certainly, choose the second. It's better to live somehow than not to live at all."

There ensued a lively discussion. The banker who was then younger and more nervous suddenly lost his temper, banged his fist on the table, and turning to the young lawyer, cried out:

"It's a lie. I bet you two millions you wouldn't stick in a cell even for five years."

"If you mean it seriously," replied the lawyer, "then I bet I'll stay not five but fifteen."

"Fifteen! Done!" cried the banker. "Gentlemen, I stake two millions."

"Agreed. You stake two millions, I my freedom," said the lawyer.

So this wild, ridiculous bet came to pass. The banker, who at that time had too many millions to count, spoiled and capricious, was beside himself with rapture. During supper he said to the lawyer jokingly:

"Come to your senses, young man, before it's too late. Two millions are nothing to me, but you stand to lose three or four of the best years of your life. I say three or four, because you'll never stick it out any longer. Don't forget either, you unhappy man, that voluntary is much heavier than enforced imprisonment. The idea that you have the right to free yourself at any moment will poison the whole of your life in the cell. I pity you."

And now the banker, pacing from corner to corner, recalled all this and asked himself:

"Why did I make this bet? What's the good? The lawyer loses fifteen years of his life and I throw away two millions. Will it convince people that capital punishment is worse or better than imprisonment for life? No, no! all stuff and rubbish. On my part, it was the caprice of a well-fed man; on the lawyer's pure greed of gold."

He recollected further what happened after the evening party. It was decided that the lawyer must undergo his imprisonment under the strictest observation, in a garden wing of the banker's house. It was agreed that during the period he would be deprived of the right to cross the threshold, to see living people, to hear human voices, and to receive letters and newspapers. He was permitted to have a musical instrument, to read books, to write letters, to drink wine and smoke tobacco. By the agreement he could communicate, but only in silence, with the outside world through a little window specially constructed for this purpose. Everything necessary, books, music, wine, he could receive in any quantity by sending a note through the window. The agreement provided for all the minutest details, which made the confinement strictly solitary, and it obliged the lawyer to remain exactly fifteen years from twelve o'clock of November 14th, 1870, to twelve o'clock of November 14th, 1885. The least attempt on his part to violate the conditions, to escape if only for two minutes before the time freed the banker from the obligation to pay him the two millions.

During the first year of imprisonment, the lawyer, as far as it was possible to judge from his short notes, suffered terribly from loneliness and boredom. From his wing day and night came the sound of the piano. He rejected wine and tobacco. "Wine," he wrote, "excites desires, and desires are the chief foes of a prisoner; besides, nothing is more boring than to drink good wine alone," and tobacco spoils the air in his room. During the first year the lawyer was sent books of a light character; novels with a complicated love interest, stories of crime and fantasy, comedies, and so on.

In the second year the piano was heard no longer and the lawyer asked only for classics. In the fifth year, music was heard again, and the prisoner asked for wine. Those who watched him said that during the whole of that year he was only eating, drinking, and lying on his bed. He yawned often and talked angrily to himself. Books he did not read. Sometimes at nights he would sit down to write. He would write for a long time and tear it all up in the morning. More than once he was heard to weep.

In the second half of the sixth year, the prisoner began zealously to study languages, philosophy, and history. He fell on these subjects so hungrily that the banker hardly had time to get books enough for him. In the space of four years about six hundred volumes were bought at his request. It was while that passion lasted that the banker received the following letter from the prisoner: "My dear gaoler, I am writing these lines in six languages. Show them to experts. Let them read them. If they do not find one single mistake, I beg you to give orders to have a gun fired off in the garden. By the noise I shall know that my efforts have not been in vain. The geniuses of all ages and countries speak in different languages; but in them all burns the same flame. Oh, if you knew my heavenly happiness now that I can understand them!" The prisoner's desire was fulfilled. Two shots were fired in the garden by the banker's order.

Later on, after the tenth year, the lawyer sat immovable before his table and read only the New Testament. The banker found it strange that a man who in four years had mastered six hundred erudite volumes, should have spent nearly a year in reading one book, easy to understand and by no means thick. The New Testament was then replaced by the history of religions and theology.

During the last two years of his confinement the prisoner read an extraordinary amount, quite haphazard. Now he would apply himself to the natural sciences, then he would read Byron or Shakespeare. Notes used to come from him in which he asked to be sent at the same time a book on chemistry, a text-book of medicine, a novel, and some treatise on philosophy or theology. He read as though he were swimming in the sea among broken pieces of wreckage, and in his desire to save his life was eagerly grasping one piece after another.

II

The banker recalled all this, and thought:

"To-morrow at twelve o'clock he receives his freedom. Under the agreement, I shall have to pay him two millions. If I pay, it's all over with me. I am ruined for ever. . . ."

Fifteen years before he had too many millions to count, but now he was afraid to ask himself which he had more of, money or debts. Gambling on the Stock-Exchange, risky speculation, and the recklessness of which he could not rid himself even in old age, had gradually brought his business to decay; and the fearless, self-confident, proud man of business had become an ordinary banker, trembling at every rise and fall in the market.

"That cursed bet," murmured the old man clutching his head in despair. . . . "Why, didn't the man die? He's only forty years old. He will take away my last farthing, marry, enjoy life, gamble on the Exchange, and I will look on like an envious beggar and hear the same words from him every day: 'I'm obliged to you for the happiness of my life. Let me help you.' No, it's too much! The only escape from bankruptcy and disgrace — is that the man should die."

The clock had just struck three. The banker was listening. In the house every one was asleep, and one could hear only the frozen trees whining outside the windows. Trying to make no sound, he took out of his safe the key of the door which had not been opened for fifteen years, put on his overcoat, and went out of the house. The garden was dark and cold. It was raining. A damp, penetrating wind howled in the garden and gave the trees no rest. Though he strained his eyes, the banker could see neither the ground, nor the white statues, nor the garden wing, nor the trees. Approaching the garden wing, he called the watchman twice. There was no answer. Evidently the watchman had taken shelter from the bad weather and was now asleep somewhere in the kitchen or the greenhouse.

"If I have the courage to fulfill my intention," thought the old man, "the suspicion will fall on the watchman first of all."

In the darkness he groped for the steps and the door and entered the hall of the garden-wing., then poked his way into a narrow passage and struck a match. Not a soul was there. Some one's bed, with no bedclothes on it, stood there, and an iron stove loomed dark in the corner. The seals on the door that led into the prisoner's room were unbroken.

When the match went out, the old man, trembling from agitation, peeped into the little window.

In the prisoner's room a candle was burning dimly. The prisoner himself sat by the table. Only his back, the hair on his head and his hands were visible. Open books were strewn about on the table, the two chairs, and on the carpet near the table.

Five minutes passed and the prisoner never once stirred. Fifteen years' confinement had taught him to sit motionless. The banker tapped on the window with his finger, but the prisoner made no movement in reply. Then the banker cautiously tore the seals from the door and put the key into the lock. The rusty lock gave a hoarse groan and the door creaked. The banker expected instantly to hear a cry of surprise and the sound of steps. Three minutes passed and it was as quiet inside as it had been before. He made up his mind to enter.

Before the table sat a man, unlike an ordinary human being. It was a skeleton, with tight-drawn skin, with long curly hair like a woman's, and a shaggy beard. The colour of his face was yellow, of an earthly shade; the cheeks were sunken, the back long and narrow, and the hand upon which he leaned his hairy head was so lean and skinny that it was painful to look upon. His hair was already silvering with grey, and no one who glanced at the senile emaciation of the face would have believed that he was only forty years old. On the table, before his bended head, lay a sheet of paper on which something was written in a tiny hand.

"Poor devil," thought the banker, "he's asleep and probably seeing millions in his dreams. I have only to take and throw this half-dead thing on the bed, smother him a moment with the pillow, and the most careful examination will find no trace of unnatural death. But, first, let us read when he has written here."

The banker took the sheet from the table and read:

"To-morrow at twelve o'clock midnight, I shall obtain my freedom and the right to mix with people. But before I leave this room and see the sun I think it necessary to say a few words to you. On my own clear conscience and before God who sees me I declare to you that I despise freedom, life, health, and all that your books call the blessings of the world.

"For fifteen years I have diligently studied earthly life. True, I saw neither the earth nor the people, but in your books I drank fragrant wine, sang songs, hunted deer and wild boar in the forests, loved women. . . . And beautiful women, like clouds ethereal, created by the magic of your poets' genius, visited me by night and whispered to me wonderful tales, which made my head drunken. In your books I climbed the summits of Elbruz and mont Blanc and saw from there how the sun rose in the morning, and in the evening, suffused the sky, the ocean and the mountain ridges with a purple gold. I saw from there how above me lightnings glimmered cleaving the clouds; I saw green forests, fields, rivers, lakes, cities; I heard sirens singing, and the playing of the pipes of Pan; I touched the wings of beautiful devils who came flying to me to speak of God. . . . In your books I cast myself into bottomless abysses, worked miracles, burned cities to the ground, preached new religions, conquered whole countries. . . .

"Your books gave me wisdom. All that unwearying human thought created in the centuries is compressed to a little lump in my skull. I know that I am cleverer than you all.

"And I despise your books, despise all worldly blessings and wisdom. Everything is void, frail, visionary and delusive as a mirage. Though you be proud and wise and beautiful, yet will death wipe you from the face of the earth like the mice underground; and your posterity, your history, and the immortality of your men of genius will be as frozen slag, burnt down together with the terrestrial globe.

"You are mad, and gone the wrong way. You take falsehood for truth and ugliness for beauty. You would marvel if suddenly apple and orange trees should bear frogs and lizards instead of fruit, and if roses should begin to breathe the odour of a sweating horse. So do I marvel at you, who have bartered heaven for earth. I do not want to understand you.

"That I may show you in deed my contempt for that by which you live, I waive the two millions of which I once dreamed as of paradise, and which I now despise. That I may deprive myself of my right to them, I shall come out from here five minutes before the stipulated term, and thus shall violate the agreement."

When he had read, the banker put the sheet on the table, kissed the head of the strange man, and began to weep. He went out of the wing. Never at any other time, not even after his terrible losses on the Exchange, had he felt such contempt for himself as now. Coming home, he lay down on his bed, but agitation and tears kept him a long time from sleeping. . . .

The next morning the poor watchman came running to him and told him that they had seen the man who lived in the wing climb through the window into the garden. He had gone to the gate and disappeared. The banker instantly went with his servants to the wing and established the escape of his prisoner. To avoid unnecessary rumours he took the paper with the renunciation from the table and, on his return, locked it in his safe.

Christian Perspectives

1. Chekhov said that "a Russian story is always the story of the undoing of a life." How does "The Bet" demonstrate Chekhov's statement?
2. The lawyer's earlier opinion was that, "It's better to live somehow than not at all." Did his view change after his imprisonment?
3. Although the actual events in the story are unlikely, the message gives us something to ponder about our own lives that "go the wrong way." It was only through completely isolating himself from mankind that the lawyer saw man bartering "heaven for earth." Can we mentally, emotionally, and spiritually set ourselves apart from the mainstream and analyze what is important and what is not important? How can we do this?
4. The banker appears to be changed after he reads the lawyer's renunciation; however, why did the lawyer hide the paper "to avoid unnecessary rumors"?

Adapting to the World Without from Within

THE RIDDLE OF INEQUALITY
Paul Tillich

For to him who has will more be given; and from him who has not, even what he has will be taken away.

—Mark iv, 25

One day a learned colleague called me up and said to me with angry excitement: "There is a saying in the New Testament which I consider to be one of the most immoral and unjust statements ever made!" And then he started quoting our text: "To him who has will more be given," and his anger increased when he continued: "and from him who has not, even what he has will be taken away." We all, I think, feel offended with him. And we cannot easily ignore the offense by suggesting what *he* suggested—that the words may be due to a misunderstanding of the disciples. It appears at least four times in the gospels with great emphasis. And even more, we can clearly see that the writers of the gospels felt exactly as we do. For them it was a stumbling block, which they tried to interpret in different ways. Probably none of these explanations satisfied them fully, for with this saying of Jesus, we are confronted immediately with the greatest and perhaps most painful riddle of life, that of the inequality of all beings. We certainly cannot hope to solve it when neither the Bible nor any other of the great religions and philosophies was able to do so. But we can do two things: We can show the breadth and the depth of the riddle of inequality and we can try to find a way to live with it, even if it is unsolved.

I

If we hear the words, "to him who has will more be given," we ask ourselves: What *do* we have? And then we may find that much is given to us in terms of external goods, of friends, of intellectual gifts and even of a comparatively high moral level of action. So we can expect that more will be given to us, while we must expect that those who are lacking in all that will lose the little they already have. Even further, according to Jesus' parable, the one talent they have will be given to us who have five or ten talents. We shall be richer because they will be poorer. We may cry out against such an injustice. But we cannot deny that life confirms it abundantly. We cannot deny it, but we can ask the question, do we *really* have what we believe we have so that it

169

cannot be taken from us? It is a question full of anxiety, confirmed by a version of our text rendered by Luke. "From him who has not, even what he *thinks* that he has will be taken away." Perhaps our having of those many things is not the kind of having which is increased. Perhaps the having of few things by the poor ones is the kind of having which makes them grow. In the parable of the talents, Jesus confirms this. Those talents which are used, even with a risk of losing them, are those which we really have; those which we try to preserve without using them for growth are those which we do not really have and which are being taken away from us. They slowly disappear, and suddenly we feel that we have lost these talents, perhaps forever.

Let us apply this to our own life, whether it is long or short. In the memory of all of us many things appear which we had without having them and which were taken away from us. Some of them became lost because of the tragic limitations of life; we had to sacrifice them in order to make other things grow. We all were given childish innocence; but innocence cannot be used and increased. The growth of our lives is possible only because we have sacrificed the original gift of innocence. Nevertheless, sometimes there arises in us a melancholy longing for a purity which has been taken from us. We all were given youthful enthusiasm for many things and aims. But this also cannot be used and increased. Most of the objects of our early enthusiasm must be sacrificed for a few, and the few must be approached with soberness. No maturity is possible without this sacrifice. Yet often a melancholy longing for the lost possibilities and enthusiasm takes hold of us. Innocence and youthful enthusiasm: we had them and had them not. Life itself demanded that they were taken from us.

But there are other things which we had and which were taken from us, because we let them go through our own guilt. Some of us had a deep sensitivity for the wonder of life as it is revealed in nature. Slowly under the pressure of work and social life and the lure of cheap pleasures, we lose the wonder of our earlier years when we felt intense joy and the presence of the mystery of life through the freshness of the young day or the glory of the dying day, the majesty of the mountains or the infinity of the sea, a flower breaking through the soil or a young animal in the perfection of its movements. Perhaps we try to produce such feelings again, but we are empty and do not succeed. We had it and had it not, and it has been taken from us.

Others had the same experience with music, poetry, the great novels and plays. One wanted to devour all of them, one lived in them and created for oneself a life above the daily life. We *had* all this and did not have it; we did not let it grow; our love towards it was not strong enough and so it was taken from us.

Many, especially in this group, remember a time in which the desire to learn to solve the riddles of the universe, to find truth has been the driving force in their lives. They came to college and university, not in order to buy their entrance ticket into the upper middle classes or in order to provide for the preconditions of social and economic success, but they came, driven by the desire for knowledge. They had something and more could have been given to them. But in reality they did not have it. They did not make it grow and so it was taken from them and they finished their academic work in terms of expediency and indifference towards truth. Their love for truth has left them and in some moments they are sick in their hearts because they realize that what they have lost they may never get back.

We all know that any deeper relation to a human being needs watchfulness and growth, otherwise it is taken away from us. And we cannot get it back. This is a form of having and not having which is the root of innumerable human tragedies. We all know about them. And there is another, the most fundamental kind of having and not having—our having and losing God.

Perhaps we were rich towards God in our childhood and beyond it. We may remember the moments in which we felt his ultimate presence. We may remember prayers with an overflowing heart, the encounter with the holy in word and music and holy places. We had communication with God; but it was taken from us because we had it and had it not. We did not let it grow, and so it slowly disappeared leaving and empty space. We became unconcerned, cynical, indifferent, not because we doubted about our religious traditions—such doubt belongs to being rich towards God—but because we turned away from that which once concerned us infinitely.

Such thoughts are a first step in approaching the riddle of inequality. Those who have, receive more if they really have it, if they use it and make it grow. And those who have not, lose what they have because they never had it really.

II

But the question of inequality is not yet answered. For one now asks: Why do some receive more than others in the very beginning, before there is even the possibility of using or wasting our talents? Why does the one servant receive five talents and the other two and the third one? Why is the one born in the slums and the other in a well-to-do suburban family? It does not help to answer that of those to whom much is given much is demanded and little of those to whom little is given. For it is just this inequality of original gifts, internal and external, which arouses our question. Why is it given to one human being to gain so much more out of his being human than to another one? Why is so much given to the one that much *can* be asked of him, while to the other one little is given and little *can* be asked? If this question is asked, not only about individual men but also about classes, races and nations, the everlasting question of political inequality arises, and with it the many ways appear in which men have tried to abolish inequality. In every revolution and in every war, the will to solve the riddle of inequality is a driving force. But neither war nor revolution can remove it. Even if we imagine that in an indefinite future most social inequalities are conquered, three things remain: the inequality of talents in body and mind, the inequality created by freedom and destiny, and the fact that all generations before the time of such equality would be excluded from its blessings. This would be the greatest possible inequality! No! In face of one of the deepest and most torturing problems of life, it is unpermittably shallow and foolish to escape into a social dreamland. We have to live now; we have to live this our life, and we must face today the riddle of inequality.

Let us not confuse the riddle of inequality with the fact that each of us is a unique incomparable self. Certainly our being individuals belongs to our dignity as men. It is given to us and must be used and intensified and not drowned in the gray waters of conformity which threaten us today. One should defend every individuality and the uniqueness of every human self. But one should not believe that this is a way of solving the riddle of inequality. Unfortunately, there are social and political reactionaries who use this confusion in order to justify social injustice. They are at least as foolish as the dreamers of a future removal of inequality. Whoever has seen hospitals, prisons, sweatshops, battlefields, houses for the insane, starvation, family tragedies, moral aberrations should be cured from any confusion of the gift of individuality with the riddle of inequality. He should be cured from any feelings of easy consolation.

III

And now we must make the third step in our attempt to penetrate the riddle of inequality and ask: Why do some use and increase what was given to them, while others do not, so that it

171

is taken from them? Why does God say to the prophet in our Old Testament lesson that the ears and eyes of a nation are made insensible for the divine message?

Is it enough to answer: Because some use their freedom responsibly and do what they ought to do while others fail through their own guilt? Is this answer, which seems so obvious, sufficient? Now let me first say that it *is* sufficient if we apply it to ourselves. Each of us must consider the increase or the loss of what is given to him as a matter of his own responsibility. Our conscience tells us that we cannot put the blame for our losses on anybody or anything else than ourselves.

But if we look at others, this answer is not sufficient. On the contrary: If we applied the judgment which we *must* apply to anyone else we would be like the Pharisee in Jesus' parable. You cannot tell somebody who comes to you in distress about himself: Use what has been given to you; for he may come to you just because he is unable to do so! And you cannot tell those who are in despair about what they are: Be something else; for this is just what despair means — the inability of getting rid of oneself. You cannot tell those who did not conquer the destructive influences of their surroundings and were driven into crime and misery that they should have been stronger; for it was just of this strength they had been deprived by heritage or environment. Certainly they all are men, and to all of them freedom is given; but they all are also subject to destiny. It is not up to us to condemn them because they were free, as it is not up to us to excuse them because they were under their destiny. We cannot judge them. And when we judge ourselves, we must be conscious that even this is not the last word, but that we like them are under an ultimate judgment. In it the riddle of inequality is eternally answered. But this answer is not ours. It is our predicament that we must ask. And we ask with an uneasy conscience. Why are they in misery, why not we? Thinking of some who are near to us, we can ask: Are we partly responsible? But even if we are, it does not solve the riddle of inequality. The uneasy conscience asks about the farthest as well as about the nearest: Why they, why not we?

Why has my child, or any of millions and millions of children, died before even having a chance to grow out of infancy? Why is my child, or any child, born feeble-minded or crippled? Why has my friend or relative, or anybody's friend or relative, disintegrated in his mind and lost both his freedom and his destiny? Why has my son or daughter, gifted as I believe with many talents, wasted them and been deprived of them? And why does this happen to any parent at all? Why have this boy's or this girl's creative powers been broken by a tyrannical father or by a possessive mother?

In all these questions it is not the question of our own misery which we ask. It is not the question: Why has this happened to *me?*

It is not the question of Job which God answers by humiliating him and then by elevating him into communion with him. It is not the old and urgent question: Where is the divine justice, where is the divine love towards me? But it is almost the opposite question: Why has this *not* happened to me, why has it happened to the other one, to the innumerable other ones to whom not even the power of Job is given to accept the divine answer? Why — and Jesus has asked the same question — are many called and few elected?

He does not answer; he only states that this is the human predicament. Shall we therefore cease to ask and humbly accept the fact of a divine judgment which condemns most human beings away from the community with him into despair and self-destruction? Can we accept the eternal victory of judgment over love? We cannot; and nobody ever could, even if he preached and threatened in these terms. As long as he could not see himself with complete certainty as eternally rejected, his preaching and threatening would be self-deceiving. And who could see himself eternally rejected?

But if this is not the solution of the riddle of inequality at its deepest level, can we trespass the boundaries of the Christian tradition and listen to those who tell us that this life does not decide about our eternal destiny? There will be occasions in other lives, as our present life is determined by previous ones and what we have achieved or wasted in them. It is a serious doctrine and not completely strange to Christianity. But if we don't know and never will know what each of us has been in the previous or future lives, then it is not really *our* destiny which develops from life to life, but in each life it is the destiny of someone else. This answer also does not solve the riddle of inequality.

There is no answer at all if we ask about the temporal and eternal destiny of the single being separated from the destiny of the whole. Only in the unity of all beings in time and eternity can a humanly possible answer to the riddle of inequality be found. *Humanly* possible does not mean an answer which removes the riddle of inequality, but an answer with which we can live.

There is an ultimate unity of all beings, rooted in the divine life from which they come and to which they go. All beings, nonhuman as well as human, participate in it. And therefore they all participate in each other. We participate in each other's having and we participate in each other's not-having. If we become aware of this unity of all beings, something happens. The fact that others have-not changes in every moment the character of my having: It undercuts its security, it drives me beyond myself, to understand, to give, to share, to help. The fact that others fall into sin, crime and misery changes the character of the grace which is given to me: It makes me realize my own hidden guilt, it shows to me that those who suffer for their sin and crime, suffer also for me: for I am guilty of their guilt — at least in the desire of my heart — and ought to suffer as they do. The awareness that others who *could* have become fully developed human beings and never *have,* changes my state of full humanity. Their early death, their early or late disintegration, makes my life and my health a continuous risk, a dying which is not yet death, a disintegration which is not yet destruction. In every death which we encounter, something of us dies; in every disease which we encounter, something of us tends to disintegrate.

Can we live with this answer? We can to the degree in which we are liberated from the seclusion within ourselves. But nobody can be liberated from himself unless he is grasped by the power of that which is present in everyone and everything — the eternal from which we come and to which we go, which gives us to ourselves and which liberates us *from* ourselves. It is the greatness and the heart of the Christian message that God — as manifest in the Cross of the Christ — participates totally in the dying child, in the condemned criminal, in the disintegrating mind, in the starving one and in him who rejects him. There is no extreme human condition into which the divine presence would not reach. This is what the Cross, the most extreme of all human conditions, tells us. The riddle of inequality cannot be solved on the level of our separation from each other. It is eternally solved in the divine participating in all of us and every being. The certainty of the divine participation gives us the courage to stand the riddle of inequality, though finite minds cannot solve it. Amen.

Christian Perspectives

1. Respond to Tillich's example of the college student who comes to college "driven by the desire for knowledge." Are you that kind of student; or are you, as Tillich says, providing for the "preconditions of social and economic success"? How do you maintain a genuine search for truth without losing it?
2. Tillich confronts some very difficult theological questions by developing his argument into three parts. Identify his premise for each part. (Identify the method of development he uses for each premise: definition, cause and effect, classification, division, comparison, contrast, analogy, support, and illustration.)
3. Identify Tillich's strategies of persuasion: ethos, logos, and pathos. How does he appeal to each?
4. Our individually-oriented society makes Tillich's view of human participation unconventional. He says that as we become aware of the unity of all beings we become liberated from the "seclusion within ourselves." What does he mean?

SONNET XIX

John Milton

When I consider how my light is spent,[1]
    Ere halt my days, in this dark world and wide,
    And that one Talent which is death to hide,[2]
    Lodg'd with me useless, though my Soul more bent
To serve therewith my Maker, and present
    My true account, lest be returning chide;
    "Doth God exact day-labor, light denied."
    I fondly[3] ask; But patience to prevent
That murmur, soon replies, "God doth not need
    Either man's work or his own gifts; who best
    Bear his mild yoke, they serve him best; his State
Is Kingly. Thousands at his bidding speed
    And post o'er Land and Ocean without rest:
They also serve who only stand and wait."

1. Milton was blind when he wrote this sonnet.
2. See Matthew 25:14–36 and Luke 12:35–40.
3. Foolishly.

Christian Perspectives

1. Milton's complaint against God expecting too much of him culminates in what statement?
2. What adverb undercuts his complaint? Why would Milton call his own complaining "foolish"?
3. Patience is personified here, as if it is an exterior speaker; but if Patience is a virtue of the spirit, is it not an inward voice? And if Patience "prevent[s]" the "murmur," does Milton ever really state his complaint to God?
4. On tracing the entire dialogue, would you say this poem represents more Milton's complaint to God about his blindness, or an inward meditation in which a virtue strengthens Milton's spirit with its particular, and needed, power. Look up the etemology of *virtue* to see how it comes from words meaning power or strength (also see Luke 6:19 and Mark 5:30 in the King James Version).
5. Why is the virtue personified in the poem, patience—not goodness, love, or kindness or one of the other virtues?

THE RISK OF LOSS

M. Scott Peck, M.D.

The act of love—extending oneself—as I have said, requires a moving out against the inertia of laziness (work) or the resistance engendered by fear (courage). Let us turn now from the work of love to the courage of love. When we extend ourselves, our self enters new and unfamiliar territory, so to speak. Our self becomes a new and different self. We do things we are not accustomed to do. We change. The experience of change, of unaccustomed activity, of being on unfamiliar ground, of doing things differently is frightening. It always was and always will be. People handle their fears of change in different ways, but the fear is inescapable if they are in fact to change. Courage is not the absence of fear; it is the making of action in spite of fear, the moving out against the resistance engendered by fear in the unknown and into the future. On some level spiritual growth, and therefore love, always requires courage and involves risk. It is the risking of love that we will now consider.

If you are a regular churchgoer you might notice a woman in her late forties who every Sunday exactly five minutes before the start of the service inconspicuously takes the same seat in a side pew on the aisle at the very back of the church. The moment the service is over she quietly but quickly makes for the door and is gone before any of the other parishioners and before the minister can come out onto the steps to meet with his flock. Should you manage to accost her—which is unlikely—and invite her to the coffee social hour following the service, she would thank you politely, nervously looking away from you, but tell you that she has a pressing engagement, and would then dash away. Were you to follow her toward her pressing engagement you would find that she returns directly to her home, a little apartment where the blinds are always drawn, unlocks her door, enters, immediately locks the door behind her, and is not seen again that Sunday. If you could keep watch over her you might see that she has a job as a low ranking typist in a large office, where she accepts her assignments wordlessly, types them

175

faultlessly, and returns her finished work without comment. She eats her lunch at her desk and has no friends. She walks home, stopping always at the same impersonal supermarket for a few provisions before she vanishes behind her door until she appears again for the next day's work. On Saturday afternoons she goes alone to a local movie theater that has a weekly change of shows. She has a TV set. She has no phone. She almost never receives mail. Were you somehow able to communicate with her and comment that her life seemed lonely, she would tell you that she rather enjoyed her loneliness. If you asked her if she didn't even have any pets, she would tell you that she had had a dog of whom she was very fond but that he had died eight years before and no other dog could take his place.

Who is this woman? We do not know the secrets of her heart. What we do know is that her whole life is devoted to avoiding risks and that in this endeavor, rather than enlarging her self, she has narrowed and diminished it almost to the point of nonexistence. She cathects no other living thing. Now we have said that simple cathexis is not love, that love transcends cathexis. This is true, but love requires cathexis for a beginning. We can love only that which in one way or another has importance for us. But with cathexis there is always the risk of loss or rejection. If you move out to another human being, there is always the risk that that person will move away from you, leaving you more painfully alone than you were before. Love anything that lives — a person, a pet, a plant — and it will die. Trust anybody and you may be hurt; depend on anyone and that one may let you down. The price of cathexis is pain. If someone is determined not to risk pain, then such a person must do without many things: having children, getting married, the ecstasy of sex, the hope of ambition, friendship — all that makes life alive, meaningful and significant. Move out or grow in any dimension and pain as well as joy will be your reward. A full life will be full of pain. But the only alternative is not to live fully or not to live at all.

The essence of life is change, a panoply of growth and decay. Elect life and growth, and you elect change and the prospect of death. A likely determinant for the isolated, narrow life of the woman described as an experience or series of experiences with death which she found so painful that she was determined never to experience death again, even at the cost of living. In avoiding the experience of death she had to avoid growth and change. She elected a life of sameness free from the new, the unexpected, a living death, without risk or challenge. I have said that the attempt to avoid legitimate suffering lies at the root of all emotional illness. Not surprisingly, most psychotherapy patients (and probably most nonpatients, since neurosis is the norm rather than the exception) have a problem, whether they are young or old, in facing the reality of death squarely and clearly. What is surprising is that the psychiatric literature is only beginning to examine the significance of this phenomenon. If we can live with the knowledge that death is our constant companion, traveling on our "left shoulder," then death can become in the words of Don Juan, our "ally," still fearsome but continually a source of wise counsel. With death's counsel, the constant awareness of the limit of our time to live and love, we can always be guided to make the best use of our time and live life to the fullest. But if we are unwilling to fully face the fearsome presence of death on our left shoulder, we deprive ourselves of its counsel and cannot possibly live or love with clarity. When we shy away from death, the ever-changing nature of things, we inevitably shy away from life.

Christian Perspectives

1. In this excerpt from *The Road Less Traveled*, Peck demonstrates some of the paradoxical truths of Christianity: We must die to live: we must lose to gain. What are some ways that we are expected to live out these principles?
2. Peck says that "the attempt to avoid legitimate suffering lies at the root of all emotional illness." Therefore to adapt to the world without, we must not avoid risks in an attempt to spare ourselves pain. Compare Peck's analogy of the women to the servant in Jesus' parable in Matthew 25 who hid his talent. What were both trying to do? What happened instead?

RETURNING TO CHURCH

Dan Wakefield

Just before Christmas of 1980, I was sitting in the Sevens, a neighborhood bar on Beacon Hill (don't all these stories of revelation begin in bars?), when a housepainter named Tony remarked out of the blue that he wanted to find a place to go to mass on Christmas Eve. I didn't say anything, but a thought came into my mind, as swift and unexpected as it was unfamiliar: *I'd like to do that, too.*

I had not gone to church since leaving my boyhood Protestant faith as a rebellious Columbia College intellectual more than a quarter-century before, yet I found myself that Christmas Eve in King's Chapel, which I finally selected from the ads on The Boston Globe religion page because it seemed least threatening. It was Unitarian, I knew the minister slightly as a neighbor, and I assumed "Candlelight Service" meant nothing more religiously challenging than carol singing.

As it happened, the Rev. Carl Scovel gave a sermon about "the latecomers" to the church on a text from an Evelyn Waugh novel called "Helena." I slunk down in my pew, literally beginning to shiver from what I thought was only embarrassment at feeling singled out for personal attention, and discomfort at being in alien surroundings. It turned out that I had a temperature of 102 that kept me in bed for three days with a violent case of the flu and a fearful suspicion that church was a very dangerous place, at least if you weren't used to it.

Perhaps my flesh was rebelling against this unaccustomed intrusion of spirit. Certainly going to church was out of character for me. My chosen public image was the jacket photo of "Starting Over," my novel about a divorced man seeking salvation through drugs, alcohol and promiscuity. I proudly posed for the picture in 1973 at my new living room bar, flanked by bottles of favorite vodkas, bourbons and burgundies. It did not look like the picture of a man who was headed to church.

In the year that led to my going to the Christmas Eve service, I felt I was headed for the edge of a cliff. I could have scored at the top of those magazine tests that list the greatest stresses of life, for that year saw the dissolution of a seven-year relationship with the woman I had fully expected to live with the rest of my life. I ran out of money, left the work I was doing, the

177

house I owned, and the city I was living in, and attended the funeral of my father in May and my mother in November.

In the midst of this chaos, I one day grabbed an old Bible from among my books, and with a desperate instinct turned to the 23rd Psalm. It brought a sense of relief, and sometimes I recited it in my mind in the months that followed, but it did not give me any sense that I suddenly believed in God. It simply seemed an isolated source of solace and calm, such as any great poem might be. It certainly did not give rise to the notion of anything as radical as going to church.

After my Christmas Eve experience at King's Chapel, I didn't get up the nerve to go back again until Easter. I did not have any attacks of shivering or chills in the spring sunshine of that service, so it seemed that even as a "latecomer" and former avowed atheist, I could safely enter a place regarded as a house of God. Still, the prospect was discomforting. My two initial trips of return had been on major holidays, occasions when "regular" people went to church, simply in observance of tradition. To go back again meant crossing the Boston Common on a non-holiday Sunday morning wearing a suit and tie, a giveaway sign of churchgoing. I did it furtively, as if I were engaged in something that would not be approved of by my peers. I hoped they would all be home doing brunch and the Sunday papers, so I would not be "caught in the act." I recalled the remark of William F. Buckley Jr. in a television interview that if you mention God more than once at New York dinner parties, you aren't invited back.

To my surprise, I recognized neighbors and even some people I considered friends at church, on a "regular" Sunday. I had simply assumed I did not know people who went to church, yet here they were, with intellects intact, worshiping God. Once inside the church myself, I understood the appeal. No doubt my friends and neighbors found, as I did, relief and refreshment in connecting with age-old rituals, reciting psalms and singing hymns. There was a calm reassurance in the stately language of the litanies and chants of the Book of Common Prayer. (King's Chapel is "Unitarian in theology, Anglican in worship, and congregational in governance," a historical Boston amalgam that will be three centuries old next June.) I was grateful for the sense of shared reverence, of reaching beyond one's flimsy physical presence, while praying with a whole congregation.

I began to appreciate what was meant by the church as "sanctuary." The word itself took on new resonance for me; when I later heard of the "sanctuary" movement of New England churches offering shelter to Central American political refugees, I thought of the kind of private refuge that fortunate citizens like myself find in church from the daily assaults of business and personal pressures and worries, the psychic guerrilla warfare of everyday life.

Caught in an escalation of that kind of battle in my own professional campaigns (more painful because so clearly brought on by my own blundering), I joined the church in May 1982, not wanting to wait until the second Christmas Eve anniversary of my entry, as I had planned. I wanted the immediate sense of safety and refuge implied in belonging, being a member — perhaps like getting a passport and fleeing to a powerful embassy in the midst of some chaotic revolution.

Going to church, even belonging to it, did not solve life's problems — if anything, they seemed to intensify around this time — but it gave me a sense of living in a larger context, of being part of something greater than what I could see through the tunnel vision of my personal concerns. I now looked forward to Sunday because it *meant* going to church; what once was strange now felt not only natural but essential. Even more remarkably, the practice of regular attendance at Sunday services, which such a short time ago seemed religiously "excessive," no longer seemed enough. Whatever it was I was getting from church on Sunday morning, I wanted — needed, it felt like — more of it.

I experienced what is a common phenomenon for people who in some way or other begin a journey of the kind I so unexpectedly found myself on — a feeling simply and best described as a "thirst" for spiritual understanding and contact; to put it bluntly, I guess, *for God.* I noticed in the church bulletin an announcement of a Bible-study class in the parish house, and I went one stormy autumn evening to find myself with only the church's young seminarian on hand and one other parishioner. Rather than being disappointed by the tiny turnout, as I ordinarily would have been, I thought of the words "Where two or three are gathered together in My name, there am I in the midst of them," and I felt an interior glow that the pouring rain outside and occasional claps of thunder only made seem more vital and precious. I don't remember what text we studied that evening, but I can still smell the rain and the coffee and feel the aura of light and warmth.

Later in the season, I attended a Bible-study session the minister led for a gathering of about 20 people on the story of Abraham and Isaac, and I came away with a sense of the awesomeness and power of faith, a quality that loomed above me as tremendous and hard and challenging and tangibly real as mountains. The Bible-study classes, which I later, with other parishioners, learned to lead on occasion myself, became a source of power, like tapping into a rich vein.

Bible study was not like examining history, but holding up a mirror to my own life, a mirror in which I sometimes saw things I was trying to keep hidden, even from myself. The first scripture passage I was assigned to lead was from Luke, about the man who cleans his house of demons, and seven worse ones come. I did not have any trouble relating this to "contemporary life." It sounded like an allegory about a man who had stopped drinking and so was enjoying much better health, but took up smoking marijuana to "relax," all the while feeling good and even self-righteous about giving up the booze. It was my own story. I realized, with a shock, how I'd been deceiving myself, how much more "housecleaning" I had to do.

I was not only going to church and devoting time to Bible study and prayer during this period, I was actively engaged in purely secular programs of physical and mental therapy and "personal growth" to try to pull myself out of the pit I found myself in when I fled home to Boston in the spring of 1980. I got into an Exercycle and diet program that in six months cut my pulse rate from a dangerously stress-induced 120 to a healthy 60, and shed 20 pounds. I gave up the alcohol that I had used as regularly and purposely as daily medicine for 25 years, then gave up the marijuana that replaced it, and even threw away the faithful briar pipe I had clenched and puffed for a quarter of a century.

I used to worry about which of these addictions I kicked through "church" and which through secular programs, as if I had to assign proper "credit," and as if it were possible to compartmentalize and isolate the influence of God, like some kind of vitamin. The one thing I know about the deepest feeling connected with all my assortment of life-numbing addictions is that at some point or other they felt as if they were "lifted," taken away, and instead of having to exercise iron control to resist them, it simply felt better not to have to do them anymore. The only concept I know to describe such experience is that of "grace," and the accompanying adjective "amazing" comes to mind along with it.

I do not for a moment suggest that giving up booze or even drugs, or losing weight or reducing the heart rate is necessarily — or even desirably — a byproduct of religious experience.

For many people, such effects may not have anything to do with religion. Each person's quest is his own, with its own imperatives and directions.

I became fascinated by other people's spiritual experiences and, 30 years after it was first recommended to me, I read Thomas Merton's "The Seven Storey Mountain." I had avoided it even when the late poet Mark Van Doren, my favorite professor and Merton's former mentor at Columbia, had spoken of it with high regard, but now I devoured it, and went on to read everything else of Merton's I could get my hands on, from the sociopolitical "Conjectures of a Guilty Bystander" to the mystical "The Ascent to Truth." Most meaningful of all was a slim "meditation" by Merton, called "He Is Risen," which I found by chance in a New York bookstore; it says in matter-of-fact prose that Christ "is in history with us, walking ahead of us to where we are going. . . ."

I thought of these words walking the brick sidewalks of Beacon Hill, thinking for the first time of my life as a "journey" rather than a battle I was winning or losing that moment, on whose immediate crashing outcome the fate of the universe (i.e., the turbulent one in my own head) depended. I remembered years ago reading Dorothy Day's column in The Catholic Worker when I lived in Greenwich Village, and I appreciated now for the first time the sense of the title: "On Pilgrimage."

I cannot pinpoint any particular time when I suddenly believed in God again while all this was going on. I only know that such belief seemed as natural as for 25 or more years before it had been inconceivable. I realized this while looking at fish.

I had gone with my girlfriend of the last several years to the New England Aquarium, and as we gazed at the astonishingly brilliant colors of some of the small tropical fish—reds and yellows and oranges and blues that seemed to be splashed on by some innovative artistic genius— and watched the amazing lights of the flashlight fish that blinked on like the beacons of some creature of a sci-fi epic, I wondered how anyone could think that all this was the result of some chain of accidental explosions! Yet I realized in frustration that to try to convince me otherwise five years before would have been hopeless. Was this what they called "Conversion?"

The term bothered me because it suggested being "born again," and like many of my contemporaries, I have been put off by what seems the melodramatic nature of that label, as well as the current political beliefs that seem to go along with it. Besides, I don't *feel* "reborn." No voice came out of the sky nor did a thunderclap strike me on the path through the Boston Common on the way to King's Chapel. I was relieved when our minister explained that the literal translation of "conversion" in both the Hebrew and Greek is not "rebirth" but "turning." That's what this has felt like—as if I were walking in one direction and then, in response to some inner pull, I turned—not even all the way around, but only at what seemed a slightly different angle.

I wish I could say that this turning has put me on a straight, solid path; with blue skies above and a warm, benevolent sun shining down. I certainly enjoy better health than when I began to "turn" five years ago, but the path I am on now seems often as dangerous and difficult as the one I was following before. Sometimes it doesn't even seem like a path at all. Sometimes I feel like a hapless passenger in the sort of small airplane they used to show in black and white movies of the 1930's, caught in a thunderstorm, bobbing through the night sky over jagged mountains without a compass.

I find strength in the hard wisdom of those who have delved much deeper into the spiritual realm than I, like Henri Nouwen, the Dutch Roman Catholic theologian who wrote in a book our minister recommended, called "Reaching Out," that ". . . it would be just another illusion to believe that reaching out to God will free us from pain and suffering. Often, indeed, it

180

will take us where we rather would not go. But we know that without going there we will not find our life."

I was thrilled to meet Nouwen at lunch a few years ago, through the consideration of my friend and neighbor James Carroll, the former priest, now novelist. I told Father Nouwen I had read and appreciated his work, but that it dismayed me to read of his anguish in "Cry for Mercy: Prayers from the Genessee"; it made me wonder with discouragement what chance a neophyte had in pursuit of the spiritual, when someone as advanced as Father Nouwen experienced anguish and confusion in his relation to God (I was neglecting numerous other, even more powerful examples, such as Jesus Christ calling out from the cross). Father Nouwen answered sharply that contrary to what many people may think, "Christianity is not for getting your life together!"

About a year ago, I felt as if finally, with God's help, I was on the right track in my own journey. Then I had an experience that was like running head-on into a wall. First, shock, then a kind of psychic pain as unrelenting as a dentist's drill. And in the torment I prayed, and there was no relief, and twice I turned back to my old way of dealing with things, by trying to numb the pain with drugs. Throughout all this, I never lost faith in God, never imagined He was not there, but only that His presence was obscured. Then the storm broke, like a fever, and I felt in touch again, and in the light. I was grateful, but I also knew such storms would come again, perhaps even more violently.

I learned that belief in God does not depend on how well things are going, that faith and prayer and good works do not necessarily have any correlation to earthly reward or even tranquility, no matter how much we wish they would and think they should. I believe in God because the gift of faith (if not the gift of understanding) has been given to me, and I go to church and pray and meditate to try to be closer to His presence, and, most difficult to all, to discern His will. I know, as it says in the Book of Common Prayer, that His "service is perfect freedom," and my great frustration and anxiety is in the constant choices of how best to serve, with the particular gifts as well as limitations I've been given.

A month or so ago, I went to Glastonbury Abbey, a Benedictine monastery in Hingham, only 40 minutes or so from Boston, to spend a day and night in private retreat. I went with about 17 questions in my head about following God or the path He wills us to take. In the chapel bookstore, I saw a thin paperback volume, "Abandonment to Divine Providence," which I picked up, took to my room and devoured. It was written by an 18th-century Jesuit named Jean-Pierre de Caussade, and it sounds (at least in this new translation) as if it had been written yesterday, specifically to answer my questions. I continue to read in it almost every day, and I always find some new passage that seems to speak to the urgency of that moment. This is what I read today, when I felt again jarred and confused about what to choose and where to turn:

"So we follow our wandering paths, and the very darkness acts as our guide and our doubts serve to reassure us. The more puzzled Isaac was at not finding a lamb for the sacrifice, the more confidently did Abraham leave all to providence."

181

Christian Perspectives

1. Wakefield's essay begins with returning to church, but it is really about his journey of faith. Identify his use of setting to communicate to his concept of a journey.
2. Wakefield says that his path of faith "seems often as dangerous and difficult as the one I was following before." Do you find this statement to be true in your own life?
3. As his faith grows, Wakefield turns to Christian writings from the past, and he is surprised by their timelessness. Why is their relevance particularly surprising to Wakefield? (Remember his former impression of the church.)
4. Wakefield said that he knew he believed in God when he saw fish. How does this seemingly ordinary observation reveal an extraordinary truth about himself? (See 2 Corinthians 5:17.)

MAKING CONNECTIONS

1. Using the excerpt from Milton's *Aeropagitica* and Malcolm X's "Freedom through Learning to Read," defend the reading of secular literature in Christian schools.
2. "The Risk of Loss" demonstrates the philosophy of those who are unwilling to take risks. What are some other, less visible ways that we avoid risks?
3. Garrison Keillor and Langston Hughes respond to their childhood religious upbringing from different perspectives. Write about an experience of your own using Keillor's humor and acceptance, or Hughes' sense of disillusionment.
4. Discuss the theme of anonymity that is present in the works "I'm Nobody," and "Unknown Citizen." How are these poems indicative of themes in modern literature and popular music?
5. Write a make believe dialogue between Dan Wakefield and Matthew Arnold. What would these writers say to each other about faith?

From PARADISE LOST
John Milton

The following lines, taken from Books 11 and 12 of John Milton's *Paradise Lost,* reveal the poet's treatment of an archetypal loss and adjustment. Adam and Eve, told they must forsake Paradise, react with despair. They are promised by Michael that they may yet find grace, but his instruction must lead them to give up the security of their original home and, by obedience and experience, establish a "paradise within" where the presence of God is known in a new way.

[Michael] pronounces to Adam and Eve their exile from Paradise]

> *Adam*, Heav'n's high behest no Preface needs:
> Sufficient that thy Prayers are heard, and Death,
> Then due by sentence when thou didst transgress,
> Defeated of his seizure many days
> Giv'n thee of Grace, wherein thou mayst repent,
> And one bad act with many deeds well done
> May'st cover: well may then thy Lord appeas'd
> Redeem thee quite from Death's rapacious claim;
> But longer in this Paradise to dwell
> Permits not; to remove thee I am come,
> And send thee from the Garden forth to till
> The ground whence thou wast tak'n, fitter Soil.
>   He added not, for *Adam* at the news
> Heart-strook with chilling gripe of sorrow stood,
> That all his senses bound; *Eve,* who unseen
> Yet all had heard, with audible lament
> Discover'd soon the place of her retire.
>   O unexpected stroke, worse than of Death!
> Must I thus leave thee Paradise? thus leave
> Thee Native Soil, these happy Walks and Shades,
> Fit haunt of Gods? where I had hope to spend,
> Quiet though sad, the respite of that day
> That must be mortal to us both. O flow'rs,
> That never will in other Climate grow,
> My early visitation, and my last
> At Ev'n, which I bred up with tender hand
> From the first op'ning bud, and gave ye Names,
> Who now shall rear ye to the Sun, or rank
> Your Tribes, and water from th' ambrosial Fount?
> Thee lastly nuptial Bower, by mee adorn'd
> With what to sight or smell was sweet; from thee
> How shall I part, and whither wander down
> Into a lower World, to this obscure
> And wild, how shall we breathe in other Air

Less pure, accustom'd to immortal Fruits?
    Whom thus the Angel interrupted mild.
Lament not *Eve*, but patiently resign
What justly thou hast lost; nor set thy heart,
Thus over-fond, on that which is not thine;
Thy going is not lonely, with thee goes
Thy Husband, him to follow thou art bound;
Where he abides, think there thy native soil.
    Adam by this from the cold sudden damp
Recovering, and his scatter'd spirits return'd,
To *Michael* thus his humble words address'd.
    Celestial, whether among the Thrones, or nam'd
Of them the Highest, for such of shape may seem
Prince above Princes, gently hast thou told
Thy message, which might else in telling wound,
And in performing end us; what besides
Of sorrow and dejection and despair
Our frailty can sustain, thy tidings bring,
Departure from this happy place, our sweet
Recess, and only consolation left
Familiar to our eyes, all places else
Inhospitable appear and desolate,
Nor knowing us nor known: and if by prayer
Incessant I could hope to change the will
Of him who all things can, I would not cease
To weary him with my assiduous cries:
But prayer against his absolute Decree
No more avails than breath against the wind,
Blown stifling back on him that breathes it forth:
Therefore to his great bidding I submit.
This most afflicts me, that departing hence,
As from his face I shall be hid, depriv'd
His blessed count'nance; here I could frequent,
With worship, place by place where he voutsaf'd
Presence Divine, and to my Sons relate;
On this Mount he appear'd, under this Tree
Stood visible, among these Pines his voice
I heard, here with him at this Fountain talk'd:
So many grateful Altars I would rear
Of grassy Turf, and pile up every Stone
Of lustre from the brook, in memory,
Or monument to Ages, and thereon
Offer sweet smelling Gums and Fruits and Flow'rs:
In yonder nether World where shall I seek
His bright appearances, or footstep trace?
For though I fled him angry, yet recall'd

To life prolong'd and promis'd Race, I now
Gladly behold though but his utmost skirts
Of glory, and far off his steps adore.
      To whom thus *Michael* with regard benign.
Adam, thou know'st Heav'n his, and all the Earth,
Not this Rock only; his Omnipresence fills
Land, Sea, and Air, and every kind that lives,
Fomented by his virtual power and warm'd:
All th' Earth he gave thee to possess and rule,
No despicable gift; surmise not then
His presence to these narrow bounds confin'd
Of Paradise or *Eden:* this had been
Perhaps thy Capital Seat, from whence had spread
All generations, and had hither come
From all the ends of th' Earth, to celebrate
And reverence thee thir great Progenitor.
But this preëminence thou hast lost, brought down
To dwell on even ground now with thy Sons:
Yet doubt not but in Valley and in Plain
God is as here, and will be found alike
Present, and of his presence many a sign
Still following thee, still compassing thee round
With goodness and paternal Love, his Face
Express, and of his steps the track Divine.
Which that thou may'st believe, and be confirm'd,
Ere thou from hence depart, know I am sent
To show thee what shall come in future days
To thee and to thy Offspring; good with bad
Expect to hear, supernal Grace contending
With sinfulness of Men; thereby to learn
True patience, and to temper joy with fear
And pious sorrow, equally inur'd
By moderation either state to bear,
Prosperous or adverse: so shalt thou lead
Safest thy life, and best prepar'd endure
Thy mortal passage when it comes. Ascend
This Hill; let *Eve* (for I have drencht her eyes)
Here sleep below while thou to foresight wak'st,
As once thou slep'st, while Shee to life was form'd.
      To whom thus *Adam* gratefully repli'd.
Ascend, I follow thee, safe Guide, the path
Thou lead'st me, and to the hand of Heav'n submit,
However chast'ning, to the evil turn

My obvious breast, arming to overcome
By suffering, and earn rest from labor won,
If so I may attain.

[from Book 11]

[Michael has just completed revealing to Adam the history of mankind, ending with the
prophesy of the Second Coming of Christ.]

   . . . so shall the World go on,
To good malignant, to bad men benign,
Under her own weight groaning, till the day
Appear of respiration to the just,
And vengeance to the wicked, at return
Of him so lately promis'd to thy aid,
The Woman's seed, obscurely then foretold,
Now ampler known thy Saviour and thy Lord,
Last in the Clouds from Heavn'n to be reveal'd
In glory of the Father, to dissolve
Satan with his perverted World, then raise
From the conflagrant mass, purg'd and refin'd,
New Heav'ns, new Earth, Ages of endless date
Founded in righteousness and peace and love,
To bring forth fruits Joy and eternal Bliss.

  He ended; and thus *Adam* last repli'd.
How soon hath thy prediction, Seer blest,
Measur'd this transient World, the Race of time,
Till time stand fixt: beyond is all abyss,
Eternity, whose end no eye can reach.
Greatly instructed I shall hence depart,
Greatly in peace of thought, and have my fill
Of knowledge, what this Vessel can contain;
Beyond which was my folly to aspire.
Henceforth I learn, that to obey is best,
And love with fear the only God, to walk
As in his presence, ever to observe
His providence, and on him sole depend,
Merciful over all his works, with good
Still overcoming evil, and by small
Accomplishing great things, by things deem'd weak
Subverting worldly strong, and worldly wise
By simply meek; that suffering for Truth's sake
Is fortitude to highest victory,
And to the faithful Death the Gate of Life;
Taught this by his example whom I now
Acknowledge my Redeemer ever blest.
  To whom thus also th' Angel last repli'd:

This having learnt, thou hast attain'd the sum
Of wisdom; hope no higher, though all the Stars
Thou knew'st by name, and all th' ethereal Powers,
All secrets of the deep, all Nature's works,
Or works of God in Heav'n, Air, Earth, or Sea,
And all the riches of this World enjoy'dst,
And all the rule, one Empire; only add
Deeds to thy knowledge answerable, add Faith,
Add Virtue, Patience, Temperance, add Love,
By name to come call'd Charity, the soul
Of all the rest: then wilt thou not be loath
To leave this Paradise, but shalt possess
A paradise within thee, happier far.
Let us descend now therefore from this top
Of Speculation; for the hour precise
Exacts our parting hence; and see the Guards,
By mee encampt on yonder Hill, expect
Thir motion, at whose Front a flaming Sword,
In signal of remove, waves fiercely round;
We may no longer stay: go, waken *Eve;*
Her also I with gentle Dreams have calm'd
Portending good, and all her spirits compos'd
To meek submission: thou at season fit
Let her with thee partake what thou hast heard,
Chiefly what may concern her Faith to know,
The great deliverance by her Seed to come
(For by the Woman's Seed) on all Mankind,
That ye may live, which will be many days,
Both in one Faith unanimous though sad,
With cause for evils past, yet much more cheer'd
With meditation on the happy end.

    He ended, and they both descend the Hill;
Descended, *Adam* to the Bow'r where *Eve*
Lay sleeping ran before, but found her wak't;
And thus with words not sad she him receiv'd.

    Whence thou return'st, and whither went'st, I know;
For God is also in sleep, and Dreams advise,
Which he hath sent propitious, some great good
Presaging, since with sorrow and heart's distress
Wearied I fell asleep: but now lead on;
In mee is no delay; with thee to go,
Is to stay here; without thee here to stay,
Is to go hence unwilling; thou to mee
Art all things under heav'n, all places thou,
Who for my wilful crime art banisht hence.
This further consolation yet secure

I carry hence; though all by mee is lost,
Such favor I unworthy am voutsaf't,
By mee the Promis'd Seed shall all restore.
      So spake our Mother *Eve,* and *Adam* heard
Well pleas'd, but answer'd not; for now too nigh
Th' Arch-Angel stood, and from the other Hill
To thir fixt Station, all in bright array
The Cherubim descended; on the ground
      Gliding meteorous, as Ev'ning Mist
Ris'n from a River o'er the marish glides,
And gathers ground fast at the Laborer's heel
Homeward returning. High in Front advanc't,
The brandisht Sword of God before them blaz'd
Fierce as a Comet; which with torrid heat,
And vapor as the *Libyan* Air adust,
Began to parch that temperate Clime; whereat
In either hand the hast'ning Angel caught
Our ling'ring Parents, and to th' Eastern Gate
Led them direct, and down the Cliff as fast
To the subjected Plain; then disappear'd.
They looking back, all th' Eastern side beheld
Of Paradise, so late thir happy seat,
Wav'd over by that flaming Brand, the Gate
With dreadful Faces throng'd and fiery Arms:
Some natural tears they dropp'd, but wip'd them soon;
The World was all before them, where to choose
Thir place of rest, and Providence thir guide:
They hand in hand with wand'ring steps and slow,
Through *Eden* took thir solitary way.
                    The End
                    [from Book 12]

Christian Perspectives

1. How do Adam and Eve differ in their responses to the judgment of exile? Is Milton suggesting something about the differences in masculine and feminine values?
2. How would you respond to an uprooting from your home and country?
3. Describe what you think the "Paradise within? is.

The Authors

W. H. Auden (1907–73), a leading modern poet, was born in England but came to the United States in 1938 and became a citizen. In 1948 he was awarded the Pulitzer Prize for his long poem, "The Age of Anxiety." His early work was characterized by blithe wit, a Marxist outlook, and a knowledge of Freudian psychology. In later years, he professed Christianity.

Matthew Arnold (1822–88), English poet who was also one of the most important literary critics of his age. He was professor of poetry at Oxford for ten years. His verse exemplifies the romantic pessimism of the 19th century. His feelings of spiritual isolation are reflected in such poems as "Dover Beach."

William Blake (1757–1827) was a great English poet and painter. Blake saw vivid pictures in his mind and tried to write and draw them so other people would see what he did. He called one of his earliest books of poems Songs of Innocence. Many of them are about animals and children. "The Tiger" and "The Lamb" are two of his famous poems.

Anton Checkhov (1860–1904) was a Russian writer who began writing sketches and humorous plays in order to support himself and his family while he was in medical school. After he finished his medical course, he turned to serious writing, which he found more desirable than a medical career. Critics have noted a sense of scientific objectivity in Chekhov's work. He presents his characters' pettiness, weaknesses, and faults, but does not moralize about them.

E. E. Cummings (1894–1962), American poet and painter, born in Cambridge, Massachusetts. He helped invent what has been termed 'pop art," and has used his playful imagination to create ingenious poetic forms. Cummings' verse has been described as a "combination of Thoreau's controlled belligerency, the elitism of a privileged Bostonian, and the brash abandonment of a Bohemian."

Emily Dickinson (1830–1866) was born in Amherst, Massachusetts, where she lived a quiet, retiring life. Her father was a prominent lawyer who was active in civic affairs; thus she had the opportunity to meet many distinguished visitors. Before she was thirty she lived a life filled with friendships, parties, and church functions. But after she reached 30 she began to withdraw from public activities, and the last years of her life she lived as a virtual recluse. She is considered as one of the greatest poets in American literature, but her fame was posthumous. Six volumes of her poetry were published after her death. Only seven of her poems were published during her lifetime.

Robert Frost (1847–1963) was born in San Francisco but moved to Massachusetts at the age of 10. He worked as a bobbin boy in a cotton mill, as a cobbler, a schoolteacher, a farmer, and a journalist, and was a professor in several universities. His poems, which reflect his New England roots, deal with man's fears and tragedies and ultimate acceptance of his burdens. The homey details of his poems often have deep symbolic significance. He received many honors in his lifetime, including four Pulitzer prizes.

Thomas Hardy (1840–1928), English novelist and poet, was one of the great English writers of the 19th century. Hardy's characters, for the most part, were drawn from the poorer rural classes, are sympathetically and humorously portrayed. Hardy's poetry is unadorned and unromantic. Its pervasive theme is man's futile struggle against cosmic forces that cannot be avoided or changed.

George Herbert (1593–1633), English metaphysical poet, was of a noble family and an ordained Anglican priest. His poems combine a familiarity with and reverence for religious experience. His verse is characterized by a quietness of tone, precision of language, and metrical versatility.

Gerard Manley Hopkins (1844–89) was born in England but spent most of his life in Ireland. He was a priest and teacher of Greek. Hopkins is considered by many as a forerunner of twentieth-century poetry. His first volume of poems was published nearly thirty years after his death.

Langston Hughes (1902–1967) was born in Joplin, Missouri. He first gained public attention as the "busboy poet" and was later known as the Poet Laureate of Harlem. he developed subjects from Negro life and racial themes that contributed to the strengthening of black consciousness and racial pride.

Garrison Keillor (1942–) writer and broadcaster from Minnesota. he gained recognition by enthralling his radio listeners with affectionate yarns about and parodies of small-town life more than a decade ago. His program, A

Prairie Home Companion is broadcast coast to coast on American Public Radio. His book <u>Lake Wobegon Days</u> is a comic work of fiction combining aspects of the personal memoir, the anecdotal novel, and local history.

Martin Luther King, Jr., (1928–68), American clergyman and civil rights leader who was born in Atlanta, Georgia. In 1956 he organized a boycott of Montgomery's city bus lines that succeeded in greatly reducing discrimination against Negroes. he then founded the Southern Christian Leadership Conference. He was awarded the Nobel Peace Prize in 1964, and was shot and killed by an assassin's bullet in 1968.

C. S. Lewis (1898–1963) was born in Belfast, Ireland. At the time of his death, he was a professor of medieval and renaissance literature at Cambridge University. He is known for both his literary scholarship and his ability to explain (often with wit) Christian beliefs. he wrote the famous <u>Screwtape Letters</u> and a series of allegorical fantasies for children set in the mythical kingdom of Narnia. He also wrote a number of poems, essays, and nonfiction books.

Richard Lovelace (1618–1657), one of the English cavalier poets. He is remembered for two melodic and much-quoted lyrics, "To Althea, from Prison," and "To Lucasta, Going to Wars."

Malcolm X (1925–1965), a leader in equal rights movement for blacks in the 1950's who was transformed from Malcolm Little, a street "hustler," to a leader of the Black Muslims. He was assassinated in New York City in 1965.

John Milton (1608–1674) was one of the greatest of all English poets. When he was very young he began to study Latin, Greek, and Hebrew. Many of his poems are filled with names and statements taken from ancient Latin, Greek, and Hebrew literature. His most famous sonnet is about his blindness. (He became blind when he was 46.) His greatest work was his long poem, <u>Paradise Lost</u>. It was about the original sin of Adam and Eve in the Garden of Eden.

Flannery O'Connor (1925–64), American author born in Savannah, Georgia. She is regarded for her bizarre imagination, uncompromising moral vision, and superb literary style. Her fiction treats contemporary Southern life in terms of comedy and tragedy. She was the victim of a type of lupus and spent the last ten years of her life as an invalid. Her fiction reflects her strong Roman Catholic faith. Her characters, although often deformed in both body and spirit, are impelled toward redemption.

Wilfred Owen (1893–1918), English poet who served as a company commander during World War I and was killed in France one week before the armistice. Owen's poetic theme is the horror and pity of war. His strong verse transfigures traditional meters and diction.

Scott Peck is a psychiatrist in private practice in Connecticut. He was educated at Harvard University and Case Western Reserve. He served in administrative posts in the government during his career as a psychotherapist. He has written two best-selling books, <u>The Road Less Traveled</u> and <u>People of the Lie</u>.

Plato, who was born in Greece about 427 BC and died in 347 BC, was one of the greatest philosophers of all time. As a young man he became a pupil of Socrates, another great philosopher and teacher. When Plato was about 40, he settled in Athens and founded the first university—the Academy. He spent his time there lecturing and writing <u>dialogues</u>—the conversations from which his philosophy can be learned. In the <u>Republic</u> and the <u>Laws</u>, Plato discusses the problems of government. Plato's teachings influenced his pupil Aristotle.

Edwin Arlington Robinson (1869–1935) attended Harvard for two years until his family ran out of money. He was fond of portraying failures, reprobates, and heavy drinkers—the characters with whom he populated his semifictitious Tilbury Town (modeled after Gardiner, Maine, where he grew up). Robinson, who viewed life with stoic pessimism, combined tight stanzas with colloquial Yankee language in his New England landscapes long before Robert Frost.

Dorothy L. Sayers (1893–1957), English writer who was one of the first women to receive a degree at Oxford. Sayers is considered one of the masters of the detective story. She is known for her brilliantly plotted novels, religious drama, and theological essays.

Percy Bysshe Shelley (1792–1822), One of the great English poets of the romantic period. The son of a prosperous squire, Shelley's life was dominated by his desire for social and political reform. Many of his beliefs were modeled after the ideas of Plato. Twentieth century critics recognize his wit, his gift as a satirist, and his influence as a social and political thinker.

Aleksandr Solzhenitsyn (1918–   ), Soviet author who now lives in the United States. Although acclaimed by literary critics and readers in Russia and abroad as "the only living classic in Russia," his later works, including two major novels, <u>Cancer Ward</u> and <u>The First Circle</u> were banned in Russia because they were considered too critical of Soviet society. He was the winner of the 1970 Nobel Prize in literature.

Jonathan Swift (1667–1754), English writer who was famous as a writer of satire. After Swift graduated from college he became a priest in the Church of England. Many of Swift's satires are concerned with the political questions and leading political figures of his day.

Henry David Thoreau (1817–62), American author and naturalist who is remembered chiefly for his beliefs that men should live simply, conforming their lives to nature. He was born in Concord, Massachusetts, and studied at Harvard. He lived for two years in a small hut beside "Walden Pond," where he devoted himself to writing and nature study. One of his most important works, "Civil Disobedience," grew out of an overnight stay in prison—a result of his conscientious refusal to pay a tax that supported the Mexican War, which he thought represented an effort to extend slavery. He advocated civil disobedience as a means of protesting the actions of government that one considers unjust.

Paul Tillich (1886–1965), a philosopher and theologian, was born in Germany and educated at the Universities of Berlin, Tubingen, Halle, and Breslau. An ordained minister of the Evangelical Lutheran Church, he taught theology at several German universities, and was teaching philosophy at the University of Frankfurt in 1933 when he was dismissed because of his opposition to the Nazi regime. At the invitation of Reinhold Niebuhr, he came to the United States and joined the faculty of Union Theological Seminary. He was later a professor at Harvard and the University of Chicago. In his writings he aimed at a correlation of the questions arising out of the human condition and the divine answers drawn from Christian revelation.

Mark Twain—pseudonym of Samuel Langhorne Clemens (1835–1910), American author who was born in Floria, Missouri. He worked as a printer and a newspaper reporter, and briefly as a riverboat pilot on the Mississippi. As humorist, narrator, and social observer, Twain is unsurpassed in American Literature.

John Updike (1932–) was born in Shillington, Pennsylvania, and is a graduate of Harvard University. His work, which includes novels, short stories, poetry, and drama, usually deals with the tensions, frustrations, and tragedies of contemporary life.

Dan Wakefield (1932–) American novelist, author of <u>Starting Over</u> (1972), <u>Going All the Way</u> (1970), <u>Home Free</u> (1977), <u>Under the Apple Tree</u>, and <u>Selling Out</u> (1985).

William Wordsworth (1770–1850), one of the great English poets and a leader in the romantic movement in england. Wordsworth's personality, as well as his poetry, was deeply influenced by his love of nature. His earlier work shows the poetic beauty of commonplace things and people.

Index

AUTHORS AND TITLES

Adventures of Huckleberry Finn,
  The, 95
Aeropagitica, 157
Allegory of the Cave, 155
Arnold, Matthew: Dover Beach,
  30
Auden, W. H.: The Unknown
  Citizen, 151

Bet, The, 163
Blake, William: The Tiger, The
  Lamb, 162, 163

Channelled Whelk, The, 101
Checkhov, Anton, The Bet, 163
Collar, The, 152
cummings, e. e.: next to of course
  god america i, 135

Dickinson, Emily: Those—Dying,
  Then; God Is a Distant Stately
  Lover, I'm Nobody, 28, 91, 150
Dogma Is the Drama, The, 50
Donne, John: Holy Sonnet XIV,
  89
Dover Beach, 30
Dulce et Decorum Est, 132

Easter Wings, 87
Ecclesiasticus, 136

Freedom through Learning to
  Read, 144

God Forgotten, 27
God Is a Distant Stately Lover, 91
God's Grandeur, 86

Hardy, Thomas: God Forgotten,
  27
Herberg, Will: Religiosity and
  Religion, 33
Herbert, George: Easter Wings,
  The Pulley, 87, 88
Holy Sonnet XIV, 89
Hopkins, Gerald Manley: God's
  Grandeur, Pied Beauty, The
  Windhover, 86, 87, 90
Huckleberry Finn, 95
Hughes, Langston: Salvation, 53

I'm Nobody, 150

Keillor, Garrison: Lake Wobegon
  Days, 141
King, Martin Luther, Jr.: Letter
  from Birmingham Jail, 121

Lake Wobegon Days, 141
Lamb, The, 163
Letter from Birmingham Jail, 121
Lewis, C. S.: What Are We to
  Make of Jesus Christ, Theol-
  ogy, Excerpt from Mere Chris-
  tianity, 81, 83, 106
Lindbergh, Anne Morrow: Chan-
  neled Whelk, 101
Lovelace, Richard, To Lucasta,
  Going to the Wars, 133
Malcom X: Freedom through
  Learning to Read, 144
Mere Christianity, Excerpt from,
  106
Milton, John: Aeropagitica,
  Sonnet XIX, Paradise Lost,
  157, 174, 183
Modest Proposal, A, 113

next to of course god america i,
  135

O'Connor, Flannery: Revelation,
  36
Owen, Wilfred: Dulce et Decorum
  Est, 132
Ozymandias, 29

Paradise Lost, 183
Peck, M. Scott: The Risk of Loss,
  175
Pied Beauty, 87
Pigeon Feathers, 55
Psalm 8, 85
Pully, The, 88

Religiosity and Religion, 33
Returning to Church, 177
Revelation, 36
Riddle of Inequality, The, 169
Risk of Loss, The, 175

Salvation, 53
Sanger, Margaret: The Turbid
  Ebb and Flow of Misery, 109
Sayers, Dorothy L: The Dogma Is
  the Drama, Toward a Chris-
  tian Aesthetic, 50, 71
Shelley, Percy: Ozymandias, 29
Solzhenitsyn, Aleksandr: The
  Templeton Address: Men
  Have Forgotten God, 21
Sonnet XIX, 174
Swift, Jonathan: A Modest
  Proposal, 113

Templeton Address, The: Men
  Have Forgotten God, 21
Thoreau, Henry David: Where I
  Lived and What I Lived for, 97
Theology, 83
Those Dying Then, 28
Tiger, The, 162
Tillich, Paul: The Riddle of Ine-
  quality, 169
To Lucasta Going to the Wars,
  133
Toward a Christian Aesthetic, 71
Turbid Ebb and Flow of Misery,
  The, 109
Twain, Mark: Huckleberry Finn,
  95

Unknown Citizen, The, 151
Updike, John: Pigeon Feathers, 55

Valediction Forbidding Mourning,
  A, 134

Wakefield, Dan: Returning to
  Church, 177
What Are We to Make of Jesus
  Christ?, 81
Where I Lived and What I Lived
  For, 97
Windhover, The, 90
Wordsworth, William: The World
  Is Too Much with Us, 105
World Is Too Much with Us, The,
  105

Index of Terms

Agreement, 11
Allusion, 14
Analogies, 10
Analysis, 15
Audience, 2

Cause and Effect, 9
Central Consciousness, 13
Character, 23
Classification, 10
Climax, 13
Comparison, 10
Conflict, 13
Contrast, 10
Coordination, 14

Definition, 9
Description, 8
Descriptive Summary, 4
Diction, 14
Division, 10

Ethos, 12
Evaluation, 6

Execution, 6, 7
Exposition, 8

Hypothesis, 7, 12

Illumination, 6, 7
Illustration, 10
Images, 14
Incubation, 6, 7

Juxtaposition, 15

Logos, 12

Narration, 8

Parallelism, 15

Omniscient Author, 13

Paraphrase, 4
Pathos, 11
Persona, 2
Personal Response, 5
Plagiarism, 4
Plot, 13

Point of View, 13
Preparation, 6, 7
Process, 8
Purpose, 2

Resolution, 13, 15 Rhetorical Situation, 2

Setting, 13
Strategy, 11
Structure, 1, 15
Subject, 2
Subordination, 14
Summarize, 4
Support, 10
Symbols, 14
Synthesis, 4. 6

Theme, 15
Thesis, 3, 4

Verification, 6, 7, 8
Voice, 2